D0204202

Propaganda

MEDIA AND SOCIETY SERIES

J. Fred MacDonald, General Editor

Propaganda

A Pluralistic Perspective

Edited by Ted J. Smith III

Media and Society Series

PRAEGER

New York
Westport, Connecticut
London

Library of Congress Cataloging-in-Publication Data

Propaganda : a pluralistic perspective / edited by Ted J. Smith.
p. cm.—(Media and society series)
Bibliography: p.
Includes index.
Contents: Social responses to twentieth century propaganda / J.
Michael Sproule — Propaganda and order in modern society / J. Fred
MacDonald — Western and totalitarian views of propaganda / Randall
L. Bytwerk — Propaganda as a form of communication / Victoria
O'Donnell and Garth S. Jowett — Propaganda and the technique of
deception / Ted J. Smith III — Active measures in contemporary
Soviet strategy / Roy Godson — Propaganda and the law / J. Justin
Gustainis — Ideology and propaganda / Nicholas F. S. Burnett —
Deceptive advertising and the power of suggestion / J. David
Kennamer — Smoke and mirrors / Stanley B. Cunningham — The
rhetoric of nuclear education / J. Michael Hogan and David Olsen.
ISBN 0-275-92743-1 (alk. paper)
1. Propaganda. 2. Communication. I. Smith, Ted J. II. Series.
P301.5.P73P76 1989
303.3′75—dc20 89-33975

Copyright © 1989 by Ted J. Smith III

All rights reserved. No portion of this book may
be reproduced, by any process or technique, without
the express written consent of the publisher.

Library of Congress Catalog Card Number: 89-33975
ISBN: 0-275-92743-1

First published in 1989

Praeger Publishers, One Madison Avenue, New York, NY 10010
A division of Greenwood Press, Inc.

Printed in the United States of America

The paper used in this book complies with the
Permanent Paper Standard issued by the National
Information Standards Organization (Z39.48-1984).

10 9 8 7 6 5 4 3 2 1

P
301.5
.P73
P76
1989

Contents

Propaganda

Introduction
Ted J. Smith III

One of the most distinctively human traits is our persistent attempt to use language to influence the course of events and the behavior of others. The form of these attempts varies greatly, ranging from prayer and incantation to command and exhortation. Regarding the last of these, it has been common throughout recorded history to distinguish between appeals that seek mutual benefit and those that are essentially manipulative. The terms used to express this distinction, however, have varied by time and culture. In the age of Classical Greece, Aristotle contrasted rhetoric, which can be both rational and ethical, with sophistic, which is neither. In twentieth-century America, the distinction has been drawn less clearly, but it is probably best captured by the contrast between persuasion and propaganda.

There has always been great popular interest in manipulative communication. This is quite understandable given that few people enjoy the prospect of being used for the benefit of another. In this century, with the advent of the broadcast media and other powerful new communication technologies, increasing government centralization and activism, the spread of militant ideologies such as fascism and Marxism, and the growth of sophisticated methods of advertising and public relations, these concerns have become acute. Thus, in popular parlance, propaganda is used as a clearly negative term to denote deliberately deceitful appeals, especially those directed to a mass audience, and there has long been widespread popular interest in identifying and understanding propaganda in order to avoid its manipulative effects.

For much of this century, scholarly usage and interest paralleled popular. Beginning in the years immediately following World War I, deceitful propaganda was the object of numerous humanstic and scientific studies; by the 1940s, units in propaganda analysis—which focused on paradigmatic examples drawn from fascism, Marxism, and advertising—were a common feature of high school and college curricula. But the scholarly view of propaganda, always diverse, continued to evolve, and by the mid–1960s a new conception had emerged which was not merely different from but in some ways hostile to the traditional popular conception.

Opinions differ on the precise reasons for this change. I argue below that one factor was a widespread shift in the political sensibilities of American intellectuals which led to a rejection of the older approach to propaganda, especially when focused on Marxist appeals, as simplistic at best and reactionary at worst. Another cause was the spread of relativistic views of truth which rendered problematic the central distinction between honest and deceitful communication. But perhaps the most important factor was the publication in 1965 of an English translation of Jacques Ellul's book *Propaganda*. He argues there that propaganda is best seen as a ubiquitous social phenomenon, integral to the operation of technological societies and all-pervasive in its effects. Full of fascinating inversions of earlier beliefs (e.g., that education, far from being a defense against propaganda, is actually its prerequisite), and broadly compatible with the contemporaneous emergence of Neomarxist analyses of false consciousness and hegemony, it had a profound impact on the study of propaganda. On the one hand, it inspired a number of subtle and sophisticated studies, typically of propaganda in the Western democracies. On the other hand, it set in motion an immense expansion of the domain of propaganda in which traditional distinction between conscious and unconscious, intentional and unintentional, personal and social, persuasive and informative, even mendacious and veracious communication were blurred or discarded. Perhaps for this reason, the study of propaganda entered a period of decline: Courses and units on traditional propaganda analysis disappeared from academic curricula and published research, while arguably of higher quality, diminished markedly in quantity. There matters rested until recently.

In the last several years, there has been a dramatic resurgence of scholarly (and popular) interest in propaganda. Aside from its scope, this outpouring of scholarship is noteworthy in at least two respects. First, it displays a strong theoretical and definitional emphasis, devoted primarily to refining and extending both the more recent sociocultural (i.e., Ellulian) and the traditional rationalistic approaches to the subject. Second, although the resurgence includes contributions from a wide variety of academic disciplines, it is centered in the field of communication studies and reflects in particular the assumptions and methods of rhetorical scholarship. The result is a level of conceptual clarity and critical rigor sometimes missing from earlier work. The purpose of this book is to reintroduce the study of propaganda and to extend its development. To these ends, it arrays a number of contemporary theoretical perspectives, identifies and explores several key issues in propaganda analysis, and exemplifies the application of the two major research traditions.

More specifically, the first six chapters focus on theoretical and definitional concerns. In the first, Michael Sproule provides a history of American propaganda analysis from a humanistic perspective by tracing four "social responses" to the subject. The next five chapters develop a range of different theoretical positions. Professor MacDonald, arguing from a broad historical and cultural perspective, examines the integrative function of propaganda in the age of mass societies. Randall Bytwerk uses an explicitly Ellulian perspective to distinguish among Nazi, Soviet, and Western species of propaganda. Victoria O'Donnell and Garth Jowett develop an intermediate position which locates propaganda relative to informative and persuasive communication and identifies "white," "gray," and "black" variants of the craft. My essay attempts to reestablish the traditional rationalistic and popular view of propaganda by defining it as deceitful communication and arraying the techniques of deception on which it is based. Finally, Roy Godson examines the range of Soviet "active measures," including both propaganda and "disinformation" techniques.

The remaining essays are narrower in scope. Chapters 7, 8, and 9 focus on several key issues in propaganda research. Professor Gustainis uses the recent legal controversy over the classification of three Canadian films as "political propaganda" to ground an examination of the First Amendment issues involved in the use of such labels. Nicholas Burnett uses the same controversy to exemplify the interrelationships between propaganda and ideology. And David Kennamer applies Grice's notion of "conversational implicatures" to explicate the deception technique of suggestion as found in commercial advertising.

The final two chapters provide detailed examples of the two general approaches to propaganda analysis. Professor Cunningham shows the value of Ellul's controversial "indistinguishablility" thesis in an analysis of a major nonproduct advertising campaign sponsored by the R.J. Reynolds Tobacco Company. Michael Hogan and David Olsen exemplify the traditional rationalistic approach to propaganda by providing a detailed rhetorical analysis of a nuclear education curriculum developed by the National Education Association.

In selecting these essays, my goal was to provide the broadest possible range of viewpoints within the inevitable constraints of space and availability. But the collection is far from exhaustive. In particular, while several authors discuss the Soviet Marxist approach to propaganda, there is no fully sympathetic explication of it. This omission is not from want of trying. A year of discussion and correspondence with various members of the Soviet embassy staff in Washington and the Union of Journalists in Moscow produced an agreement that the Soviets would provide an article on their view of propaganda to be published unedited in this book. Six months later, a Union representative cabled that the article was ready and asked to whom it should be sent. Unfortunately, it never arrived, and scores of inquiries to the embassy and the Union went unanswered. Perhaps it was a casualty of the ideological uncertainties engendered by glasnost and perestroika. In any event, those interested in pursuing the subject can find detailed treatments of the traditional Marxist view in the entries on "Propaganda" and "Agitation" in the *Great Soviet Encyclopedia*.

Finally, it must be noted that several of the articles (my own in particular) are likely to be seen as politically controversial. I see no reason to apologize for this. Propaganda analysis has always been inextricably intertwined with political issues and perspectives, and it is difficult to see why this should not be made explicit. More important, the study of propaganda leads directly to a range of profoundly important issues, including the nature of truth, the morality of social influence, the role of the press in a democratic society, and the possibility of rational discourse. With so much at stake, passionate controversy is both inevitable and valuable. My goal in this book was to initiate those debates, not settle them, and it is in that spirit that the reader is asked to judge its merits.

1 Social Responses to Twentieth-Century Propaganda
J. Michael Sproule

Whatever happened to propaganda? That venerable, disapproving term for social influence, prominent during the inter-world war period, gave way in recent decades to such rhetorical euphemisms as communication and information. As a serious expression for inquiries about persuasion, however, propaganda has enjoyed a rehabilitation of late, and has gained such semantic cousins as doublespeak and disinformation. Does this linguistic ebb and flow tell us anything important about the practice and theory of social influence? Indeed, it does. Vicissitudes of terminology among students of political rhetoric are the visible signs of an underlying four recognizable but seldom differentiated schools of thought on modern mass communication: the humanist, professional, scientific, and polemical perspectives.

Each of the four perspectives on propaganda has experienced periods of dominance and decline both within society at large and in academe. All of them may best be regarded as social responses to the conflict between traditional American democracy and modern practices and techniques of social influence. The perspectives each give a characteristic answer to a question critical for a society which prides itself on democratic political practice: How may citizens make informed decisions about political problems when their knowledge of those problems is influenced by the very elites they are supposed to control?

The rise of the modern communication industry has posed problems for traditional democratic theory which assumes that citizens independently are able to gather sufficient information to participate in political society. America's idealized political heritage is that of a rural republic in which citizens, intimately acquainted with their small-town neighbors, managed local affairs from personal knowledge, and elected fellow townspeople to deal with a comparatively small number of state and national issues. Although nineteenth-century America saw differences in ethnic background and language, the majority of the nation's people participated in an agricultural economy that homogenized family income and social interest. The basis of this traditional image of an agrarian democracy began to break down in the mid–1800s due to the rise of large cities that were fed by immigration and were home to emerging industrialization. Increasingly stratified in income and social position, and housed in urban centers, citizens relied more than before on their newspaper to provide knowledge of political issues. Citizens now depended more than ever on the competence and good will of those who controlled the channels of public communication. American political theorists were slow to recognize the significant implications of communication practices for democratic institutions. The late nineteenth-century's premier writer on American government, James Bryce, still pictured American public opinion as essentially homogeneous, with the electorate acting "directly and constantly upon its executive and legislative agents" (1899, vol. 2, p. 263).

World War I provided the context for the discovery of how new communication technologies and techniques were altering the traditional picture of American democratic practice as involving informed control by an independent citizenry. The war years brought an unprecedented level of national mobilization that included establishment of an official agency of mass persuasion called the Committee on Public Information (CPI). The CPI eschewed the heavy-handed press censorship characteristic of the European belligerents, preferring to establish an all-pervasive system of communication that touched citizens at every possible point in their lives. While the Committee prepared and sent out millions of pamphlets giving reasoned official views of the war, the full CPI program was organized around short, dramatic war appeals that were easily available to those who might not take the time to request or even read detailed official guidance on the Great War.

Reflecting the crusading spirit of the CPI's leader, progressive journalist George Creel, the Committee at every point set before the public the Wilson Administration's view of an idealistic war fought to ensure the worldwide triumph of democracy. Within this broad, optimistic rhetorical framework, two darker themes occasionally held center stage: the condemnation of Germany and Austria for alleged war atrocities, and encouragement for citizens to act as rhetorical vigilantes against disloyal utterances. Glancing at the morning newspaper, an ordinary citizen might begin the day by reading articles based on official CPI press handouts or on interviews with government officials conducted or arranged by CPI press spokesmen. If the citizen scanned the paper's editorial cartoon, it is possible that the picture was based on a theme suggested to the artist by the Creel

Committee's *Bulletin for Cartoonists*. If the newspaper of choice were a rural weekly, it was often the case that the war story was one written by the CPI staff itself and sent to the paper in a form ready for printing. The Committee further advanced wartime themes by means of advertisements placed in popular periodicals through donations of business organizations. These ads usually contained attention-grabbing art prepared by the CPI's staff of nationally renowned artists and texts written by the best copywriters loaned by top advertising agencies.

The influence of the CPI was felt in the daily routines of Americans. In the workplace, and on the streetcar and train, the worker would likely glance at CPI war posters and would often find in his or her pay envelope a pro-war flyer. If the family had children in school, it is likely that the citizen would encounter wartime messages appearing in the academic curriculum via the CPI's *National School Service* bulletin. During the weekly trip to the movie house, the citizen and his family might occasionally watch one of the CPI's several war films, which enjoyed blanket bookings, and probably would listen often to one of the CPI's 75,000 official Four Minute Men speakers who delivered short talks to audiences based on weekly themes set in Washington. If the family took in the state fair or resided in a large metropolitan area, it is possible that the members saw exhibits of American material and watched reenactments of front-line action at one of the CPI's several war expositions. And if the family's ancestry were not English, the members might be the recipients of messages from one of the CPI's many Americanization Committees that were established for dozens of the nation's minority groups (Mock and Larson 1939; Vaughn 1980).

Between the declaration of war and the Armistice, the nation generally accepted the wartime preachings of the CPI at face value. Not everyone fully shared the official view of the war, but the largest group of potential naysayers, German-Americans, either got on the wartime bandwagon or kept prudently silent. A number of socialists spent time in jail for speaking against the war (Chafee 1941); and a few disaffected intellectuals, such as Randolph Bourne, wrote disapprovingly of the spectacle of the nation's opinion leaders outdoing themselves to echo the tune of the CPI (Bourne [1917] 1965, pp. 191–203). While the war years saw few challenges to the CPI's monopoly of the public forum, however, postwar conditions soon provided a context in which the wartime persuasions came to be seen in a more sinister light.

The view that the mass media, driven by modern advertising and public relations techniques, might themselves constitute a new and worrisome political phenomenon called propaganda emerged gradually in the months after the Armistice of November 1918. The term propaganda itself had entered the general public lexicon some months before the U.S. entry into the war. By 1915, U.S. newspapers were providing reports of sabotage and secret bribes conducted by German agents and sympathizers in the United

States. Often based on information revealed by investigations of the U.S. Secret Service, these accounts gave instances of efforts to win support for the German cause through purchase of American newspapers and subsidies for pro-German groups, together with sporadic episodes of sabotage of American munitions plants and merchant ships carrying supplies to the Allies. These reports helped to fix in the public consciousness a specter of "The German Propaganda."

While agents and sympathizers of Britain and France also organized propaganda campaigns in the United States, only the German effort was treated in exposé fashion, largely because of the care of the pro-Ally campaigners to avoid association with covert activities (Irwin 1935). Further, the heavy-handedness of German self-justifications underscored their propagandistic nature, for example, the effort to minimize with technical legalisms the loss of more than 1,000 civilian lives in the submarine sinking of the British passenger liner, *Lusitania*. In contrast, the natural sympathy of Americans for countries suffering from German invasion helped mask the self-serving nature of the pro-Ally arguments (Viereck 1930).

The public's wartime perspective on propaganda was a restricted and isolated one. The phenomenon was understood as dishonest communication orchestrated in underhanded campaigns by a foreign enemy. The idea that appropriation of the communication industry by domestic institutions and groups constituted a pervasive social propaganda had not yet entered popular consciousness. After the Armistice, however, the notion of propaganda as a general social problem became established. A series of postwar developments caused the odious rubric, previously reserved for pro-German communication, to be transferred both to the wartime campaigns by the Allied powers and to the Wilson Administration's own Committee on Public Information.

Several factors established the context for a new view that the modern methods of persuasion could be inherently propagandistic. The first of these was the postwar revisionist thinking about the origins of the war. Revisionist interpretations were set in motion by the opening of the war archives of Bolshevik Russia and the defeated Central Powers, Germany and Austria. As commentators diffused revelations from the war archives, Americans increasingly saw their erstwhile allies as sharing guilt for the war. Assertions by the CPI that the war began as a simple German-Austrian plot now took on the appearance of propagandistic half-truths (Sproule 1987). Related to reapportionment of war guilt was the new tendency to reject wartime atrocity tales. CPI publications, as well as other official and semiofficial war commentaries, often confidently presented the Germans as wantonly slaughtering and mutilating civilians; but postwar books and articles persuasively discounted these stories. Whereas most Americans had accepted wartime atrocity tales as gospel, the debunking of these stories showed that falsehood could gain the aura of truth when presented by a governmental bureau that presided over all channels of public communication (Seldes 1929, p. 435; Ponsonby 1928).

Disillusionment with the high human costs of the war was another factor helping to open the public to the existence of wartime propaganda. Postwar books by such war correspondents as Philip Gibbs revealed that the front-line reporters had voluntarily censored their dispatches so as to emphasize the heroism and enthusiasm of the troops, and to inflate the competence of the military machine. Now focusing on the horror and stupidity of the war, the postwar books showed how news had been seasoned by propaganda as reporters and editors endeavored to give their articles the tone approved by wartime leaders (cf. Gibbs 1915; 1920).

A final factor promoting postwar propaganda consciousness was disillusionment with the terms of the Versailles Treaty. Progressives were especially outraged by various punitive terms that, rather than set up a solid new structure for democracy, took wealth and territory from the Central Powers and enriched America's former allies in ways that created new causes for war (Goldman 1966, pp. 265–68). Americans were now prone to see the Great War as yet another imperialistic undertaking. These impressions led to a general rejection of Wilsonian idealism and internationalism, two linchpins of the CPI's wartime message.

Now that the central claims of the CPI were overturned, it was but a simple extrapolation to see the CPI itself as an office of propaganda. Postwar conditions helped paint a picture of the Creel Committee as an agency that hoodwinked the public by confidently transforming wishful thinking, ignorance, and half-truths into a self-serving dogma designed to fuel the Wilson Administration's war policies. A new image of modern propaganda began to emerge as Americans understood how the mass media might be captured by spokesmen whose unchallenged facts could better be characterized as distortions.

THE HUMANIST RESPONSE

New perspectives on the war caused major American intellectuals to assemble lessons from the record of the wartime communication agencies. The earliest commentators on propaganda were humanists and progressives who saw propaganda as an obstacle for widespread participation in modern democratic life. A month after the Armistice, John Dewey, one of the most enthusiastic articulators of the Wilsonian vision of the Great War, now focused on the "intellectual paternalism" of the wartime practices of guiding public opinion. Contending that "shaping public opinion has become an essential industry," Dewey (1918, p. 216) expressed concern that the war had both accelerated and made permanent the practices of official and centralized communication. Citing instances of continued efforts of government officials to manipulate public opinion concerning Germany,

Dewey worried over the influence that propaganda continued to hold upon the wellspring of democracy, public opinion. Progressive journalist Will Irwin (1919, p. 54), who for a time directed the CPI's program of overseas propaganda, echoed Dewey's concern that the efforts of special-interest propagandists "to slant, to bias, to color the news" showed no signs of abating after the Armistice.

By the early 1920s, the critiques of wartime communication by disillusioned progressives were maturing into a general humanist perspective on persuasion that came to be known as propaganda analysis. The propaganda analysts voiced concerns that democracy was imperiled by the ability of special interests to use the new methods of persuasion in ways that frustrated traditional political participation, and this framework became the dominant perspective on modern persuasion during the 1920s and early 1930s. The major early theorist of propaganda analysis was the journalist, Walter Lippmann. From personal experience as a wartime U.S. military propagandist, Lippmann (1922) wrote of how authorities were able to manipulate the news in ways supportive of official policies. Lippmann revealed the conscious distortions in French war communiques, messages that doled out information strategically to create the proper state of mind in the French public. Showing that the success of Wilson's Fourteen Points was due to their propagation by means of the new media, Lippmann announced a new age of politics through communication. Throughout his book, Lippmann showed that the traditional relationship of a self-governing people to their government was permanently changed by modern propaganda.

Following the lead of Lippmann, further accounts of propaganda's entry into the news columns were penned regularly during the 1920s and 1930s. Upton Sinclair ([1920] 1936) provided an autobiographical account of how newspapers gave more favorable coverage to the wealthy than to reformers, a book enthusiastically read by journalists who chaffed under pressures from editors and publishers to color the news. Walter Lippmann and Charles Merz (1920) caused quite a stir with their analysis of how anti-Bolshevik biases led to inaccuracies in *The New York Times*' reports of the Russian Civil War. George Seldes (1929) contributed an influential report of how propaganda by foreign governments worked its way into articles in U.S. newspapers. Will Irwin (1936) reprised this problem, and also discussed propagandistic influences on domestic news by the publicity departments of the Democratic National Committee and the New Deal.

Beyond the frequent focus on propaganda in the news, humanist social scientists and popular writers scrutinized the social agents and agencies of the new phenomenon. Walker (1927) and others analyzed the machinations of press agents, who tried to get their self-serving editorials accepted as news by the nation's editors. Wohlforth (1930) and others focused on efforts by government agencies to win space in news columns. Commentators exposed notorious episodes of propagandistic bribery, such as the campaign of the National Electric Light Association against publicly owned power plants (Seligman 1930). An influential report by the nation's teachers revealed the endeavor of interest groups to work their special points of view into the curricula of the public schools (National Education Association 1929).

Writers belonging to the school of propaganda analysis generally shared the goal of the progressives to increase citizen participation in politics. Viewed from this perspective, propaganda was inherently problematic for democracy, since the access of society's powerful interests to the communications media was not necessarily proportional to the merits of their proposals. Concerned that one-sided paid publicity campaigns and various manipulations of the news were distorting the public's ability to sort out issues and arguments, the propaganda critics emphasized education as a means to help citizens break through the smoke screens of biased communication. In an influential monograph, Biddle (1932, pp. 7–13) gave one of the clearest articulations of how society might respond to the new persuasions through emphasis on a humanistic education in critical thinking. Biddle explained that the Great War revealed modern propaganda to be essentially an endeavor to mask the selfish interests of the persuaders with emotional appeals that avoided argument. Biddle observed that the competition of propagandas did not minimize the danger to democracy, for the welter of competing claims "tends to diminish independent, critical intelligence." Similarly, he described efforts to legislate against dishonest advertising as an incomplete response to the social ethics of modern communication, given the ability of the propagandist to skillfully insert messages in the general news. The solution, Biddle wrote, was a "direct attack upon gullibility itself," that is, to replace the educational system's reliance on providing "ready-made conclusions" with a curriculum that enabled students "to think critically about the nation's affairs."

Propaganda analysis, with its progressive, humanistic vision of an educated citizenry intelligently sifting through competing claims, was the dominant social response to modern propaganda during the 1920s and 1930s. An intellectual movement of considerable strength, propaganda analysis spawned a vast literature during the inter-world war period. The movement culminated in the formation of the Institute for Propaganda Analysis in 1937. The Institute widely diffused antipropaganda thinking from higher education to the public schools and to the reading public. Propaganda analysis declined during the 1940s and 1950s, decades more concerned with national security than social self-criticism. But the humanist social response to modern persuasion has never disappeared, and has often surfaced in the years since the Vietnam War. Since the 1960s, the concern that propaganda is diminishing democracy has been reflected in popular books that have exposed, for example, media manipulations in the 1968 presidential campaign (McGinniss 1969) and the systematic use of lying as a tool of government (Wise 1973). The desire to combat propaganda has underlaid such educational efforts as the Public Doublespeak program of the National Council of Teachers of English.

THE PROFESSIONAL RESPONSE

The worries of the progressive propaganda analysts reflected only one strain of American thought relevant to modern communication. Other perspectives emerged in the 1920s and 1930s to offer alternate suggestions as to how American society should view and adjust to the practices of modern social influence. Important among these alternative perspectives was the thinking of the new communication professionals themselves. Having their own activities and interests to defend, the propaganda workers labored to reconcile their craft with American democracy. The professional perspective, which views propaganda as an essentially harmless refinement on the traditional American marketplace of ideas, was first clearly articulated during the 1920s by important spokesmen of the domestic propaganda industry.

At the turn of the century, it would have been presumptuous to depict the nation's collection of newspapers, independent promoters, press agents, and patent medicine copywriters as an "industry" of communication; however, the Great War had advanced the coalescence of these rhetorical precursors into an increasingly integrated engine of social influence. The success of the CPI gave visibility to the infant professions of advertising and public relations.

Through their work with the CPI, advertisers had demonstrated their ability to influence public perception and action (Lee [1937] 1973, pp. 455 ff.). Former employees of the CPI, such as Edward L. Bernays, found that they could make a living in public relations by applying to domestic issues their wartime talents for news promotion. Rather than send out handouts, as did the press agents of old, the postwar public relations specialists now conducted grass roots campaigns, based on specially created events and organizations (Bernays 1923; 1928). The development of commercial radio in the 1920s, together with the increased use of market research into the attitudes of consumers, rounded out the four corners of the American opinion industry. Commercial broadcasters now used research to identify programs of greatest popular appeal (Hurwitz 1983, pp. 97 ff.). Provided with an audience of unprecedented size, advertisers refined their appeals on the basis of insights into the consumer's mind supplied by market research surveys (Lockley 1950).

The new communication professionals were naturally concerned about assaults on their craft from a humanist, progressive coalition largely centered in the nation's universities. Convinced that their activities were beneficial to society, the professionals sought to show how their work was consistent with, even helpful to, democratic life. Central to the position of the professionals was the claim that propaganda was not only necessary for a complex society, but that the phenomenon benefited society by providing the material upon which public opinion could be based. Bernays, a public relations counselor who became the chief spokesman for the professional viewpoint, argued that propaganda would always exist "where leaders need to appeal to their constituencies" (1928, p. 109). Bernays emphasized that his own craft of public persuasion carried a positive social value in that it "brings to the public facts and ideas of social utility which would not so readily gain acceptance otherwise" (1923, p. 216). In this vein, Bruce Bliven (1926) enthused, "Let's Have More Propaganda!"— arguing that only the free circulation of opposing views would enable citizens to act intelligently. Bernays, too, offered "open competition" as the best social response to modern persuasion (1928, pp. 11–12).

While minimizing the alarms raised by humanists about the concentration of so much power in the hands of the new communication elite, the professionals did acknowledge the potential for abuses of persuasive power. The professionals suggested that they themselves could best handle such a danger through codes of professional practice. The notion that professionalism was the best solution to problems of propaganda was articulated by Ivy Lee, one of the earliest public relations practitioners, who admitted to only one danger of propaganda, namely its proclivity to hide its source. Contending that "failure to disclose the source of information" (1925, p. 23) was the sole social danger of propaganda, Lee suggested the solution of having newspaper editors insist upon knowing the sources of the material they considered for publication. Such disclosure would protect democracy, Lee believed, because the nation's readers would be able to sort through propaganda and decide what arguments were in their best interests (1925, p. 38).

Bernays, too, expressed confidence that professionalism could serve as a trusted guardian of a democracy influenced by propaganda. He presented the ethical persuader as occupying a crucial middle ground between the public and the special pleader, that is, the client of professional public relations. Describing public relations as an art of adjusting the client's view to that of the public, and the public's to the client, Bernays characterized modern persuasion as a two-way street in which the interests of both the client and the public were served. Contending that public relations professionals had, in fact, improved the responsiveness of business to the public interest, Bernays recommended ethical self-monitoring by communications professionals as the answer to potential abuses of the modern powers of social influence (1923, pp. 56–57, 215–17; 1928, pp. 62 ff.).

Since the 1920s, humanists have continued to question whether propaganda could actually serve two masters, that is, meet the needs of both the special pleader and the public. At a 1925 gathering of journalism teachers, a professor asked Ivy Lee whether it was "ethical for a publicity man to ever send anything to the papers for publication that he believes serves his client, but does not serve the reader." In replying, Lee (1925, pp. 36–38) stuck firmly to his view that revealing the source is the key issue in propaganda, and that readers would be able to decide for themselves what served their interests. Similary, in a public debate with Bernays on the question of "Does Propaganda Menace Democracy?" Ferdinand Lundberg took issue with Bernays' contention that "everybody in America is free to use propaganda." Lundberg asserted that propaganda could never be "freely" circulated, because the propaganda of ideas now required the vast resources available to social elites, groups that had shown their ability to act contrary to the public interest (Bernays and Lundberg 1938, p. 343). In recent years, the 1930s humanist critique is best echoed by Alfred McClung Lee (1973), who warns that intellectuals may become hired purveyors of socially dangerous positions, and Jacques Ellul (1965) who elaborates on how the noisy competition of propagandas creates a confusing blather that evokes apathy in receivers (pp. 254–57).

Whatever worries remain about the practice of modern propaganda, the absence of twentieth-century restraint on communication practitioners shows that American society has at least tacitly accepted the assurances of the professionals that propaganda does not menace democracy. Consistent with the view that disclosure affords protection, political action committees funnel ever-increasing monies into political campaigns, and efforts to equalize spending or paid television exposure by political candidates has won little support. There is at least some evidence that the nation has been served by reliance on the good will of professionals. If one compares today's journalism to that portrayed by such early propaganda analysts as Irwin, Sinclair, Lippmann, and Seldes, it is clear that the goal of the propaganda critics to purify the news has at least in part succeeded. Seldes (interview with author, May 12–13, 1984) notes the improvement and the corresponding irony of today's right-wing political attacks on journalism. But issues of alleged deficiencies in professional practice by agencies of the communication industry continue to surface, as shown by the long-standing controversy over the social ethics of violence in television programs (Rowland 1983). Under a system of professional self-policing, each generation will face anew the question of the extent to which the professionals are able to serve their own interests simultaneously with meeting the needs of their society.

THE SCIENTIFIC RESPONSE

In American higher education of the 1930s a third perspective on social influence, the scientific, emerged as humanists and social scientists increasingly differentiated themselves along the lines of historical-critical versus statistical-experimental scholarly methodologies. The researchers who viewed themselves as scientists of society began to perceive a conflict between critical, qualitative propaganda analysis and scientific, quantitative communication research. Communication scientists labored to develop a literature consciously separate from that of their humanist colleagues. Private foundations supported the diffusion of statistical-communication research in several fields of social science (Sproule 1987).

Harold D. Lasswell, the political scientist, is representative of the social researcher who forsook critical studies because of a growing belief that true knowledge about persuasion could be had only through quantitative methods (Lasswell and Leites 1949, pp. 40–52). With support of the Rockefeller Foundation, Lasswell became a pioneer in statistical content analysis. Lasswell, as well as other scientists of communication, increasingly treated propaganda as a neutral phenomenon whose nature and effects might be examined and objectively quantified. Academic researchers carried out laboratory experiments to examine the short-term effects of propaganda materials on audiences, and independent consultants developed for broadcasters and businesses the survey method of marketing research.

In addition to carrying the stigma of nonquantification, propaganda studies possessed a second characteristic prejudicial to their compatibility with new twentieth-century notions about social science. Usually containing either an explicit or implicit call for reform, propaganda analysis was rooted in the progressive ideology that called for new measures to enhance citizen participation in society. Proposals for social reform, however, were increasingly seen as nonacademic, according to the analogy being drawn between social and natural science research. The view that an interest in reforming the status quo rendered the researcher biased, and therefore unfit to conduct scientific research in persuasion, is shown in the case of psychologist Hadley Cantril. President of the Institute for Propaganda Analysis, Cantril was also in charge of securing renewal from the Rockefeller Foundation of a grant to Princeton University for quantitative research on the effects of radio. Sensing the conflict between his two academic hats, Cantril (1938) begged off from signing an article in the Institute's bulletin that compared the social organization of broadcasting in the United States, Britain, and Germany. Cantril believed that his connection to even an implicit questioning of the structure of American broadcasting would compromise his application for foundation-supported research. He was probably correct, for private foundations in the late 1930s were increasingly anxious to avoid connection with proposals for social change. Such reformist projects not only threatened the tax-exempt status of the foundations, but also tended to embroil the foundations in embarrassing social controversies (Sproule 1987).

The desire of the private foundations to avoid controversial social research was adroit given the increasing anticritical social atmosphere of the late 1930s. By the end of the decade, American opinion leaders were increasingly bothered by perceived threats from Europe's fascist and communist countries, as well as from the domestic supporters of those totalitarian ideologies. As Europe raced into war, the American social atmosphere changed from one of social self-criticism, prevalent during the early Depression years, to that of social solidarity. The onset of wartime mobilization gave statistical-experimental communication research a chance to prove its social utility at the same time that the new mood worked against critical inquiries into the aims and methods of special-interest groups. The scientific perspective on social influence was confirmed as distinct from its humanist parent during the war years. Beginning in 1941, Harold Lasswell set up a group, sponsored by the Library of Congress, to analyze Axis communications by means of statistical content analysis. At the same time, the Army established a research branch that brought in top statistical researchers to conduct surveys and experiments to aid the Army in training and general operations. The work of the Lasswell and Army research groups was chronicled in postwar books and helped establish statistical-experimental communication research as the legitimate approach to social influence in academic social science (Lasswell and Leites 1949; Stouffer et al. 1949).

Whereas the earlier academic propaganda studies had been reformist inquiries, the publications of the communication scholars characterized the researcher as a neutral observer. Whereas propaganda analysis critically scrutinized whose interests were served by a propaganda campaign, and what the persuasion portended for society, the communication researchers focused on quantifying the success of persuaders. During the postwar years, communication researchers touted their focus on measurable persuasive effect as providing reliable knowledge that could serve the needs of the nation's policymakers, as had been the case during World War II.

In eschewing the issues of social ethics favored by the humanist propaganda researchers, the position of the communication scientists agreed with the professional view that propaganda posed no social problem because of competition. Lasswell (1933, vol. 12, pp. 522–26) characterized propaganda as an amoral phenomenon that provided democratic leaders with an alternative to violence as a means to coordinate society for action. Given the social neutrality of propaganda, the proper role of the communication scientist was to provide apolitical, certified knowledge about persuasion that could help society's persuaders. Indexes of *Psychological Abstracts* show the postwar tendency to conduct social research under the more neutral rubrics of communication and information instead of the more value-laden term of propaganda. The humanistic approach to communication took a peripheral cultural position, existing on the fringes of social science, percolating in the modest revival of classical rhetoric in the field of speech, and gaining occasional visibility from works of such popular writers as Vance Packard (1957).

THE POLEMICAL RESPONSE

While the humanists, professionals, and scientists were forming and presenting their views, a fourth way of looking at techniques of twentieth-century social influence—the polemical—was organizing on the sidelines. To take a polemical approach to social influence is to argue that particular advocates or groups are discredited because they allegedly act as mere propagandists for an idea, individual, or group held in general disrepute. This form of propaganda analysis is characterized by its emphasis on attacking political opponents through weak proofs that establish an often vague connection between an opponent and a social devil term.

The use of propaganda analysis for partisan political purposes probably is inherent to a society characterized by the give and take of political attack. Sometimes it is easier to win points by casting aspersions on the source or mode of presentation of an argument than it is to rebut the argument itself. Certainly the use of polemical propaganda analysis can be seen in the efforts all World War I belligerents to discredit each other's persuasions. But as practiced in twentieth-century America, the first important instance of polemical propaganda analysis may be found in a 1918–1919 hearing by the Senate Judiciary Committee chaired by Senator Overman (U.S. Congress, Senate 1919). This first major polemical excursion into propaganda began as a response to reports of pro-German propaganda activity among brewers, German-American societies, and religious congregations. The foray into Bolshevik propaganda came later as a congressional response to the postwar Red Scare.

The Overman Committee hearings show certain similarities to humanistic propaganda analysis. The committee's endeavor to expose self-serving and behind-the-scenes influence by brewers and distillers was consistent with the interest and approach of mainstream propaganda analysts. But whereas the humanist writers tended to focus on the morality of the actual aims and techniques of propagandists, the Overman Committee report clearly exhibits the essential nature of the polemical response to propaganda—namely, the use of vague proofs to attack political enemies through innuendo and guilt by association.

In the report of the Overman Committee, the legal and moral right of German-Americans to support the cause of the Central Powers—before American entry into the war—is transformed into an ex post facto proof of disloyalty. The report intones that "It is in evidence before the committee that certain branches of the Lutheran Church were particularly active in defending the German cause during our period of neutrality, not only by means of religious teachings, but by work through the secular societies, especially the subsidiary organizations of the German-American Alliance" (1, pp. viii-ix). Mere advocacy of a position is here treated as constituting disloyalty because the advocate failed to anticipate that the cause supported might later be anathematized. The Overman Committee seemed unaware of the possibility that native American pro-German propagandists might legitimately have viewed their work as beneficial to the United States as, for instance, a help to avoiding entry into a costly war.

Beyond the ex post facto form of guilt by association, the Overman report shows a second way of discrediting prewar American advocacy of the German cause, in this case by connecting all pro-German advocacy to the propaganda and sabotage work of certain of Germany's agents. While the Overman Committee legitimately focused on the pre–1917 campaign of industrial sabotage orchestrated by Germany, the committee frequently connected the illegal activities to sincere and legitimate sympathy and public support by German-Americans for their ancestral land. Here advocacy of a cause by Americans is tarred by a blanket identification of such native propaganda with machinations of agents serving a foreign power. To the committee, any connection between the German Embassy and pro-German advocacy rendered all pro-German propaganda inherently illegitimate. No effort was made to distinguish links between German agents and Americans that might be indirect or unknown to the Americans from agreed-upon secret subsidies designed to further the ends of a foreign government. To the extent that the committee report further mixes propaganda activities by German agents with their work in sabotage of American plants and ships, the report unfairly links all forms of pro-German advocacy to clearly illegal acts. The Committee took the same loose analytic approach when dealing with Bolshevik propaganda and that by the domestic liquor industry.

In 1930, the U.S. House heeded the admonition of Congressman Hamilton Fish that another investigative response to propaganda, in this case pro-communist advocacy, was necessary. The Fish Committee hearings followed the basic pattern of political propaganda analysis established by the Overman report. Legitimate inquiry into clearly suspicious activities of domestic groups and foreign agents was freely mixed with efforts to discredit political opponents through innuendo and guilt by association. The Fish Committee heard from a large number of witnesses, mostly representatives of national patriotic societies, police officials, and school administrators, individuals inclined to provide rhetorical support for the Committee's purpose of rooting out leftist radicalism.

Representative of the hearings is the testimony of H. Ralph Burton, Washington attorney and counsel to the Daughters of the American Revolution. Burton estimated that some two million communists and communist sympathizers lurked in the United States, a figure obtained by summing membership of organizations which, Burton contended, "in one way or another, advocate the principles of the communists" (U.S. Congress, House 1930: Part I, 3, pp. 13–14). Included in Burton's net were all atheist and pacifist groups as well as those he believed taught "opposition to our national defense activities," since all allegedly contributed to "the same objective" of a general social breakdown. Not all the Representatives agreed completely with Burton; for instance, Carl Bachmann of West Virginia thought the estimate of two million was high given the total vote for communist candidates of around 15,000 in 1928. Nevertheless, testimony reflected the kind of vague guilt by association that the Fish Committee attracted and encouraged. In a hostile statement to the committee, Roger Baldwin (U.S. Congress, House 1930: Part I, 4, pp. 405–408) of the American Civil Liberties Union attacked the group for naively assuming that propaganda rather than social conditions caused revolution. Baldwin contended that the hearings had been dominated by hysterical and ignorant officials and professional patriots, and he charged that the investigation was but a rationalization for chairman Fish's stated desire for deportation laws and an end to trade with the USSR.

The pursuit of partisan political attack under the guise of propaganda analysis became institutionalized in the United States through the work of the House Un-American Activities Committee (HUAC). This committee was initially chartered in 1934 for a special investigation into pro-Nazi propaganda, under the leadership of John McCormack and Samuel Dickstein. The 1934 investigations generally emphasized such appropriate targets as the clearly illegal subversive work of the Silver Shirts—a domestic Nazi-style paramilitary organization—and the suspicious connections between domestic Nazi propaganda and the public relations firm of Byoir, Dickey, and Lancaster. However, the work of the committee did produce human casualties among persons, such as Ivy Lee, who were not directly linked to fascist propaganda. Lee was summoned to testify in executive session for his having accepted retainers to represent German trade interests. Although Lee evidently convinced the McCormack-Dickstein committee that he had neither directly advised the German government nor participated in German propaganda, the committee released to the press the Lee testimony, and Lee found himself the target of stories branding him as a Nazi adviser. Lee's biographer attributes Lee's untimely death of a brain tumor some months later to his anxiety over the reports (U.S. Congress, House 1934, pp. 175–93; Heibert 1966, pp. 286–310).

HUAC was reactivated in 1938 under the leadership of Congressman Martin Dies of Texas. Dies contended that his committee would take a "judicial attitude," require "specific proof," and avoid both smears and attacks of persons with whom he and the others disagreed (U.S. Congress, House 1938, vol. 1, pp. 2–3). However, the Dies committee quickly attained a reputation for flimsy political headline-hunting conducted under the guise of congressional inquiry. For instance, the committee attacked the work of the Consumers Union as un-American, ostensibly because CU opposed advertising; but evidently the scrutiny was motivated by a personal antipathy toward the Union by J. B. Matthews, Dies' chief investigator (Katz 1977, pp. 192–201). Similarly, Matthews' announcement that HUAC was conducting a theretofore unrevealed "investigation" of the Institute of Propaganda Analysis was clearly a political counterattack leading only to headlines instead of actual hearings (Sproule 1987).

Under Dies and his successors, HUAC became a permanent committee, examining propaganda and covert activities with relatively little regard for sound evidence and with heavy doses of political attack. When Senator Joseph McCarthy later honed polemical propaganda analysis to a fine art, this social response to modern communication became a high point in the American political landscape. With the passing of HUAC and McCarthy, the polemical perspective on propaganda has become less prominent. No longer institutionalized in a congressisonal committee, polemical propaganda criticism is now widely diffused in attacks by political groups on their opponents' advertising and media techniques. Further, as an alternative to academic media criticism, polemical propaganda analysis has become increasingly privatized in organization and respectable in operation. Two well-known right-wing vehicles of propaganda criticism, Accuracy in Media and Accuracy in Academia, are now joined by the new publication, *Propaganda Review,* which takes a more left-of-center perspective. While usually polemical in tone and purpose, the reports of such groups often show a close connection to humanistic criticism by conforming to reasonable standards of evidence and analysis.

In the 1920s and 1930s, four distinct perspectives on social influence emerged as humanist writers, professional propagandists, social scientists, and politicians offered alternative visions of how society should treat the phenomenon of modern persuasion. Greater recognition of the differences among the four social responses to propaganda will help today's writers and educators make sense of society's ever-ambiguous relationship to the voices of its media. What for example should be the proper mix of humanism, scientism, and professionalism in today's communication education? A relevant contemporary political question might be the predicted future nature of the U.S. government's office of disinformation as a humanist, scientific, professional, or polemical agency. As scholars and writers become more aware of the intellectual roots and recurring controversies of modern social influence, our culture will be better able to intelligently respond to its organizations of communication.

REFERENCES

Bernays, E. L. 1923. *Crystallizing Public Opinion.* New York: Boni and Liveright.
———. 1928. *Propaganda.* New York: Liveright.

Bernays, E. L., and F. Lundberg. 1938. Does Propaganda Menace Democracy? A debate. *Forum* 99:341–45.

Biddle, W. W. 1932. *Propaganda and Education*. New York: Teachers College, Columbia University.

Bliven, B. 1926. Let's Have More Propaganda! *World Tomorrow* 9 (December): 254–55.

Bourne, R. [1917] 1965. Twilight of Idols. In *The World of Randolph Bourne,* ed. L. Schlissel, pp. 191–203. New York: Dutton.

Bryce, J. 1899. *The American Commonwealth*. 3rd ed. 2 vols. New York: Macmillan.

Cantril, H. D. 1938. Letter to Clyde Miller, February 1. Papers of the Institute for Propaganda Analysis, privately held, Short Hills, N.J.

Chafee, Z. 1941. *Free Speech in the United States*. Cambridge, Mass.: Harvard University Press.

Dewey, J. 1918. The New Paternalism. *New Republic* 17 (December 21): 216–17.

Ellul, J. 1965. *Propaganda*. New York: Knopf.

Gibbs, P. 1915. *The Soul of the War*. London: Hinemann.

———. 1920. *Now It Can Be Told*. New York: Harper & Brothers.

Goldman, E. 1966. *Redezvous with Destiny*. New York: Knopf.

Hiebert, R. E. 1966. *Courtier to the Crowd*. Ames: Iowa State University Press.

Hurwitz, D. L. 1983. Broadcast Ratings. Ph.D. dissertation, University of Illinois.

Irwin, W. 1919. "An Age of Lies." *Sunset* 43 (December): 23–25, 54, 56.

———. 1935 [?]. Let's Not be Suckers Again. Typescript, Box 1. Papers of Will Irwin, Hoover Institution Archives, Stanford, California.

———. 1936. *Propaganda and the News*. New York: Whittlesey.

Katz, N. D. 1977. Consumers Union: The Movement and the Magazine. Ph.D. dissertation, Rutgers University.

Lasswell, H. D. 1933. Propaganda. In *Encyclopaedia of the Social Sciences*. Vol. 12, ed. E. R. A. Seligman, pp. 521–28. New York: Macmillan.

Lasswell, H. D., and N. Leites. 1949. *Language of Politics*. Cambridge, Mass.: M.I.T. Press.

Lee, A. Mc. [1937] 1973. *The Daily Newspaper in America*. New York: Octagon.

———. 1973. *Toward Humanist Sociology*. Englewood Cliffs, N.J.: Prentice-Hall.

Lee, I. L. 1925. *Publicity*. New York: Industries Publishing.

Lippmann, W. 1922. *Pubic Opinion*. New York: Macmillan.

Lippmann W., and C. Merz. 1920. A Test of the News. *New Republic,* supplement, 23 (August 4): 1–42.

Lockley, L. C. 1950. "Notes on the History of Marketing Research." *Journal of Marketing* 14:733–36.

McGinniss, J. 1969. *The Selling of the President 1968*. New York: Trident.

Mock, J. R., and C. Larson. 1939. *Words that Won the War*. Princeton, N.J.: Princeton University Press.

National Education Association. 1929. *Report of the Committees on Propaganda in the Schools*. N.p.

Packard, V. 1957. *The Hidden Persuaders*. New York: David McKay.

Ponsonby, A. 1928. *Falsehood in War-Time*. New York: Dutton.

Rowland, W. D. 1983. *The Politics of TV Violence*. Beverly Hills, Calif.: Sage.

Seldes, G. 1929. *You Can't Print That!* Garden City, N.Y.: Garden City.

Seligman, E. R. A. 1930. "Propaganda by Public Utility Corporations." *Bulletin of the American Association of University Professors* 16:349–68.

Sinclair, U. [1920] 1936. *The Brass Check*. Rev. ed. New York: Albert and Charles Boni.

Sproule, J. M. 1987. Propaganda Studies in American Social Science: The Rise and Fall of the Critical Paradigm. *Quarterly Journal of Speech* 73:60–78.

Stouffer, S., E. A. Suchman, L. C. DeVinney, S. A. Star, and R. M. Williams, Jr. 1949. *The American Soldier*. 2 vols. Princeton, N.J.: Princeton University Press.

U.S. Congress, House. 1930. Special Committee to Investigate Communist Activities in the United States. *Investigation of Communist Propaganda*. 71st Cong., 2d sess. 5 parts.

U.S. Congress, House. 1934. Special Committee on Un-American Activities. *Investigation of Nazi Propaganda Activities and Investigation of Certain Other Propaganda Activities*. 73rd Cong., 2d sess.

U.S. Congress, House. 1938. Special Committee on Un-American Activities. *Investigation of Un-American Propaganda Activities in the United States*. 75th Cong., 3d sess.

U.S. Congress, Senate. 1919. Subcommittee of the Judiciary Committee. *Brewing and Liquor Interests and German and Bolshevik Propaganda*. 66th Cong., 1st sess. 3 vols.

Vaughn, S. 1980. *Holding Fast the Inner Lines*. Chapel Hill: University of North Carolina Press.

Viereck, G. S. 1930. *Spreading Germs of Hate*. New York: Liveright.

Walker, S. 1927. Men of Vision. *American Mercury* 10 (January): 89–93.

Wise, D. 1973. *The Politics of Lying*. New York: Vintage.

Wohlforth, R. 1930. Catch 'em Young—Teach 'em Rough. *New Republic* 33 (October 22):257–58.

2 Propaganda and Order in Modern Society

J. Fred MacDonald

Propaganda is an omnipresent, intrusive aspect of modern life. Massive in its presumptions and purposes, propaganda has made the present century a time of unprecedented human direction. Never have so many been so controlled by so few. While there may be little flattery in being called a propagandist, a multitude of such professionals have employed imbalanced argumentation, dishonesty, disinformation, exaggeration, or whatever is necessary to maneuver the broad audience toward desired points of view. Ironically, whether one considers it abhorrent deceit or benign necessity, propaganda has played—and continues to play—a constructive role in contemporary society.

The word propaganda quickly conjures up stereotyped images of distorted information being fed for partisan advantage to ignorant, gullible people. In the popular interpretation, propaganda is exploitative lying, calculated deception leading individuals to perfidy and nations to wickedness. In particular, it is perceived as the technique of "the enemy" that is especially evident to citizens in the liberal-democratic West in the record of Communist and Fascist communication. From Lenin's credo that "truth" must be shaped to serve political ends, to the "Big Lie" espoused so openly by Dr. Josef Goebbels, propaganda is popularly understood as the perverse tool of dangerous leaders seeking to indoctrinate through methodologies dependent upon prevarication.

Such an interpretation possesses elements of truth. Propaganda is manipulative and sometimes deceitful. Propaganda does seek predetermined reaction in the mass audience, and it is frequently predicated on the philosophy that ends justify means. Moreover, in an era of myriad forms of electronic communication—where amoral technology facilitates indoctrination and catalyzes desired response, where mass audiences can be assembled quickly, where social-political-economic-cultural-intellectual elites can "inform" millions efficiently and authoritatively—propaganda is an omnipresent and seductive reality. However, perhaps because it is also an emotional reality, the popular interpretation fails to include much that is fundamental to understanding the social function of propaganda.

Stripped of stereotyped negative connotations, propaganda is little more than the principal methodology of persuasion operative in a society that is technological, urban, and populous. What seems obvious in one-party authoritarian states is only more subtle in liberal-democratic nations. Indeed, propaganda is an integral part of all modern civilizations. In Western nations there may be rivalrous lines of propaganda locked in competition for social acceptance, political loyalty, or customer approval; but such situations may be no less calculated in their intent than mass communication in an autocratic regime where reality is often shaped to fit a monolithic party line. In authoritarian states the principal function of propaganda is to legitimize and reinforce the power of the ruling elite; in democratic regimes propaganda functions primarily to convince and manipulate. In either political context, however, propaganda plays a critical role in the preservation of order.

In the so-called "Free World" (a manipulative, self-congratulatory term originated by those in the anticommunist West to denigrate their competition behind the East European "Iron Curtain" and the East Asian "Bamboo Curtain"), an aspirant for political office citing statistics—whether accurate or not—to support his own candidacy is a propagandist. A clergyman exhorting the heavens to cast out Satan and reorient government toward Christian moral goals is propagandizing. Propaganda is in children's TV cartoons where muscular superheroes battle intergalactic oppressors in the name of a commonly understood definition of "justice." It exists in bourgeois detective stories which continually preach that "crime doesn't pay" and that the forces of law and order are working successfully to protect life, liberty, and private property. Even commercial advertisements are propagandistic: interpretive communications from the well-honed propaganda factories that advertising agencies have become. It is no coincidence that in the Spanish-speaking world the word for advertisement is "propaganda."

In the modern world all mass communication is persuasive. Here choices between politically permissible points of view constitute public opinion; and social freedom, democracy, dictatorship, and totalitarianism are themselves value-laden terms by which to measure the range of propagandistic diversity tolerated with a particular state. The phenomena usually recognized as propaganda—the heavy-handed film, posters, radio, television, and mass publications of Communists and Fascists—are little more than confrontational expressions of rivalrous persuasions, abrasively obvious in the way in which their self-serving points of view contrast with perceived objective realities in liberal-democratic states.

Manipulating the traditions and historic commonalities within a nation, propaganda reiterates mutually respected values, skews events and phenomena to harmonize with the national viewpoint, and reaffirms the correctness of national policies and goals. Even when contentious major political parties seek the support of the electorate, it amounts to competition among varying sociopolitical interpretations, each communicated assuringly through party propaganda. The citizen here is left to decide which partisan "truth" to accept.

The hymns to the secular state that are national anthems, required pledges of allegiance to the state, enshrined treasured artifacts, holidays commemorating national heroes—these are solemn aspects of present-day existence. They bind citizens to the "purpose" or "mission" of the nation. They are also propagandistic rituals that shape the individual and forge a common citizenship. From public education which takes children from parents and private institutions in order to indoctrinate them in verities approved by government, to the national popular culture which subverts regionalism and entertainingly disseminates acceptable points of view, propaganda readies the individual for citizenship in the national polity—and reaffirms constantly the essential rectitude of that harmonious relationship.

Not only does propaganda amalgamate the individual with the modern state, it defines for the citizen the place of his or her state in the world. Certainly, language differences help demarcate and isolate the individual within a particular sociopolitical arrangement. Traveling diagonally from one corner of Europe to another, for example, a voyager may pass through many contiguous states—Denmark, the Netherlands, Germany, Poland, Czechoslovakia, Hungary, Yugoslavia, Rumania, Bulgaria, Greece, Turkey—set apart from one another by different languages.

Not only is each state distinguished from its neighbors by exoteric languages, but over time particularized national existence has created idiosyncratic points of view which shape the ways in which individual states and their citizens understand themselves and the rest of the world. Each nation possesses a historic corpus of attitudes, beliefs, and material interests through which it explains and legitimizes its existence. Whether based upon Marx or Mohammed, Buddha, Abraham, or Christ, apartheid, socialism, bourgeois democracy, or military authority, all modern states speak from the framework of their distinct mind note.

In a fashion which is both self-defensive and self-congratulatory, leadership in each contemporary political state seeks to communicate (consciously or unconsciously) its particular understanding in terms conforming to its national perspective. Although most of the world saw it as naked aggression, the Japanese in the 1930s understood their military expansion into East Asia as divinely sanctioned and honorable. In the Soviet Union, "news" from the West is considered distortion and subterfuge unless it meshes with the interpretation of the state.

Milton Mayer (1955) has described how citizens of National Socialist Germany never felt themselves to be tyrannized victims of Nazi totalitarianism; instead, they thought they were free. In the United States, two multimillion-dollar sports franchises compete in four to seven baseball games every October and the winner is proclaimed champion of the *world*. While varying in their significance, such examples indicate ways in which national perspectives often do not translate as truth outside the nation of origin.

Propaganda has deep historical roots. While some scholars have traced persuasive communication as far back as the biblical temptation of Adam by Eve, the institutionalized indoctrination that is modern propaganda had its earliest manifestation in the *Congregation de propaganda fide* created in the seventeenth century by Pope Gregory XV. Coming late in the Counter-Reformation, this Congregation for the Propagation of the Faith was an official bureau of the Church, the purpose of which was to spread Roman Catholicism—its theology, social institutions, and political power—throughout the world. More significantly, through this office the Church introduced to Western politics the model of the bureaucratic organization intent upon the premeditated and intensive persuasion of a large population toward a predetermined conviction.

From the prototype has developed the present reality of pervasive propaganda—whether organized by government or competitive private interests—as integral to modernity. In fact, such propaganda is not without important social function. This is a condition born of the interplay of historical, industrial-technological, and cultural forces.

HISTORICAL DEVELOPMENTS

The rise of the commoner, the "mass man," to power in the twentieth century undermined traditional institutions of social control. Tied to earlier economic and political realities, these institutions were intricate, agrarian-based arrangements that subjugated sizable numbers—indeed, the vast majority of the population—and carefully regulated the relative freedom of a small ruling minority.

From the Urals to the Atlantic, order in Europe was maintained through traditional social prescriptions. In Tsarist Russia, serfdom committed most of the citizenry to forms of manorial servitude, while an elite of old-nobility boyars, Christian church leaders, and eventually a landed gentry contended for shares of power in a society crowned historically with an aristocracy of immense authority. In Western Europe, the agricultural subordination of the peasantry was enhanced through an industrial-technological revolution whose material achievements were created by a new, but subjugated and exploited urban working class.

In accepting Western systems as a blueprint for its industrial future, Japan in the mid-nineteenth century quickly subverted traditional agrarian institutions and weakened centuries of accepted social controls. Such rapid transition to technological modernity created an expanding new social class that was urban and industrial and in need of regulation appropriate to the new society.

One of the most oppressive forms of agrarian social control flourished in the United States where, for more than three centuries, legal slavery turned millions of people of African ancestry into possessions of propertied Caucasians. Strategically, such regulation ended only as Northern industrialism with no need for slave labor eroded the agrarian ascendancy vital for the perpetuation of involutary servitude. Tactically, this slavery ended because in waging civil war against the slave-holding South the industrial North needed black troops. As might be anticipated, emancipation of blacks into a hostile white world led quickly to alternative forms of repressive social regulation ranging from official Jim Crow laws to murderous vigilantism practiced by whites.

Although in preindustrial times these arrangements were more or less oppressive, they exercised social control. Long-accepted formulas—institutionalized loyalty commanded by divine-right monarchy; feudal legacies rigidly situating each person within the social scheme; approved religion urging social passivity and promising personal improvement in an afterlife; plantation owners and overseers whose word had the force of law; even the quiet resignation of the oppressed—created, maintained, and justified domestic order. Obedience in these societies came not from constant indoctrination but from conditioned popular acceptance of hierarchy and regimentation, and adaptation to the relative political impotence of the average citizen.

When kings or emperors made war, and the "one, true" Church sanctified the battle, dutiful foot soldiers battled out of a loyalty to majesty as well as to prescriptive social traditions. Agrarian workers needed no persuading to buy from the company store or its equivalent. Slaves usually required little specialized convincing to accept their lot. Certainly, there were instances of definance and even rebellion, but the force of tradition could always be reinforced by the force of arms; and soldiers and serfs, citizens and slaves could even be executed under law were their insubordinations sufficiently flagrant. Even the new class of industrial workers could be disciplined—from summary discharge to arrest, imprisonment, and even execution by established police systems—should its private grumblings become public recalcitrance or organized resistance.

In the twentieth century, however, Western humanity has faced a profound social challenge. In an age of expansive democratic arrangements, where the common man has come to power under the auspices of "isms," there has been perforce an acute necessity for fashioning new and relevant means of establishing control and predictability. Rootless in his usurpation of power, and so much larger in numbers than those he replaced, mass man has had to convince himself and others—and it is an ongoing process accomplished through propaganda—that his modern constructs are best. Nothing less than the social, political, and economic organization of modern life is held together through this propaganda.

For the industrial world in flux, this has been an era of democratic excess. Emerging from centuries of oppressive order, the generic "mass man" of the present has slipped suddenly from the limitations and obligations imposed by tradition, only to embrace with scant preparation a social freedom demanding stability and sophisticated self-regulation in order to survive. In 1930 the Spanish critic Jose Ortega y Gasset limned this development when he wrote in *The Revolt of the Masses* ([1930] 1961, pp. 102–03):

Now, the mass-peoples have decided to consider as bankrupt that system of standards which European civilization implies, but as they are incapable of creating others, they do not know what to do, and to pass the time they kick up their heels and stand on their heads. Such is the first consequence which follows when there ceases to be in the world anyone who rules; the rest, when they break into rebellion, are left without a task to perform, without a programme of life.

Elitist, conservative, and "cultured," Ortega denounced the barbarous potentialities of democratic man freshly loosened via world war and social revolution. He saw it especially in destructive Fascism which in Italy sprang politically from the moral and economic bankruptcy of bourgeois Italian republicanism—but aesthetically from those Futurist artists of the century's first decade who proclaimed their intoxication with speed and emotion and their disdain for order and rationalism.

As harbingers of the excesses of mass man, the Futurists proclaimed the victory of action over reason. Museums and academies were of the old and were to be undermined, smashed, flooded, or incinerated. This was the age of the new and young and nihilistic—a time to appreciate the roar of motors, the heat of raging furnaces, and "the beauty of speed" epitomized in the racing automobile "with its hood adorned with great tubes like serpents with exploding breath . . . [for] a racing motor car which seems to run on machine-gun fire is more beautiful than the Winged Victory of Samothrace."

Above all the Futurists, as would their Fascist progeny, glorified military combat. War, wrote the painter Filippo Tommaso Marinetti in 1909, was "the only health giver of the world—militarism, patriotism, the destructive arm of the Anarchist, the beautiful Ideas that kill, the contempt for women" (Cited in Coates and White 1970, vol. 2, pp. 340–41).

There were other, less spiritual signs of the democratization of Western society. Social revolution in Tsarist Russia destroyed the autocracy legitimate for centuries. As various political factions sought to establish order and justify their own preeminence, the result was a vicious civil war and decades of Communist Party purges resulting in the contemporary Soviet authoritarian state.

The emergence of an Imperial Japan that was capitalistic, technological, and expansionist further eroded preindustrial social controls and produced an era of military autocracy and international aggression for which Japanese citizens—and much of the world—paid dearly in World War II. And in the United States concerns over an unpredictable future led Caucasian males to resist until 1920 the right of white American women to participate in federal elections. And well into the second half of the twentieth century, both sexes of whites resisted the de facto enfranchisement of African-Americans and other racial minorities.

Democratic mass man reached his nadir in Adolf Hitler and the National Socialism of interwar Germany. An art-school dropout and military underachiever, Hitler ruled a nation which in an earlier order had produced the likes of Beethoven, Hesse, and Goethe, Frederick the Great and von Clausewitz. Now, in the name of a mythic race whose physical characteristics neither he nor his henchmen possessed, this vulgar man turned racial hatred into national policy. Brutality became patriotism, and nationalism—so devoutly embraced by democratic humanity as a substitute for the traditions of Church, Monarchy, and Empire—became justification for unprecedented destruction of human life.

Propaganda as a social adhesive must be understood within the context of the emancipation of the masses. Whether emanating from the state or business corporation, the church, school, voluntary organization, or the like, propaganda is the persuasive communication directing mass man. Whether in Imperial Japan or Nazi Germany, a Marxist-Leninist Soviet Union or a Democrat-Republican United States, mass man learns from it and defines himself through it. He is moved to conform via propaganda, and he seldom makes decisions without having been approached through it.

Certainly, in the liberal-democratic states, propaganda is the rhetoric of modern politics, stirring emotions to direct public opinion. Voting citizens from Canada, France, Japan, the United States, and elsewhere regularly encountered their governmental leaders "selling" themselves on television—seeking the right physical appearance, the correct phrase, the proper tone to ensure popular acceptance of their programs. Public relations, a modern fine art, has become a critical aspect of all levels of political process. The advertising agency, too, has emerged as a vital part of modern sociopolitical organization.

In the United States, for example, an effective advertising agency is now mandatory for any political campaign. Dwight Eisenhower discovered the importance of the ad agency when in 1952, as the first presidential candidate in U.S. history to peddle himself via television spots, he employed Batten, Barton, Durstine & Osborn to convince the electorate. In 1960 Kennedy hired Guild, Bascom & Bonfigli to help in the struggle against Richard Nixon. In 1964 Lyndon Johnson used manipulative commercials from Doyle Dane Bernbach while Barry Goldwater used those fabricated by Erwin Wasey, Ruthraff and Ryan, Inc. Such is the nature of propaganda that advertising personnel responsible for promoting fried chicken, automobiles, beer, and perfume now hawk U.S. political candidates to a constituency well used to drawing personal conclusions based on the truth as propounded in 30- or 60-second television spots. The French scholar Jean-Paul Gourévitch (1986, p. 35) termed this reality of government by television a "télécratie" or teleocracy, an appropriate neologism that appreciates the effectiveness of television as a medium of propaganda.

Mass man is educated and controlled through propaganda. His civic values are filtered through school boards, party committees, state legislatures, courts of law, and other forums intending to preserve orthodoxy. The communications media through which daily he is informed—whether via formal news broadcasts or through the many formats of popular entertainment—frame the world to complement the historic national understanding that he has learned. Little he usually hears, sees, or reads, has not been prepared by experts committed to the system and familiar with its "language."

While degrees of dissent may be permitted within the various national arrangements, true radicals are always in the minority. Their critiques are either suppressed by the authorities or they are nationally disdained as threatening curiosities or unpatriotic subversions. For a regime to allow revolutionaries unfettered access to the mass media is for that regime to surrender its propaganda monopoly and, therefore, part of its legitimacy.

INDUSTRIAL-TECHNOLOGICAL DEVELOPMENT

While historical developments account for the emancipation of the mass man and the need for new levers to ensure obedience and predictability, the motive force driving such change has been modern industrial-technological development. It has precipitated structural revolution in traditional societies and has made possible the success of propaganda as an effective means of necessary social control. In this regard, significant events of political import such as the Emancipation Proclamation, the Great War of 1914–18 with its subsequent sociopolitical revolutions, and the decolonization movement in the decades after World War II merely delivered obvious final blows toppling anachronistic arrangements and leaving mass man to fend for himself.

The Industrial Revolution that began in eighteenth-century Western Europe radically altered the relationship between citizen and state. Abandoning the countryside for futures in burgeoning industrial cities, laborers found traditional agrarian values unsuitable for their new needs. New grievances were articulated in innovative philosophies as diverse as liberalism, democracy, republicanism, trade unionism, Marxism, Marxism-Leninism, anarchism, anarcho-syndicalism, Fascism, and National Socialism. Even established institutions, from the Church to the State, addressed the pressing new social concerns, preferring, at best, reformist legislation and moral pronouncement to the more passionate appeals for armed upheaval.

Importantly, the industrial-technological revolution which created the necessity for political change also produced the means of preserving social stability during and after such transition. The delivery of mass propaganda could never have been effective were it not for the perfection of the technology of mass media and communication. Electrification in general, but specific developments such as wireless broadcasting, phonography, photographic reproduction, facsimile; plus the telephone, tape recorder, and especially television—the medium described by screenwriter Paddy Chayefsky in his cinematic masterpiece *Network* as "the most awesome goddamn propaganda force in the whole godless world"—have made possible effective communication between a single source and a mass audience.

Once mass man was organized and open to centralized persuasion, propaganda became the rhetoric of the state. Whether it was sublime actors like Adolf Hitler and Franklin D. Roosevelt using radio to form and then spark national will—or Winston Churchill in film, print, or broadcast motivating the anti-Axis struggle; or, less effectively, Ronald and Nancy Reagan on American television urging a war against illegal narcotics—whatever the source, the partisan message was propagated quickly, widely, and convincingly.

It is significant, moreover, that the widespread availablity of modern communication technology has made possible in the nonindustrial world a quicker movement toward institutions of mass control than was the case in the West. With transistor radios, picture magazines, computers, and videocassette recorders, subversive ideas cross borders where traditional controls are still decentralized and weak. The reactionary revolution of the Ayatollah Khomeni was primarily a struggle by traditional religious forces against influential foreign values entering Iran with the importation of Western industrialization. Where most technologically advanced nations have been strong enough to resist foreign encroachment into their culture and social tradition, Western styles and perspectives propagate an alluring subterfuge that challenges classical values in much of the preindustrial Third World.

Mass communication technology has resulted in a quantum leap in mass controllability. Where only a century ago Dostoevsky marveled at the social control possible through the miracles and mysteries manipulated by the Christian Church, in the mid-twentieth century Aldous Huxley and George Orwell described in the modern totalitarian state a technology of social control with immensely more powerful means of creating and ensuring orthodoxy.

Through its control of the flow of public ideas and information via the mass media, the modern state to one degree or another sets the national agenda and delimits the participation of the citizenry in the realization of that agenda. In the Soviet Union, control of all media is straightforwardly governmental. In the United States, capitalistic corporations with close economic, ideological, and personal ties to government possess and operate the media of mass communication subject to governmental regulations. And in the United Kingdom there exists a mix of libel laws restricting print, indirect government ownership in the case of the British Broadcasting Corporation, and government-regulated private broadcasting.

In all instances, however, there is an orthodoxy to be respected, and laws and traditions restrict the communication of the full range of alternative perspectives on the truth. Whether it be a commissar warning against deviation from the party line, or an American television executive ignoring political malcontents because their ideas are threateningly radical—or worse yet, boorish—every system exerts controls over access to its mass media, controls whose propagandistic values are evident.

CULTURAL DEVELOPMENT

The development of popular culture is a direct result of the emergence of mass man and the technologies of mass communication. As the culture of the multitude, popular culture is necessarily of, by, and for the average. Substantially, popular culture is little more than traditional folk art produced and delivered to the mass audience. It is no coincidence, therefore, that popular culture has been the substance in which propaganda has flourished.

It would be easy to produce a list of examples illustrating the highpoints of statist propaganda in popular culture. From the war songs of Tin Pan Alley in 1917–18, to the films of Leni Riefenstahl in the 1930s, to the contemporary Soviet exploitation of sports for political glorification, states have exploited popular culture to impress the world with the vitality of their systems and to convince their own citizens of the strength and rectitude of their respective regimes. But propaganda is communicated by all forms of popular culture and these need not be as obvious as "Over There," *Triumph of the Will,* or Olga Korbut.

Just as folk tales dating beyond the time of Aesop conveyed value-laden morals, so too is relevant sociopolitical communication an integral part of popular culture. In the United States—the premier producer of mass entertainment appreciated throughout the world—the genres which have amused audiences for years have also propagandized a distinct sociopolitical philosophy.

In some cases, the propaganda from Hollywood was related to a specific need in time. In the 1930s, musicals danced and sang away the Depression; social dramas underscored the necessity for human perseverance; crime stories taught that outlawry would end inevitably in painful reformation, imprisonment, or death; and love stories suggested that economic hard times could be survived with enough kisses and hugs.

Similarly, in the early 1940s, war dramas showed heroic Yanks fighting to protect loved ones. While they might die on celluloid to defend abstract notions of freedom and justice, in person Hollywood stars lent their talents to raising public morale and defense dollars.

Other genres of entertainment have transcended time and continued to propagate their didactic messages well after their first appearances. No type of American entertainment has been more enduring or manipulative than the Western. Whether in literature, film, popular music, radio, or television, in the United States the Western has communicated a set of values that are deeply patriotic. In the Western, brave white forefathers settle the wilderness, defeat anarchistic outlaws, tame unruly aboriginals, and transplant ever-westward the civilized values shared by the audience as the common national perspective. The Western projects a past that never happened that way; its goal is not historical reconstruction, but the shaping of the past to appeal to the present.

Capitalists might find justification in the initiative and individuality demonstrated by Western heroes. Patriots could enjoy the image of selfless American forefathers evident in the genre. Children could shape their lives according to the moral code of cowboy champions. And adults facing personal or national calamity could take courage in the invincibility suggested by these stories of nationalistic pioneers who, themselves, overcame grave threats to expand and protect the American Eden.

By the late 1950s, fully one-quarter of all sound movies made in the United States had been Westerns. Whether they were B Westerns or first-rate productions, these films communicated a sociopolitical value system to mass audiences locked in Depression, World War, then an aggressive new role in a postwar East-West rivalry. On television by the late 1950s, moreover, the Western blossomed again as the first choice in entertainment by Americans locked in a cold war with a communist adversary.

This national preoccupation with the Western seemed to reach its culmination in two separate, but related, events: the Vietnam War in which those trained by countless hours of cowboy mythology delivered via the mass media went again into the wilderness to save the good guys from those outlaws who would take over their towns and destroy their freedom; and in the awarding in 1980 of the Presidential Medal of Freedom to John

Wayne, the movie actor whose roles in Western motion pictures projected an ennobling image of the selfless common man whose altruism in assisting the downtrodden was matched only by his faith in the mythic American way of life. As the cultural historian Loren Baritz has described it, these themes came together frequently on the battlegrounds of Southeast Asia (1985, pp. 51–52):

It is astonishing how often American GIs in Vietnam approvingly referred to John Wayne, not as a movie star, but as a model and a standard. Everyone in Vietnam called dangerous areas Indian country. Paraphrasing a bit of Americana, some GIs painted on their flak jackets THE ONLY GOOD INDIAN IS A DEAD ONE. They called their Vietnamese scouts Kit Carsons. These nineteen-year-old Americans, brought up on World War II movies and Westerns, walking through the jungle, armed to the teeth, searching for an invisible enemy who knew the wilderness better than they did, could hardly miss these connections. One after another said, at some point, something like "Hey, this is just like a movie."

While this inquiry has focused principally on the propaganda which binds citizen to society and state, and state to the community of nations, this does not suggest that propaganda is limited to these relationships. Indeed, modern social life is replete with propaganda at all levels of social interaction. From the commercials for consumer products that occupy much broadcasting time and cover subway stations, public buses, taxicabs, and highway billboards, to government health directives and political speeches delivered via the mass media, the average citizen in the industrialized world—and, particularly, in the Western industrialized world—is bombarded by contrastive points of view, each claiming to be true, each seeking acceptance. Today, propaganda, itself, has become a pervasive, vital industry.

Historically, propaganda has been the modern response to the social-political-economic reevaluations that took place in the twentieth century. It has made sustained order possible in mass society. Through its power of persuasion, propaganda has offered the method by which to reorganize, consolidate, and govern. And via its ability to condition, it has forged in each political arrangement a stabilizing consensus.

Certainly, propaganda has proved to be an imperfect and sometimes reprehensible mechanism of control. It often has produced results that have been physically and morally disastrous. But once able to prescribe and justify what it prescribed, propaganda has afforded new leaders a necessary mechanism for human management. Despite the controversy it has engendered, propaganda has been strategic to the survival of mass man and the civilization he now rules.

REFERENCES

Baritz, L. 1985. *Backfire: A History of How American Culture Led Us into Vietnam and Made Us Fight the Way We Did*. New York: Morrow.

Coates, W. H., and H. V. White. 1970. *The Ordeal of Liberal Humanism. An Intellectual History of Western Europe*. Vol. 2. New York: McGraw-Hill.

Gourévitch, J.-P. 1986. *La politique et ses images*. Paris: Mediatheque Edilig.

Mayer, M. 1955. *They Thought They Were Free. The Germans 1933–1945*. Chicago: University of Chicago Press.

Ortega y Gasset, J. [1903] 1961. *The Revolt of the Masses*. London: Unwin.

3 Western and Totalitarian Views of Propaganda

Randall L. Bytwerk

In August 1940, during Britain's gravest peril, a *Punch* cartoon portrayed three phlegmatic Britains in a pub, two patrons and the publican, listening to Radio Berlin announce: " . . . meanwhile, in Britain, the entire population, faced by the threat of invasion, has been flung into a state of complete panic. . . . " (Balfour 1979, frontpiece). A cartoon of like ilk could never have appeared in Hitler's Germany, where listening to foreign radio stations was a serious offense, sometimes punished by death.

In 1985 the United States spent about $146 million for Voice of America and Radio Liberty broadcasts to the Soviet Union and Eastern Europe. The Soviets spent an estimated $300 million jamming those broadcasts (Harper's index 1986, p. 11). Jamming of Western broadcasts has now ceased, but the transmitters as yet have not been dismantled. Although Americans familiar with the scope of Radio Moscow's activity sometimes view with alarm, no one has seriously proposed imitating Soviet jamming.

These two examples illustrate one of many differences between democratic and totalitarian propaganda. Whether Marxist or fascist, totalitarian propagandists fear the power of the enemy's propaganda more than do their democratic colleagues.

There are other differences, differences to some so sizeable that the term "propaganda" loses its defining power if applied to such disparate phenomena. Jacques Ellul's definition of propaganda (1965, p. 61), a wide one, seems to some so all-encompassing that everything becomes propaganda. But if he is correct in maintaining that there are essential similarities between all forms of modern propaganda, a broad definition is appropriate.

Ellul's argument is partially one of result: Forms of modern communication which have the same result are propaganda, even if their underlying theories are substantially different. Thus, the title of his book would better be translated *Propagandas,* a plural that French allows more readily than English. In classic Ellulian prose, he asserts: "The means employed to spread democratic ideas make the citizen, psychologically, a totalitarian man. The only difference between him and a Nazi is that he is 'a totalitarian man with democratic convictions', but those convictions do not change his behavior in the least" (1965, p. 256).

To demonstrate that is no small task; Ellul does not quite succeed in his own extensive discussions of the subject. I do not propose to do it here either. I do intend to examine some differences between democratic and totalitarian propaganda, and to see how those differences influence the respective views of domestic and foreign propaganda. With a clearer view of how propaganda is seen from differing perspectives, I think Ellul's broad definition of propaganda becomes more defensible.

THE TOTALITARIAN PERSPECTIVE

Although the Nazis and Marxists are sometimes thought to make the same kind of propaganda—and although there are striking similarities—their propagandas display substantial differences, differences that it is unwise to ignore, as Germany's Chancellor Kohl discovered when in 1986 he compared Gorbachev to Goebbels, observing that both were experts at public relations ("Ich bin von . . . " 1986, p. 19). The resulting international discussion was lively.

Hitler's discussion of propaganda in *Mein Kampf* is blunt, displaying no high regard for the intellectual abilities of the masses. A familiar passage, for example, asserts (1943, p. 180):

All propaganda must be popular and its intellectual level must be adjusted to the most limited intelligence among those it is addressed to. Consequently, the greater the mass it is intended to reach, the lower its purely intellectual level will have to be. . . . The art of propaganda lies in understanding the emotional ideas of the great masses and finding, through a psychologically correct form, the way to the attention and thence to the heart of the broad masses.

A key principle of Nazi propaganda was emotional appeal. Since it was most important to get the basic ideas across, propaganda had to be flexible, able to say one thing in the city and another in the country, as Goebbels put it.

Eugen Hadamovsky, one of the few Nazi theorists, defines propaganda as "the will to power" (1933, p. 10). Although he adds that it must always be subsidiary to an idea, Nazi ideas clearly are not as developed as Marxist-

Leninist theory. In the same way, propaganda was—from the Nazi perspective—far more an art than a science. Granted, there were basic principles one had to know, but beyond a certain point, truly effective propaganda depended on the inborn ability of a genuis, not the abilities of a scientist. The Nazi literature on propaganda stresses technique rather than theory.

Information must then be carefully controlled, since clever enemy propaganda can easily deceive the masses. From the Nazi perspective, it was proper to conceal information or prohibit listening to foreign broadcasts, since the information, even if accurate, could mislead the readily misleadable masses.

It was also very important to understand public opinion. Goebbels gives remarkable space in his diaries to worries about how to deal with public reactions to the latest rationing measures, or to bombing raids, or to antismoking campaigns. Tens of thousands of pages of Nazi public opinion reports survived the war. Although they are typically not of Gallup quality (those too honest in reporting public dissatisfaction to their superiors encountered difficulty), they demonstrate a powerful concern with what the masses were thinking.

The task of the press was to support the general propaganda campaign. Hadamovsky writes (1933, p. 100): "The German intellectuals active in public opinion should speak not of freedom, rather of self-discipline and responsibility. The press should not be the ultimate value to which they pay homage, rather they should serve the nation with their ability and strength." Objectivity was a dangerous concept, first since it was impossible to be objective, second because the result could damage the concretely existing nation for the benefit of abstract principle.

Thus, from the Nazi standpoint, propaganda was essentially the same, regardless of who made it. Nazis, of course, saw themselves at an advantage, given the perceived strength of their ideology. But they saw enemy propagandists as using the same techniques and methods, methods which could appropriately be borrowed. Since Goebbels assumed his opponents were attempting to use the same tools he was using, he could shock his subordinates by praising the way in which Churchill had handled Dunkirk (Bramsted 1965, p. 429). A self-proclaimed master of the art of propaganda, Goebbels respected those able to move the masses. The Nazis freely admitted to learning from the Catholic Church, the Marxists, Allied propaganda of World War I, and any number of others.

Marxist-Leninist propaganda sees itself sees itself differently. According to the *Great Soviet Encyclopedia,* "Communist propaganda is a scientifically based system of intellectual activity. The activity is subdivided into propaganda and agitation. According to the familiar quotation from Plekanov, "the propagandist conveys *many* ideas to one or a few persons, an agitator conveys *only one or a few ideas,* but to a *great mass of people*"

(Agitation 1973–83, vol. 1, p. 137). Propaganda is deeper, the particular concern of party members and agitators, whereas agitation puts the material in a more popular form. The *Great Soviet Encyclopedia* explains the goal of agitation in this manner (Agitation 1973–83, vol. 1, p. 137):

The CPSU uses agitation for the communist education of the workers, for heightening their political consciousness, for explaining the meaning of current events to the working masses, and for mobilizing and organizing them to fulfill the tasks facing the Party, the working class, and all the people.

Since propaganda is scientifically based, it must be accurate: "The information in agitation should be theoretically correct and based on reliable sources and scientific facts . . . " (Agitation 1973–83, vol. 1, p. 138). Note the first requirement: Information must be theoretically correct. It is consistent with Marxist-Leninist theory to suppress information which has a false theoretical base, since even accurate information cannot be rightly understood if it comes from a false theoretical perspective.

A post-glasnost article in *Pravda* stresses that socialist journalism requires "a scientific analysis of life's phenomena, a profound knowledge of affairs, ideological convictions, and constructive judgments on the part of the author" (Makhrin 1987, p. 3). Thus there are severe penalties in Soviet bloc nations for passing on information of public record. The penal code of the German Democratic Republic, for example, allows two- to twelve-year prison terms for collecting and disseminating nonsecret information if it is likely to assist those hostile to the socialist community (Lacqueur 1985, p. 243). Although the German Democratic Republic some years back gave up the attempt to stop its citizens from watching television programs from the Federal Republic, and even provides Federal Republic channels in cable systems, speaking publicly about what one sees can be a penal offense.

The perceived scientific base limits Soviet propaganda's flexibility. The Nazis produced livelier propaganda because of their conviction that it was not a scientific activity following as closely as possible a comprehensive theory. Soviet propaganda, on the other hand, must be able to at least argue that all its content is theoretically justifiable. Even in 1987, a speaker at the Sixth Congress of the Soviet Union of Journalists could say: "We must be deeply committed to communist ideals and confident in the party program as if it were our own life creed. Even the slightest deviations from this bring about mistakes and losses whose correction and recovery take decades" (From the position . . . 1987, p. 3).

Marxist-Leninist press theory can consistently deny the press to anyone not holding the proper theories. Yevgeny Prokhorov, writing in *Zhurnalist,* the Soviet trade organ for journalists, makes the argument as clearly as one could wish (1976, p. 76): "The Marxist concept of press freedom in the framework of the socialist system calls for complete freedom to be granted to communist journalism, and for the liquidation of the bourgeois press."

It is much harder for Marxist-Leninists to admire enemy propaganda than it was for the Nazis. Since propaganda goes far beyond technique, the technical skillfulness of the enemy is a cause for anger more than admiration. Western propaganda is portrayed as a collection of disreputable techniques designed to mislead the masses. It emphasizes emotional and irrational appeals, methods entirely inconsistent with the scientific, rational nature of Marxist propaganda. A clear statement comes from A. Panfilov, who analyzes Western radio propaganda (1981, p. 79):

All these definitions [from Western sources] are clearly more of [*sic*] less synonymous. Their gist is not that propaganda constitutes a difficult struggle to form a person's world outlook and his political and other convictions, i.e., to form an immeasurably complex set of human knowledge based on the laws of objective reality. In the bourgeois theoreticians' interpretation, propaganda is a purely mechanical manipulation of "impulse situations" that should provoke an equally mechanical reaction.

A more recent Soviet writer claims Western broadcasting aimed at Czechoslovakia has an insidious goal: "to arrange things so they [young people] will get bogged down in vague discussions about the meaning of life, and then slide into futile self-analysis, morose reflection, and social apathy." The article accuses Western propagandists of appealing to the emotions rather than the reason of the audience, and concludes that to combat such propaganda, it is necessary to be "vigilant and unswerving" (Chausov 1987, p. 5).

Western, or bourgeois, propaganda is, then, inherently defective. Its purpose is to render the masses willing to accept a society that advances the interests of the capitalist class rather than their own. Soviet propaganda, to the contrary, is said to follow a policy of strict truthfulness.

Soviet theorists tend to assume that they and their Western counterparts work in similar ways—that is, consciously conducting their activity to support their political system. Since capitalism is obsolete, an historical truth allegedly sensed by Western propagandists, its case is inherently weak. Western propagandists must resort knowingly to lies. A common Soviet claim is that Western propagandists consciously adopt Nazi techniques: "Washington studied closely and adopted the Nazi technique of the 'Big Lle.' Goebbels's diaries, in several volumes, have been translated and published in the United States. The Hoover Institution not only stores but also widely uses Nazi propaganda archives" (Grachev and Yermoshkin 1984, p. 76). Panfilov is surprised that, "after bourgeois theoreticians have thus spoken and written about propaganda, they themselves are distressed both about it being discredited and the fact that the notion of 'propaganda' is closely associated with that of a 'lie' in the USA and other capitalist countries" (1981, p. 79).

But most Western theorists are not starting from the same point in their analysis. David Benn accurately observed that Western work on propaganda comes from a psychological or sociological direction, but Soviet propaganda "has been a sub-branch of ideology rather than of the social sciences. The vast Soviet literature on the subjects has been overwhelmingly concerned with correctness of content and methods of organization" (1986, p. 113). Thus, until recently the Soviets have had surprisingly little interest in public opinion, a matter to which the Nazis devoted enormous energy (Kershaw 1983), since Marxist-Leninist propaganda by definition serves the interest of the working class. As the *Great Soviet Encyclopedia* observes (Propaganda 1973–83, vol. 24, p. 270):

The central task of communist propaganda is to instill in the toilers the Marxist-Leninist world view, lofty ideological and political qualities, and the norms of communist morality and to encourage conscious, creative participation by all in the process of the socialist and communist transformation of society. The degree to which these goals are realized is the overall criterion of the effectiveness of communist propaganda, and the general index of this effectiveness is the level of public activity of the masses.

The effectiveness or ineffectiveness of propaganda is *visible*. If the masses are not responding as theory demands, propaganda and agitation are being improperly conducted. Correct propaganda, by definition, would have the results theory predicts, since it is simply persuading the masses to act in their own best interests.

The effects of Gorbachev's *glasnost* campaign are yet unclear, although it must be remembered that the policy's goal is not to implement Western-style freedom of the press, but rather to help remove imposing barriers to economic and social development through more open discussion of difficulties. *Glasnost* is an attempt to broaden the permissible range of discussion while remaining within the framework of Marxist-Leninist theory. Adopting Western views on the press would require fundamental restructuring of that theory, an unlikely prospect. The problem the Soviets face is that relatively open criticism, once begun, is difficult to keep in comfortable bounds.

Nazi and Marxist-Leninist propagandas, in summary, have major theoretical differences. That does not mean the practice is always that different. Anyone who compares, say, the Nazi newspaper, the *Völkischer Beobachter,* with the German Democratic Repubic organ *Neues Deutschland* will have little difficulty finding similarities. In the same way, a line in a German Democratic Republic song announces "The party is always right," a line which fifty years ago would have read "The Führer is always right." But those similarities should not be allowed to conceal the great differences.

VIEWS OF PROPAGANDA IN THE WEST

At least since the First World War, making propaganda has been a disreputable practice in the West. The term is not often precisely defined (indeed, attempts to define it precisely are never successful), but most people seem to feel about it like the classic operational definition of pornography by Supreme Court Justice Potter Stewart: "I can't define it, but I know it when I see it." Propaganda is seen as the attempt to consciously mislead the audience; fascists and Marxists are the archetypical examples of "bad men speaking well." The preferred description refers to the competition of ideas, truth resulting from free speech, or similar phrases, for a process which, though clearly better than the totalitarian alternative, is hardly as successful as often maintained.

Ellul argues at length that propaganda is as widespread in Chicago as in Kiev. But it is not always the same kind of propaganda. Whereas, for example, the Soviets, though not the Nazis, have often simply disregarded public opinion, such disregard is much harder in the West. A problem comes in what kind of public opinions (another word for which we should more readily use the plural) are heeded. All opinions are not equal. In the free marketplace of ideas, some ideas are freer, that is, more likely to be heard, than others.

This is not only the result of allegedly wicked capitalists controlling the media in ways serving their interests; it is a consequence of allowing people choice. Ellul demonstrates that modern mass societies are simultaneously individualistic societies. That is, the individual, removed from the moorings of family and faith, is likelier to accept the perceived attitudes of "everybody else," or to accept peculiar ideas restoring him to lost certainty.

Part of the reason for Ellul's unpopularity among many scholars may be his claim that intellectuals are the most susceptible to modern propaganda (1965, pp. 110–13). Faced with the most choice, they may be under the greatest pressure to resolve uncertainty by adopting strong ideology. Certainly anyone wishing to begin a strange group or promote an ideology is more successful on university campuses than on factory floors. The Bhagwan, formerly resident in Oregon, for example, drew followers almost uniformly well educated.

Public opinion in the West is more clearly driven by the public than in totalitarian states. That is not an unmixed blessing. Western democratic states, drawing on Christian roots, began with a consistent world view. Because humanity was by nature prone to evil, government, being composed of people, was also so inclined. Humans were nonetheless, as divine creations, of value. This dual view of man, as a creature both divine and depraved, encourages journalists to seek out the base as a check on evil and a spur to good. Modern democracies have largely lost their theological anchors but the critical impulse remains strong. Thus, criticism in the West is often now only that, pointing out undeniable evil without giving a convincing view of the world as it ought rightly be.

In the same way, the individual is freer to express less admirable thoughts and drives. Thus, modern communication in the West falls prey to what I call the Adolf Hitler Theory of the mass media. The *1986–87 Books in Print* lists nearly 100 books on Adolf Hitler, less than fifty on Winston Churchill, a man whose public career spanned three times as many years. There is a fascination with the minutiae of Hitler's life that Churchill's memory escapes; a remarkable number of popular fiction paperbacks carry a swastika on the cover. The evil of Nazism has powerful attraction.

Popular television and films focus more on violence and sex than are perhaps justified by their actual frequency. Take pornography, for example. Fifty years ago in the United States, pornography was tamer, both less accessible and acceptable than now. The character of humanity has not since declined; rather, it is easier and safer to indulge. And given the opportunity, most of us will indulge. Unrestrained market-driven mass communication inherently produces abominations. This is no brief for censorship; rather, it is an observation that communication in a culture of uncertain values produces unpleasant consequences. And democracies today are less certain of their values than they were fifty years ago.

Totalitarian societies, to the contrary, have the advantage of an ideology which defines humanity (or at least the part to which the audience belongs) as good, and provides an absolutist code of ethics. Americans who read *Pravda* for the first time are surprised by the vehemence and frequency of social criticism. Soviet newspapers receive 200,000 letters from readers daily, many of which are critical (Facts and Figures 1986, p. 1). Some are printed, even followed up. All such criticism, however, assumes the essential validity of the system. What is wrong is that citizens are not correctly following the precepts of Marxism-Leninism; when they do, problems will disappear. In the same way criticism in democracies once assumed truth was knowable and able to be agreed upon, a confidence many no longer feel.

Although the West is no longer as confident of its values as it once was, most people retain the conviction that Gresham's law does not apply to the free marketplace of ideas. A great evil of totalitarian propaganda is therefore seen as the unwillingness to allow other points of view to be heard. Thus, Smith observes (1985, p. 173): "In a highly authoritarian polity, the regime tries to monopolize for itself all opportunities to engage in propaganda, and often it will stop at nothing to crush any kind of counterpropaganda." His language suggests the reprehensibility of the behavior.

Similarly, the revelations in 1986 of an American disinformation campaign directed against Libya aroused indignation, unflattering comparisons being made to similar Soviet attempts, though from a Marxist-Leninist standpoint, as Bittman (1985) observes, disinformation is an acceptable strategy.

Westerners have contradictory views of totalitarian propaganda, sometimes granting it an effectiveness that the totalitarians themselves would be only to be too pleased to have, other times wondering how it can have any success at all. As Benn observes (1985, p. 112):

Propaganda is sometimes referred to as a Soviet 'secret weapon'; or as an instrument of 'thought control'—which presupposes a substantial degree of official success in shaping public opinion. Yet at other times Soviet communication is assumed to be absurdly crude, inept and dreary; and it is said that in fact no one in Russia believes in Marxism-Leninism any longer.

The contradiction shows up often. On the one hand, Soviet bloc mass media are presented as dreadful stuff, often evidenced by what happens when, as in the German Democratic Republic, people have the option to choose Western media. On the other hand, the Nazis persuaded much of the rest of the world that *Triumph of the Will* was typical of the German reaction to Nazism, and Gorbachev's "charm offensive" seems more effective in Western Europe than in the Soviet Union.

Part of the reason for the contradiction, perhaps, lies in Ellul's distinction between sociological and political propaganda. Although the campaigns of the moment may be disbelieved or doubted, the overall force of propaganda is powerful. People have strong reasons to want to believe in the rightness of their society. Ellul maintains that propaganda is in large part self-inflicted, that is, modern propaganda is less the result of sinister propagandists manipulating the masses than of a desire on the part of the masses to have the world make sense (1965, pp. 118–19).

Several anecdotes support the argument. In 1945, at the end of the Third Reich, newsprint shortages were severe. Goebbels' propaganda ministry proposed putting out newspapers every other day to save paper. The regional propaganda offices strongly opposed the cutback, arguing that it would be better to publish one-page newspapers every day (Reichsministerium 1945). The public need for information, even unreliable information, was desperate. According to Shlapentokh, a Soviet defector, *Pravda* journalists were surprised and distressed to learn from a readership survey that the most hard-line commentator among them, whose views were the clearest, was also the most popular (Benn 1985, p. 115). Consider the Gulf of Tonkin, the *Mayaguez* incident, Grenada, KAL 007, and the bombing of Libya, all cases in which American public opinion changed very quickly, consistent with a general view of the rightness of American conduct. I am less interested in whether the particular case was correct or not than in the speed with which public opinion turned.

CONCLUSION

Is propaganda too broadly defined in Ellul's work? I think not. If the only word one has for large woody plants is "tree," one has difficulties. The differences between an oak and a bristlecone pine are not minor. But if one distinguishes between deciduous and coniferous trees, oaks and beeches, spruces and pines, the word "tree" remains useful to distinguish those things from, say, seahorses. In the same way, propaganda is the collective name for a variety of phenomena, which have enough in common to render a generic term useful.

Ellul considers Soviet, Chinese, and U.S. propaganda "entirely different" in type and methods, but argues that regardless of who makes modern propaganda, regardless of their techniques, propaganda produces similar effects, that propaganda for democracy destroys the basis of what it is attempting to maintain (Ellul 1965, pp. ix-xviii). Although I lack the space to trace his argument here, it is not easily dismissed.

Neither Ellul nor I would argue that "everything is propaganda." Indeed, Ellul specifically notes many things that are not propaganda, ranging from simple dialogue to the Christian sermon, from election campaigns to the influence of a strong family. Nor does the argument require the claim that Soviet and U.S. propagandas are equally reprehensible.

Nonetheless, propaganda is in no danger of running short in our world. And I submit that Ellul is correct in arguing that its presence is a threat to the democratic ideals most in the West maintain (1965, pp. 232–57). The results of propaganda, whether East or West, Nazi or Democratic, are unsettlingly similar.

I close with two examples. In 1984 Radio Moscow announced that the Hitler diaries affair was a CIA plot "intended to exonerate and glorify the Third Reich" (Harris 1986, p. 377). At the same time, *Stern* founder Henri Nannen was telling *The New York Times* that the affair was probably the work of East German agents attempting "to spread disinformation and destablize the Federal Republic" (Harris 1986, p. 388). His charge was widely thought plausible.

The second example. Seymour Hersch's recent book on the flight of KAL 007 finds that both sides were more eager to make propaganda than to find out what really happened. He concludes with this comment: "Those in Washington who chose to increase international tension, and their counterparts in Moscow who responded in kind, were acting in ignorance of the facts and the realities" (1986, p. 250). But both were responding consistently with the view of the enemy their propagandas encourage.

Fifty years ago Leonard Doob closed his book on propaganda with an uncertain prognosis (1935, p. 412):

[I]f everyone remains gullible and the willing victims of intentional and unintentional propagandists, the task of finding and then establishing new social values becomes almost impossible. More people must simply puncture the truths in the "lies" which they accept, and appreciate the truths in the "lies" which they reject. Only then will they be able to destroy the evil and buncombe of society; only then will they be ready to recognize the leaders whose values and whose propaganda are neither deceptive nor illusory; only then will they be immune to a doctrine like Fascism. This should be possible—but is it?

The answer is less certain today.

REFERENCES

Agitation. 1973–83. *Great Soviet Encyclopedia*. Vol. 1:137–38. New York: Macmillan.

Balfour, M. 1979. *Propaganda in War: 1919–1945*. London: Routledge & Kegan Paul.

Benn, D. W. 1985. Soviet Propaganda: The Theory and the Practice. *The World Today* 41:112–15.

Bittman, L. 1985. *The KGB and Soviet Disinformation: An Insider's View*. Washington, D.C.: Pergamon-Brassey's.

Bramsted, E. K. 1965. *Goebbels and National Socialist Propaganda: 1925–1945*. E. Lansing: Michigan State University Press.

Chausov, L. 1987. "Truth versus Fiction." *Pravda* (translated by Associated Publishers), March 16, 5.

Doob, L. W. 1935. *Propaganda: Its Psychology and Technique*. New York: Henry Holt.

Ellul, J. 1965. *Propaganda: The Formation of Men's Attitudes*. Translated by K. Keller and J. Lerner. New York: Knopf.

Facts and Figures. 1986. *Pravda* (translated by Associated Publishers), May 5, 1.

From the Position of Openness. 1987. *Pravda* (translated by Associated Publishers), March 16, 3.

Grachev, A., and N. Yermoshkin. 1984. *A New Information Order or Psychological Warfare*? Translated by D. Beliavsky. Moscow: Progress Publishers.

Hadamovsky, E. 1933. *Propaganda und Nationale Macht*. Oldenburg, Germany: Gerhard Stalling.

Harper's Index. 1986. *Harper's* July, 11.

Harris, R. 1986. *Selling Hitler*. New York: Pantheon.

Hersh, S. M. 1986. *"The Target is Destroyed."* New York: Random House.

Hitler, A. 1943. *Mein Kampf*. Translated by R. Mannheim. New York: Houghton Mifflin.

"Ich bin von mehr Leuten gewählt als Hitler." 1986. *Der Spiegel,* November 10, 17–24.

Kershaw, I. 1983. *Public Opinion and Political Dissent in the Third Reich*. Oxford: Oxford University Press.

Lacqueur, W. 1985. *A World of Secrets: The Uses and Limits of Intelligence*. New York: Basic Books.

Makhrin, Y. 1987. Journalist's Duty Commands. *Pravda*, February 9, 3.

Panfilov, A. 1981. *Broadcasting Pirates or Abuse of the Microphone: An Outline of External Political Radio Propaganda by the USA, Britain and the FRG.* Translated by N. Bobrov. Moscow: Progress Publishers.

Prokhorov, Y. 1976. The Marxist Press Concept. In *International and Intercultural Communication,* ed. H. Fischer and J. Merril, pp. 51–58. New York: Hastings House.

Propaganda. 1973–83. *Great Soviet Encyclopedia.* Vol. 24:269–70. New York: Macmillan.

Reichsministerium für Volksaufklärung und Propaganda. 1945. Activity Report, 24 January. National Archives Microfilms T–580, roll 682.

Smith, B. L. 1985. Propaganda. *Encyclopedia Britannica.* 15th ed. Vol. 26:166–174.

4 Propaganda as a Form of Communication

Victoria O'Donnell
and Garth S. Jowett

Propaganda is a form of communication. In this essay, we examine propaganda as communication; define propaganda; examine different forms of propaganda, including disinformation, which is receiving considerable attention from the media; differentiate propaganda from persuasive and informative communication, other forms of communication with which propaganda is frequently confused; and present a purpose-centered model of propaganda. If propaganda studies are to be enhanced, we believe that there is a need to truly understand what propaganda is and to be able to evaluate it in a modern context free from value-laden definitions.

COMMUNICATION DEFINED

Communication has been defined quite simply as that which happens when A communicates to B about X (Sereno and Mortensen 1974, p. 73). A and B may be persons, groups, or social and political systems. A is commonly referred to as a "sender" and B as a "receiver." Communication is often face-to-face interaction, but it also may be mediated interaction where A communicates to B through C about X. Here C is a mediator through which the message must pass before it reaches B. A news story that is broadcast over radio or television to the public is an example of mediated communication. The story comes from a source (A), is encoded by a news writer (C), altered to fit production standards of the station and limits of the medium (other Cs), and is received by the public (B).

Communication theorists have also developed transactional models that describe communication as a process in which "participants create and share information with one another in order to reach mutual understanding" (Rogers and Kincaid 1981:63). In other words, A and B share information in order to mutually understand X. This view of communication emphasizes relationships between or among senders and receivers that lead them to converge toward or diverge away from one another in their understanding of ideas. If communication efforts are successful, A and B will have a mutual understanding about X. Some models of communication are not transactional because they emphasize the one-way flow of messages that disallows immediate feedback.

The elements in most communication models are (1) a sender, (2) a message, (3) a channel, and (4) a receiver. Other important elements are (5) feedback and (6) the effects of the message. These six elements occur within a context, both in a specific and immediate sense as well as within the sociocultural framework of the times.

A HISTORICAL CASE STUDY

Let us examine an example of World War II propaganda that will enable us to see its communicative elements, isolate the specific characteristics of propaganda, and lead us to a definition of propaganda.

During World War II, many "freedom" radio stations operated illegally inside Germany or from bordering countries with the avowed purpose of opposing Hitler and Nazism. Germany, in turn, operated radio stations pretending to be "freedom" stations in bordering countries with the hidden purpose of deceiving her enemies and lowering their morale. One such station operated in France from the autumn of 1939 until the spring of 1940. The host of this station was a man called Ferdonnet who pretended to be a patriotic Frenchman whose love of country had prompted him to warn his fellow Frenchmen to save France before it was too late (Roetter 1974, p. 103). Using the technical resources of Radio Stuttgart, his talks reached the French soldiers in the Maginot Line and beyond into France. Speaking the jargon of the common people, he voiced their complaints about the war and repeated gossip about Paris. He presented his arguments in an intelligent way, playing on the doubts and suspicions of his listeners. For example, he sympathized with the men's crowded and damp conditions in the Maginot Line while telling them that their superior officers were dining at a well-known restaurant. He described the fine, six-course lunch that the officers ate with mouth-watering descriptions of every dish. Why, he asked, did they put up with such miserable conditions and distasteful rations during the cold winter when the British soldiers were in French towns, spending money, and enjoying the cafes and the French women? The French soldiers were already miserable due to the conditions in the Maginot Line, and they were bitter about the differences in pay between British soldiers and themselves. Playing on their doubts and suspicions, Ferdonnet told them that they were being shamelessly exploited by being made to fight England's war and were being treated as subjects of a British colony. He taunted them and prodded them to support a "new" government for France, one that would not kowtow to the British.

This radio broadcast, pretending to be pro-France, was actually "black," that is, deceitful, propaganda designed to weaken the morale of the French soldiers. The French soldiers and other French people who listened to the broadcasts, however, knew that it was a pro-German broadcast and saw through the disguise. Nevertheless, during the winter of 1939–40, it was common practice for the French people to listen to Ferdonnet. They knew he would be more entertaining than their own official radio broadcasts, and, although they knew he was pro-German, they were not repelled. Many of the things he said, they had already said to each other. Even though they knew they were listening to propaganda disguised as patriotic persuasion, they felt the way Ferdonnet wanted them to feel—bitter against the British and discouraged about their conditions. Ferdonnet articulated their own discontentment very well.

Let us examine this historical example in order to see what elements of propaganda are apparent:

1. The *purpose* of the German broadcast was not to save France, as Ferdonnet stated, but it was a *deliberate* attempt by Germany to lower the morale of the French soldiers. The major goal of Germany's propaganda in 1939 was to stress the invincibility of the Wehrmacht and the hopelessness of Britain and France's cause. Germany also wanted to suggest that, despite her superiority, the possibility of talks and negotiation still existed. This ploy, Germany hoped, would engage the sympathy of the people in the neutral countries of Norway, Denmark, Holland, and Belgium who sincerely believed that peace could be achieved and divert any suspicions of the neutral countries about Germany's true intentions toward them. However, the real target audience in this campaign to convince people that Germany's goal was peace was the people of France. Germany wanted to win control of the western European continent and felt that this could be achieved if France's resistance could be broken.

The German message that was mediated through Ferdonnet was designed *to achieve a response that was not necessarily in the best interest of its audience, but a response that would have furthered the desired intent of the propagandist*.

2. This deliberate attempt to weaken France was *systematic*. Ferdonnet's broadcasts were a regular stream of talks and commentaries over a period of several months. He became a familiar voice on the air, and French soldiers and civilians tuned in regularly.

3. The broadcasts were deliberate and systematic communications designed *to shape the perceptions* of the French people about their situation, about their confidence in the French government, about the lot of the poor compared to the rich, and to reinforce the doubts and suspicions of the French soldiers about their role compared to the British.

Ferdonnet's arguments were not new, for they were the same ones that many loyal and patriotic French people voiced as they sat around and argued about the government and the war. What Ferdonnet was doing is known as "resonance," voicing the beliefs and feelings that already exist in the audience. Resonance is a technique whereby the receivers of a message do not perceive the themes of the messages to be imposed upon them from an outside authority to which they are required or committed to defer. Rather the receivers perceive the arguments of the message as having come from within themselves. In this way, the propagandist functions as an alter ego to the receiver, "someone giving expression to the recipient's own concerns, tensions, aspirations, and hopes. . . . Thus, propaganda . . . denies all distance between the source and the audience" (Kecskemeti 1973, p. 264).

4. Resonance was also used to *manipulate the cognitions* or thoughts of the French people. The soldiers, in particular, had been experiencing harsh conditions on the Maginot Line. The winter of 1939–40 had been extremely cold and damp, and the soldiers were forced to stay there without leave. Ferdonnet told them that the men who worked in the French tax offices had been exempted from military service, unlike ordinary French citizens. This plus Ferdonnet's comments about the French officers getting leave and eating in wonderful restaurants and the more highly paid British soldiers spending their money in French cafes and on French women heightened feelings of bitterness and manipulated the thoughts of the French soldiers. Roetter traces the argument (1974, pp. 105–06):

Why, Ferdonnet asked, was France fighting Britain's war—the war of a crumbling, plutocratic, decadent empire? . . . Were there, he enquired rhetorically, any British soldiers in the Maginot Line? Of course not—the British knew better than to entomb themselves. They lived in comfortable billets, their pay—as everyone knew—was better. . . . It was altogether a grim situation for France. The only way out was a change in her leadership. There was a little time left yet, but not much.

If successful, Germany's propaganda would have caused the French soldiers to intensify the bitterness and resentment that they already felt and to turn them against their own government and allies.

5. The ultimate goal of Germany was *to direct the behavior* of the French soldiers, perhaps to get them to desert, turn against their officers, or to be nonsupportive of the British. The French people as well might have been less diligent in their support of the war. It was during this period that a French farmer wrote a letter to the BBC to ask if a British soldier could take over the duties of his son in the French army because he needed his son to work on his farm (Roetter 1974, p. 106).

6. Although the French saw through the propaganda and knew that Ferdonnet was a voice in behalf of Germany, they found listening to him more palatable than listening to the official French broadcasts, which they

found boring. People are capable of recognizing propaganda for what it is, and they are not necessarily repulsed by it. Nor are they likely to do anything self-destructive because of it.

PROPAGANDA DEFINED

Propaganda is a form of communication involving the sending of a message to a receiver. Because propaganda is often disseminated through the mass media, or because the true source is often concealed, it tends to be mediated communication. Our definition of propaganda focuses on the communicative process and on the purpose of the propagandist. As described in the case study of Ferdonnet's broadcasts in France, propaganda has a selfish purpose weighted in favor of the propagandist and not necessarily in the best interest of the receiver.

We define propaganda as *the deliberate and systematic attempt to shape perceptions, manipulate cognitions, and direct behavior to achieve a response that furthers the desired intent of the propagandist* (Jowett and O'Donnell 1986, p. 16). This definition is purpose-centered because propaganda seeks to control and to deliberately alter or maintain the balance of power in a way that is favorable to the propagandist.

Propaganda, Institutions, and Ideology

The propagandist is almost always an institution: a government, a corporation, a religious organization, or an educational establishment. Institutional propaganda has as its purpose to propagandize an ideology to an audience which the propagandist sees as having similar objectives. The appearance of similarity of objectives makes the views of the propagandist more viable. For example, Germany wanted to convey an ideology of strength and invincibility while attempting to achieve the objective of weakening France's resistance. An ideology is a set of ideas, beliefs, values, attitudes, practices, and representations that constitutes a comprehensive framework for dealing with and influencing social, economic, and political reality. Ideology is a form of consent to a social order and conditions and rules within the social order. This includes assigning roles to gender, racial, religious, national, and social groups.

When propaganda is used to maintain the legitimacy of an institution and its activities, it is known as *integration propaganda,* for it reinforces the positions and interests represented by officials who sponsor and sanction propaganda messages. Propaganda may also be used to stimulate the masses to act, to overthrow an old order, or to bring about significant change. This is known as *agitative propaganda,* for it seeks to arouse people to action. In either case, the purpose of propaganda is to gain acceptance of the institutional ideology. Propaganda may seek to get people to accept institutional attitudes, to engage in certain patterns of behavior—voting, contributing money, joining groups, demonstrating for or against causes, deserting armies, buying products, and so on. Whatever the desired response, it is implemented to serve the ends of the propagandist, not necessarily the people who engage in responsive behavior. This is why our definition focuses on purpose. Josef Goebbels, Minister of Information for the Third Reich and master of propaganda techniques, reportedly said that propaganda had no fundamental method, only purpose—the conquest of the masses.

Origins of the Word "Propaganda" and its Negative Connotations

The word "propaganda" was originally developed by an institution, the Roman Catholic Church. In Latin, it meant "to propagate" or "to sow." Pope Gregory XV used it in 1622 when he established the "Sacra Congregatio Christiano Nomini Propaganda," or, as it was more commonly known, the "Sacra Congregatio de Propaganda Fide," meaning the Congregation for the Propagation of the Faith. The Church used propaganda to integrate its ideology and to oppose the Reformation.

Here was an example of an institution that openly sought to maintain its domination of the balance of power in the struggle with the forces of the Protestant Reformation. The explicit purpose of the Sacra Congregatio de Propaganda Fide was to carry the faith to the New World as well as to revive and strengthen it in Europe. In 1627, Pope Urban VIII founded the Collegium Urbanum, the seminary that served as a training ground for propaganda. The methods to be used by the missionaries were left to their discretion, but the purpose was to get the people to accept the Church's doctrines. Until this time, "propaganda" did not have negative connotations; however, as Qualter (1962, pp. 4–5) pointed out, the Roman Catholic origins of the word gave it a negative connotation in the Protestant countries that it does not have in Catholic countries. Thus, although the word "propaganda" began as a somewhat neutral term, it derived negative shades because of institutional and ideological differences.

Today, "propaganda" tends to have pejorative and dishonest meanings. It is often associated with lies, deceit, psychological warfare, and even brainwashing. Actually, there are different forms of propaganda which are described as white, gray, or black in relationship to an acknowledgment of the source of propaganda and the accuracy of information that is communicated.

Forms of Propaganda

White propaganda comes from a source which is identified correctly and communicates accurate information. Because there is no attempt to conceal the source, this form of propaganda is also called "overt" propaganda. For example, what listeners hear on Radio Moscow and the Voice of America is reasonably close to the truth, and they know that the source is the Soviet Union or the United States. The information is presented in such a way, however, that the sender is associated with the "best" ideas and the "best" ideology. White propaganda attempts to build credibility with the audience, for this could have usefulness at some point in the future.

The Liberty Weekend celebration of July 4, 1986, was an excellent example of white propaganda. While ostensibly a great outpouring of enthusiasm for the one-hundredth anniversary and refurbishing of the Statute of Liberty, the celebration provided an ideal opportunity to extol the virtues and strengths of the American "way of life." Television broadcasts of the events of the weekend, the parade of the tall ships, the lighting of the statue, the concerts, and the fireworks display, emphasized the concept of American political "freedom" and the opportunities found in an open society such as the United States. There was no need to deliberately contrast this with the lack of freedom in closed societies, for it was clearly implied. The broadcasts, exported to many other countries, became a well-managed form of white propaganda. Reactions to the broadcasts differed in different parts of the world. Some people found them moving and appropriate in tone, while others were offended by their blatant and chauvinistic nationalism.

Gray propaganda is when the source may or may not be correctly identified and when the accuracy of information is uncertain. When the Soviet Union sent massive air and ground forces into Afghanistan on December 24, 1979, seeking to replace one communist-controlled government with another, more closely allied with Moscow, Radio Moscow attempted to justify the action as an invitation from the Afghanistan government to intervene in a civil war. After that, there was virtually no coverage in any of the Soviet media. When Mikhail Gorbachev became the general secretary of the Communist Party, Soviet coverage of activity in Afghanistan became increasingly detailed but in a one-sided and inaccurate way. On December 25, 1985, Soviet television presented a documentary entitled, "Afghanistan: The Revolution Cannot Be Killed." This program gave the impression that the Afghan War had been started by outsiders, showing routes leading from Pakistan and Iran into Afghanistan and using film clips that suggested that the guerrillas were acting as mercenaries. One captured bandit, identified as a Turkish national, said he had been sent to carry out a mission for the CIA. The program closed with shots of pro-Soviet Afghan troops being hailed by the crowds and a song about the Afghan homeland (Ebon 1987, p. 345).

Gray propaganda is often used to embarrass an enemy or competitor. The Voice of America did not miss an opportunity to derogate the Soviet Union following the invasion of Afghanistan. While the emergence of glasnost has created the appearance of more cooperation between the two countries, both the United States and the Soviet Union continue to embarrass each other by creating spy scares. For example, American journalist Nicholas Daniloff was arrested in Moscow on August 30, 1986, and charged with spying not long after a Soviet United Nations employee, Gennadi F. Zakharov, had been arrested in America by the FBI for receiving classified documents from an agent. Both sides issued statements to the world press justifying their actions.

Black propaganda is when a false source is given and lies, fabrications, and deceptions are spread by the propagandist. Because the source is concealed, this is also known as "covert" propaganda (Shultz and Godson 1984, pp. 36–39). Black propaganda is the "Big Lie," including all types of creative deceit. This is the form of propaganda that the general public most commonly understands as being "true" propaganda. It is black propaganda that makes the headlines and captures the public's imagination, especially as such activities are glamorized within the context of revealing wartime exploits. This is a unique form of communication, consisting of the deliberate attempt to hide the real identity of the sender of the message (the propagandist) and also providing false information.

The success of black propaganda depends on establishing a strong degree of credibility for both the supposed source and the content of the message. To be successful, the receiver of the propaganda must have sufficient reason to believe that *this* source could and did send *this* message. The propagandist using techniques of black propaganda is careful to choose both sources and messages that will be received within the social, cultural, and political framework of the target audience. If the receiver cannot perceive the messages as relative to the apparent source, the propaganda attempt will fail.

Disinformation

To ensure the highest possible reception of the congruence of source and message, the specialized form of black propaganda known as "disinformation" has been refined in the twentieth century. The world was adopted in 1955 from the Russian term "dezinformatsia," taken from the name of a division of the KGB devoted to black propaganda. It means "false, incomplete, or misleading information that is passed, fed, or confirmed to a targeted individual, group, or country" (Shultz and Godson 1984, p. 37). The term should not be confused with the word "misinformation" because it has a much more deliberate and complex goal. The techniques of disinformation are subtle and sometimes highly effective variations of black propaganda, often using news stories deliberately designed to weaken adversaries, or to present them in a negative light, but passed off as real and from credible sources.

One current example involves the unusually broad disinformation campaign aimed at convincing the world that the AIDS virus was genetically engineered in an American military laboratory while researching biological warfare. This campaign began with the publication of the story in the October 1985 issue of the Soviet weekly *Literaturnaya Gazeta*. The article quoted heavily from the Indian pro-Soviet newspaper *Patriot*. Placing a story in a foreign news source before taking it up in the Soviet press is a standard disinformation ploy to increase credibility. However, the Soviets had jumped the gun, and subsequent checks revealed that no such story had appeared in the Indian newspaper. Nevertheless, the story was picked up by the international press, and despite repeated protests from the U.S. government for a retraction, the Soviet press continues to keep the story alive. By April 1987, it had been reported in the press of more than sixty countries. The credibility of this false story was given an enormous boost when it appeared on the front page of the October 26, 1986 issue of the *Sunday Express* in London. The British newspapers carry much prestige internationally (regardless of their varying quality), especially in the Middle East. In recent months, subtle variations of this story have appeared in the world press, including an East German broadcast of the story into Turkey, suggesting that it might be wise to get rid of U.S. bases because of servicemen infected with AIDS.

Even the U.S. media have relayed this disinformation story. On March 30, 1987, Dan Rather read the following news item on the CBS Evening News:

A Soviet military publication claims the virus that causes AIDS leaked from a U.S. Army laboratory conducting experiments in biological warfare. The article offers no hard evidence, but claims to be reporting the conclusions of unnamed scientists in the United States, Britain, and East Germany. Last October, A Soviet newspaper alleged that the AIDS virus may have been the result of Pentagon or CIA experiments.

Subsequent attempts to get CBS to retract the story have failed. U.S. citizens traveling to other parts of the world may be surprised when confronted with this successful disinformation campaign.

Because of the deliberately deceptive nature of disinformation, open democratic political systems have difficulty accepting its existence and practice as an ongoing part of international relations. Thus, when it was revealed that the United States had engaged in a disinformation campaign aimed at the Libyan leader Muammar el-Qaddafi, the result was a public furor, and the resignation of Bernard Kalb, the Assistant Secretary of State for Public Affairs. Kalb gave his reasons: "I'm concerned about the impact of such a program on the credibility of the United States. Faith in the word of America is the pulse beat of our democracy. Anything that hurts Amer-

Figure 1
Deflective Source Model

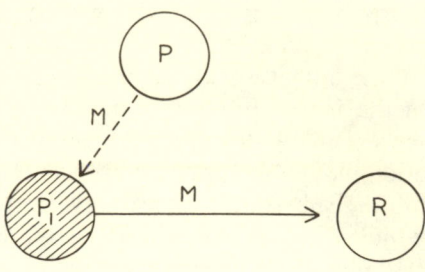

Figure 2
Legitimizing Source Model

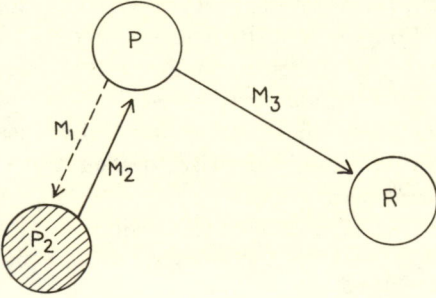

ica's credibility hurts America" (*USA Today* October 9, 1986, p. 11A). A
New York Times/CBS News Poll in late October indicated that 73 percent
of those surveyed said that it was not all right for the Administration to
lie in order to achieve a foreign policy goal (*The New York Times* October
31, 1986, p. 5). Such public sentiment does not reflect the reality of international politics, and it would be naive to suggest that disinformation is
not widely practiced by all of the major world powers.

As a communication process, the disinformation model has some rather
unique properties. As illustrated in Figures 1 and 2, there are two ways in
which it operates. In Figure 1, the propagandist (P) creates a *deflective
source* (P1) which becomes the apparent source of the message (M). The
receiver (R) peceives the information as coming directly from P1 and does
not associate it with the original propagandist (P). In Figure 2, the propagandist secretly places the original message (M1) in a *legitimizing source*
(P2). This message (now M2), as interpreted by P2, is then picked up by
the propagandist (P) and communicated to the receiver (R) in the form
M3, as having come from P2. This both legitimizes the message, and dis-
associates the propagandist (P) from its origination. With either model,
the intent is to obscure the identity of the original message originator, and

to create a greater degree of credibility for the combination of message and apparent source.

A MODEL OF PROPAGANDA

We have developed a model of propaganda (Jowett and O'Donnell 1986, p. 22) to demonstrate how propaganda uses elements of informative and persuasive communication, yet differs in purpose (see Figure 3). Figure 3 begins with communication in general, which is broken down into two types of communication, informative and persuasive. Propaganda is a unique subset of communication that incorporate characteristics of both information and persuasion.

Informative Communication

When information is used to accomplish a purpose of sharing, explaining, or instructing, this is considered to be informative communication. Once gained, information tends to reduce uncertainty about people, places, and ideas and promotes mutual understanding between sender and receiver. Generally speaking, informative communication is thought to be neutral because it is about subject matter that has attained the privileged status of being beyond dispute. Whenever information is regarded as disputable by either the sender or receiver, it is difficult for the communication process to proceed as information.

Persuasive Communication

Persuasion is communication that attempts to get the receiver to accept or adopt a new response in a voluntary fashion. O'Donnell and Kable (1982, p. 9) define persuasion as "a complex, interactive process in which a sender and a receiver are linked by verbal and nonverbal symbols through which the persuader attempts to influence the persuadee to change a response." A positive response from the persuadee might be, "I never thought of it that way, but I do now" or "I never did that before, but now I intend to."

The process of persuasion is an interactive one in which the persuadee attains fulfillment of personal needs or desires if the persuader's purpose is adopted. In order for the persuader to achieve his or her purpose, attention must be paid to fulfilling the needs of the persuadee. Both persuader and persuadee are dependent upon one another to have their needs fulfilled in the persuasive interaction. For this reason, O'Donnell and Kable (1982, pp. 4–5) call persuasion a process of "interactive dependency." Both parties approach the message-event and actively use it to fulfill their needs. Mutual reciprocity, persuader sensitivity to the persuadee's needs, and

Figure 3
A Model of Propaganda

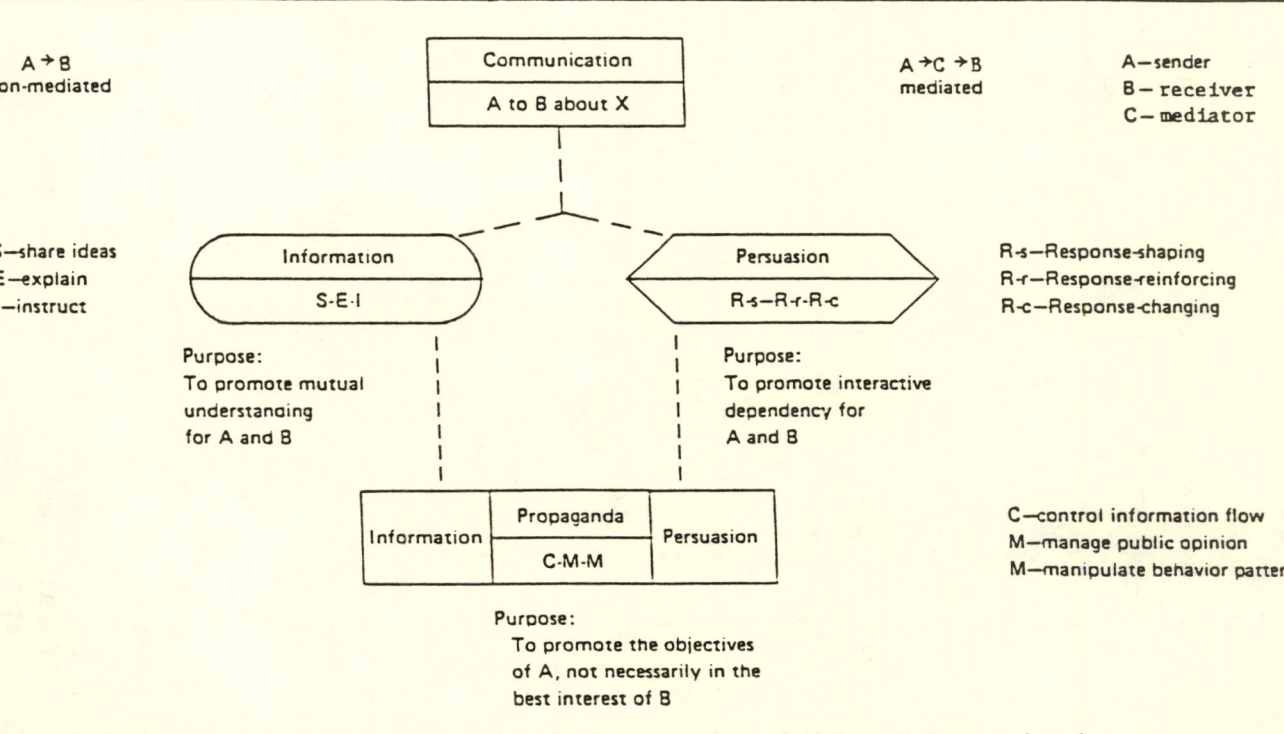

Reprinted with the permission of Sage Publications, from Garth Jowett and Victoria O'Donnell, *Propaganda and Persuasion*, p. 22.

voluntary compliance by the persuadee are the essential characteristics of the persuasion process that differentiate it from the propaganda process. Because both persuader and persuadee stand to have their actual and openly stated needs fulfilled, "persuasion" is a more respectable term than "propaganda."

Changing Responses through Persuasion. There are three types of responses attainable from a persuasive interaction: response shaping, response reinforcing, and response changing. Response shaping is similar to teaching, for the persuader attempts to get an audience to behave in a new way by providing positive reinforcement for learning the new behavior. The audience's need for positive reinforcement is filled, and the persuader's need for the desired response from the audience is filled. Response reinforcing stimulates persuadees to feel more strongly about something with which they are already in agreement. Much persuasion in today's society is response reinforcing (blood drives, fund-raising, political rallies, helping others, and so on), but people have to be motivated to go out and do these things year after year. Response changing occurs when people are influenced to move from a neutral, positive, or negative position to a different position, to change behavior, or to adopt a new behavior. This is the most difficult kind of persuasion because it involves getting people to think differently or to alter their behavior.

Voluntary Change. Whatever the desired response, practitioners of persuasion assume that the audience has access to counterpersuasion and information other than that presented by the persuader. In other words, there is a recognition that any change that occurs within the persuadee will be voluntary change. Both parties—persuader and persuadee—in the interaction perceive the change due to persuasion as mutually beneficial.

Of course, a persuader can mislead an audience regarding actual purpose. Sometimes an audience is aware of a persuader's hidden agenda, but sometimes an audience is manipulated and used without knowing it. This we regard as propaganda. Audience discovery that a propagandist is masquerading as a persuader will either alienate an audience or enable them to get some fulfillment from the communication without succumbing to the propagandist's purpose. This was the case in 1939 with the French people who knew that Ferdonnet was a propagandist for the Nazis. Their knowledge of the deception did not prevent them from listening to the broadcasts but it enabled them to resist the message.

Propaganda and Elements of Information and Persuasion

The model in Figure 3 depicts propaganda as a separate type of communication that draws upon elements of information and persuasion. Since the purpose of propaganda is to promote institutional objectives that are not necessarily in the best interest of the audience, a propagandist does not regard the well-being of the audience as a primary concern. Furthermore, the propagandist may not believe in the message that is being sent. Indeed, the propagandist is likely to be detached from the recipient to the point that his or her true identity is concealed. Identity concealment is often necessary to achieve desired objectives and goals. When the propagandist seeks to control information flow, manage public opinion, or manipulate behavior, the goals may not be achieved if the true intent or the real source were revealed.

Information. Propaganda may appear to be informative communication when ideas are shared or something is explained. The propagandist knows, however, that the purpose is not to promote mutual understanding but rather to promote the propagandist's partisan objectives. A propagandist will try to control information flow and manage a certain public's opinion by shaping perceptions through strategies of informative communication.

Altheide and Johnson (1980) make a case for what they call "bureaucratic propaganda" in which organizations, ranging from the military to television networks to evangelical crusades, release official reports containing what appears to be scientifically gathered and objective information to influential groups with the purpose of maintaining legitimacy of organizations and their activities. The information in the official reports is often contrived, distorted, or falsely interpreted, but it may never be seen by the public but rather by a congressional committee or some citizens' group and may be used for some action or program.

Persuasion. A propagandist uses the techniques of persuasion, appearing to promote interactive dependency. In reality, however, the propagandist wants to promote partisan and institutional interests, sometimes at the expense of the recipients of the propaganda, sometimes not. Ultimately the goal of propaganda is to manipulate behavior and behavior patterns. Both persuaders and propagandists seek votes, product consumption, membership in organizations, contributions, and other forms of action responses. Behavior change is not easy to bring about. Both persuaders and propagandists are well aware of this and actively seek information regarding the variables related to behavior change and predictors of behavior. The point is that the techniques of persuasion to bring about change are used by the propagandist but for a different set of objectives. The persuader seeks open and mutual fulfillment of needs; the propagandist promotes institutional objectives that are not necessarily revealed and that are not necessarily in the best interest of the audience.

We have demonstrated that propaganda is not only a form of communication but that it can be differentiated from other forms of communication by discovering its real purpose. Sometimes it is not possible to know or discover the actual purpose of propaganda without historical hindsight. It is important, nevertheless, to recognize propaganda where it exists and to examine its role and function as a separate and significant form of communication.

REFERENCES

Altheide, D. L., and J. M. Johnson. 1980. *Bureaucratic Propaganda*. Boston: Allyn and Bacon.

Ebon, M. 1987. *The Soviet Propaganda Machine*. New York: McGraw-Hill.

Jowett, G. S., and V. O'Donnell. 1986. *Propaganda and Persuasion*. Beverly Hills, Calif.: Sage.

Kecskemeti, P. 1973. "Propaganda." In *Handbook of Communication,* ed. I. D. Pool, F. W. Frey, W. Schramm, N. Maccoby, and E. B. Parker, pp. 844–70. Chicago: Rand McNally.

O'Donnell, V., and J. Kable. 1982. *Persuasion: An Interactive Dependency Approach*. New York: Random House.

Qualter, T. H. 1962. *Propaganda and Psychological Warfare*. New York: Random House.

Rogers, E. M., and D. L. Kincaid. 1981. *Communication Networks: Toward a New Paradigm for Research*. New York: Free Press.

Roetter, C. 1974. *The Art of Psychological Warfare: 1914–1945*. New York: Stein and Day.

Sereno, K. and C. D. Mortensen. 1974. *Foundations of Communication Theory*. New York: Harper & Row.

Shultz, R. H., and R. Godson. 1984. *Dezinformatsia: Active Measures in Soviet Strategy*. Washington, D.C.: Pergamon-Brassey's.

5 Propaganda and the Techniques of Deception

Ted J. Smith III

The chapters in this book demonstrate the great diversity in conceptions of the meaning of the term "propaganda." This diversity should not be surprising. Given that the term has been widely used for over 300 years in a number of different, even hostile, cultures, it is only natural that a multiplicity of meanings and nuances have evolved. Equally important, because definitions of propaganda are often linked to judgments of truth and morality, the various parties to the dispute have every incentive to insist on their preferred formulations of the term.

It should be noted, however, that extensive similarities underlie this surface diversity. Careful analysis shows that nearly all of the many definitions of propaganda can be readily divided into two groups, which represent two "root conceptions" of the term. The first of these defines propaganda as communication that is consciously or unconsciously *biased* in the sense of being one-sided. In this conception, the role of the propagandist is to build a case for a particular conclusion by arraying only those materials which lend it support. Other views and other items of evidence are either ignored or considered solely for purposes of refutation. This conception is reflected in the primary definition of the term offered by most American dictionaries. For example, the 1984 edition of *The Random House College Dictionary* describes propaganda as "1. information or ideas methodically spread to promote or injure a cause, group, nation, etc."

Portions of this chapter have appeared in *Moscow Meets Main Street* by Ted J. Smith III, © The Media Institute, 1988. Reprinted by permission.

Although the characteristic of bias is common to nearly all definitions of propaganda, different groups vary greatly in their evaluation of that trait. For some, assigning the label of "propaganda" to a message is evaluatively *neutral*. It merely describes the message as biased without saying that bias itself is either good or bad. As discussed by Professor Gustainis in his contribution to this volume, this position has been argued most fully by the U.S. Department of Justice in defense of its classification of three recent Canadian films as "political propaganda" under the provisions of the Foreign Agents Registration Act. The validity of this usage was confirmed by the Supreme Court in the case of *Meese v. Keene*.

Certain other groups see some "biased" communications as good, and therefore may imply a *positive* evaluation when they call a message "propaganda." This is most clearly the case when the "bias" is seen as supporting an established truth. For example, several papers in this volume note that propaganda originally denoted messages designed to spread Catholic doctrines. It seems reasonable to assume that this propaganda was seen as good, at least by Catholics. An additional and more recent example is provided by contemporary Marxist-Leninist ideology. As discussed in the entry on "Propaganda" in the current (1978) English-language edition of the *Great Soviet Encyclopedia*, Marxists draw a firm distinction between "bourgeois" and "communist" propaganda, with the latter depicted as wholly beneficial because it advances the cause of socialism.

Propaganda is also a positive term for many who endorse a conflict notion of truth. In this view, truth emerges from the clash of opposing positions, each of which must be presented as forcefully as possible. Because one-sided, these presentations qualify as "propaganda," but are seen as both necessary and good because they advance the search for truth. This was the view of early proponents of propaganda in public relations such as Edward L. Bernays (e.g., 1928). It is also the basis for the traditional conception of the democratic press as a "free marketplace of ideas" and for the adversarial procedures followed in Western courts of law.

Finally, many groups imply a distinctly *negative* evaluation when they refer to biased communications as "propaganda." But the reasons for such evaluations are not as obvious as they may seem. Quite frequently, those who condemn a message as "propaganda" do so in the belief that the message is not merely biased but also false. It is on these grounds that non-Catholics may reject Catholic propaganda, non-Marxists reject Marxist propaganda, and Marxists reject bourgeois propaganda. (It is also why skeptics, who deny that humans can ever know the truth, reject all confident assertions of knowledge.) We will deal with this conception of propaganda presently.

Those who see propaganda as negative *because* it is biased are usually drawn from the ranks of pluralists (who believe that there may be multiple truths) and relativists (who believe that all positions are equally true). These groups oppose propaganda because, by seeking to impose a single truth, it suppresses the recognition of other possible truths. This is, in part, the basis of the "humanist" attack on the Allied propaganda used in the First World War, as described in Michael Sproule's chapter. For example, many American humanists criticized the activities of the Committee on Public Information not simply because some messages it produced were false or exaggerated but because it harnessed the enormous powers of government and the press to the promotion of a single point of view. These concerns intensified with the growth of the broadcast media in the 1920s, and they still inform many criticisms of commercial advertising and governmental communication.

An important extension of this negative view took hold among Western intellectuals after about 1960, aided in part by the appearance of Jacques Ellul's book *Propaganda* (1965). Among other things, Ellul argues that almost all consistently biased messages should be seen as propaganda, *even if the bias is unconscious*. The immediate effect of his argument is to vastly expand the scope of the term. This is a great boon to critics of the Western democracies, for it allows huge areas of public discourse in those societies— including much of education, the arts, politics, and popular entertainment—to be labeled "propaganda" because it promulgates unreflected cultural values and assumptions. But this expansion can be purchased only at enormous cost. Virtually any message could reflect unconscious biases, and most probably do. Yet precisely because biases can be unconscious, neither the message source *nor any outside critic* can ever be certain that a given message is *not* biased. If virtually all messages either are or may be propagandistic, the term is of little meaning or use.

The second root conception defines propaganda as communication that is not merely biased but *deceitful*. In this view, the propagandist employs tricks and falsehoods to mislead his audience, and the "Big Lie" of Goebbels and the Nazis becomes the paradigm instance of the craft. Used in this sense, the term "propaganda" always implies a negative evaluation. It is also invariably partisan because it is applied only to the messages of an opponent.

Three important points should be noted at this time. First, while there may be a certain degree of overlap between the two root conceptions of propaganda, centering on the question of when, if ever, bias constitutes deceit, the basic distinction between the two seems intuitively clear. There is, after all, an obvious difference between making a case for a particular point of view and lying through your teeth. Further, the distinction has been recognized since antiquity, perhaps most clearly in Aristotle's contrast of amoral rhetoric and immoral sophistry (1941, pp. 325–29).

Second, casual observation suggests that the second root conception is very common in popular discourse. When Americans speak of "propaganda," it is often, even usually, deceitful communication to which they refer.

Third, almost everyone would agree that instances of deceitful communication exist and that it is important to identify them as such. The latter is especially true in democratic societies, which are guided in part by the judgments of ordinary citizens. If they are misled by sophistry, the state as a whole is weakened. For this reason, in the two decades immediately following World War Two, scholarly studies of propaganda abounded, and students were routinely taught to recognize and resist common propaganda techniques using examples drawn mostly from Nazi Germany and Stalinist Russia.

In short, it appears that the conception of propaganda as deceitful communication is clear, ancient, popular, and useful. Thus it is puzzling to note the virtual elimination of this usage in American intellectual circles beginning in the mid–1960s. Courses and units in propaganda analysis all but disappeared from high school and college curricula and scholarly studies of propaganda dwindled to a trickle. Most of what little remained offered Ellulian analyses of democratic "propaganda" or historical discussions of Nazi deceit. Only in the last few years has there been a resurgence of interest in the field (see, especially, Jowett and O'Donnell 1986), but much of this has centered on the narrow topic of "disinformation," or deceitful communication from a hidden source (see, especially, Shultz and Godson 1984, and Godson's chapter here).

The purpose of this chapter is to revivify the study of propaganda defined as deceitful communication. The project will require three steps: (1) a frank discussion of the reasons for the demise of propaganda studies, (2) a detailed definition of this conception of propaganda, and (3) an analysis of common propaganda techniques. Henceforth, for the sake of convenience, the term "promotion" will be used to denote communication that is merely biased; the term "propaganda" will be used exclusively in its second sense to denote deceitful communication.

THE CURIOUS DECLINE IN PROPAGANDA STUDIES

In attempting to account for the decline of scholarly interest in propaganda analysis, one thing seems clear: It cannot be attributed to any decline in the incidence of propaganda itself. In the international arena, for example,[1] there has been a constant flow of false and deceptive information from a wide range of countries and political groups. Foremost among these sources of propaganda are the various Marxist governments, including the Soviet Union, the People's Republic of China and their proteges and supporters, plus several Third World countries notable for their vehemently anti-American stance (e.g., Libya, Iran).

This flow has been documented in great detail by a number of sources, including conservative critics (e.g., Tyson 1981; Hazan 1982; Barron 1983; Pincher 1985; Ebon 1987), Marxist defectors (e.g., Bittman 1981; 1985; 1988; Shevchenko 1985; Levchenko 1988; Dzhirkvelov 1988), journalists and writers (e.g., Nagorski 1985; Oberg 1988; Daniloff 1988), government agencies (e.g., U.S. Congress, House 1980; 1982; U.S. Congress, Senate 1985; U.S. Department of State 1986; 1987a; 1987b; U.S. Information Agency 1988), and academic researchers, mostly in the field of Soviet studies (e.g., Shultz and Godson 1984; Dailey and Parker 1987; Smith 1988a). Extensive additional documentation may be found in such recurrent sources as the quarterly newsletter *Disinformation Forecast*, which began publication in 1985, Accuracy in Media's twice-monthly *AIM Report*, occasional papers produced by the Boston University Program for the Study of Disinformation (e.g., O'Donnell 1988), various publications of the Heritage Foundation (e.g., 1985) and the Ethics and Public Policy Center (e.g., Hook, Bukovsky, and Hollander 1987), and reports of the State Department's Office of Disinformation Analysis and Response, formed in 1986 as a permanent successor to its Active Measures Working Group.

As a number of these sources make clear, international Marxist (especially Soviet) propaganda activities have continued in the new age of glasnost ("openness"). Yet, paradoxically, the policy of glasnost, originated by the Sovet Union but now emulated to some degree by most countries in the Second World, also provides some of the best evidence of the nature and scope of those activities. Since 1985, revelations by Soviet leaders and official media of the actual course of Soviet history and the real state of Soviet society have grown from a trickle to a torrent. Among the most striking of these are the May 1988 announcement that final examinations in history for Soviet secondary students would be drastically shortened because of pervasive "inaccuracies" in their officially approved textbooks, and a February 1989 interview in the Soviet mass-circulation weekly newspaper *Argumenti i Facti* in which historian Roy Medvedev estimated that Stalin had been responsible for the deaths of 20 *million* Soviet citizens through executions, deliberate mass starvation, forced labor, and the rigors of penal servitude.

There is widespread disagreement among political observers about the precise significance of these disclosures. Some note that it has long been common for Soviet leaders to consolidate power by exposing the misdeeds of their predecessors and that most of the "revelations" merely confirm what many Soviet citizens and Western experts have known for years. Others argue that the disclosures are so numerous and profound that they constitute an irreversible break with the past and could function to delegitimate the ruling Marxist government and ideology. Be all that as it may, for students of propaganda their significance is manifest: Every revelation of the truth is also necessarily an admission that past official pronouncements on that topic were nothing more than open, calculated lies—in short, propaganda, in the purest and most negative sense of the term. Taken together, they establish beyond reasonable doubt that the Soviet Union has long followed a program of systematic, institutionalized mendacity of truly Orwellian proportions.[2] Nor is the phenomenon unique to the Soviet Union. Current experiments with glasnost in other Marxist countries such as Hungary and Poland are confirming very similar records of falsehood. And in the People's Republic of China, the overthrow of the so-called "Gang of Four" in 1977 was followed by the admission that many official claims made during the period of Mao Zedong's rule (1949–1976) were in fact untrue. Among these is the assertion, very widely accepted by Western intellectuals in the 1960s and 1970s, that the Chinese communists had succeeded in eradicating famine in their country.

More disturbing than the prevalence of foreign propaganda is the fact that it is accorded a prominent, even privileged, position in the news coverage provided by a number of major American media, especially network television. This is an extremely serious charge, in particular because it is directed against professional journalists who pride themselves on their objectivity, skepticism, and sophistication, and I do not make it lightly here. Detailed evidence for the claim may be found in an earlier study (Smith 1988a; see also Tyson 1981; Muravchik 1988). For present purposes, the case must rest on three examples drawn from network television news and quoted in their entirety below. The first appeared on NBC's evening newscast for August 25, 1984.

Connie Chung: The Soviet Union today has a new explanation for the downing of the Korean airliner 007 nearly a year ago. Moscow Radio now claims the plane was actually destroyed by a U.S. bomb planted on board and set off by remote control to cover up a failed spy mission.

The second comes from the CBS evening newscast of March 30, 1987.

Dan Rather: A Soviet military publication claims the virus that causes AIDS leaked from a U.S. Army laboratory conducting experiments in biological warfare. The article offers no hard evidence but claims to be reporting conclusions of unnamed scientists in the United States, Britain, and East Germany. Last October a Soviet newspaper alleged that the AIDS virus may have been the result of Pentagon or CIA experiments.

The third example is taken from an interview of Radio Moscow "commentator" Vladimir Posner aired on February 26, 1986, as part of ABC's coverage of a speech in which President Reagan sought public support for increased defense spending.

David Brinkley: Well, the President said again what other American officials have often said, and it was this: that he wants to pursue the Strategic Defense Initiative, or Star Wars, and the Soviet Union is already pursuing it and has been, he said, for 20 years. People from your side always deny that. What is the fact?

Vladimir Posner: I think that before you can deny something or you can assert something you have to be able to show it. Now if the Soviet Union has been pursuing its equivalent of SDI for 20 years, the United States should be able to provide the proof, the testing of these things up in the air, the deployment, perhaps, of some of them. What the President said is simply not true, because there is no proof of this. And as a matter of fact, never did the United States even talk about a Soviet SDI kind of activity until it was proposed by the President back in 1983. Why for 14 [*sic*] years did no one in the American administration or the American military even bring up the idea that the Soviet Union was pursuing some kind of antiballistic space defense? Why? Because it didn't exist. Why is it brought up now? Because it has to be brought up as a proof that the Americans have to do the same thing. It's not there, never was, but supposedly now it is.

Four features of these examples require comment. First, all of the Soviet statements are clearly false. The NBC report claiming that KAL flight 007 was destroyed by the United States to cover up a failed spy mission is contradicted by the audio tape of the Soviet pilot's radio transmissions, including the chilling final statement "The target is destroyed," and by the Soviet Union's own admission on September 6, 1983, that it had "terminated" the flight. The claim that AIDS is the product of U.S. biological warfare experiments is part of a long-term Soviet disinformation campaign and was identified as such at a special State Department press briefing held on November 3, 1986, almost five months before the CBS report (see also, U.S. Department of State 1987a, pp. 51–55). Finally, aside from several lesser deceits in Mr. Posner's statement, his claims that the Soviet Union is not pursuing its equivalent of the American SDI program, and that President Reagan's assertions to the contrary are therefore "not true," were contradicted by Soviet leader Mikhail Gorbachev in a November 1987 interview with NBC's Tom Brokaw in which he acknowledged that his country was conducting SDI research.

Second, it seems likely that the veteran journalists who reported or elicited these claims did so *knowing* they were false. For one thing, even at the time they were made, all of the claims were preposterous. This is obvious in the case of the NBC and CBS reports: Any informed person would have been aware of the tapes and the Soviet admission of responsibility in the KAL–007 incident and of the extensive medical evidence indicating a natural African origin for the AIDS virus. As far as Mr. Posner's denial of any Soviet SDI program is concerned, brief reflection shows this claim to be almost equally improbable. Although opinions differ on the ultimate feasibility of an effective SDI system, the question is still open. And there is no doubt that deployment of such a system could mark a qualitative change in the military balance of power because it could largely negate an opponent's arsenal of nuclear missiles. This being so, it is almost unthinkable for the Soviet Union to forego research in this area while the United States forges ahead. Aside from constituting a radical departure from Soviet arms development policies since the end of World War II, it would be grossly irresponsible for the Soviet leaders to ignore this threat to their nation's military power.

But the best evidence of foreknowledge comes from the behavior of the journalists involved. Among other accusations, all three stories assert or directly imply that American leaders have lied to the American public. Given contemporary press values, even a marginally credible accusation of official mendacity can be expected to produce an outburst of intense journalistic scrutiny. Yet nothing of the sort occurred. The claims were reported and then ignored. This is reasonable only if the journalists involved were convinced the accusations were false.

Third, despite the fact that the Soviet claims were both false and viciously anti-American, and despite the strong probability that the journalists who reported them knew they were false, all were simply relayed to the American public without any comment or challenge whatsoever. Worse, by asking Mr. Posner to adjudicate a dispute between American and Soviet views ("What is the fact?"), Mr. Brinkley clearly suggested that Mr. Posner's claims were more veracious than President Reagan's.

Fourth, it must be stressed that claims like these are a common, even routine, feature of foreign affairs coverage in the American national media.[3] In any international dispute, the standard practice of most of these media is to adopt a "neutral" stance in which the conflicting claims of the United States and its opponent are accorded more or less equal status as the two "sides" of the controversy. The sides, however, are not treated equally throughout. The claims of American leaders are typically subjected to the most minute scrutiny, and even slight errors, omissions, exaggerations, and infelicities of expression are duly noted. In contrast, the claims of hostile opponents, even when blatantly propagandistic, are typically reported without comment, as in the three examples above; on occasion, American journalists make special efforts to bolster the plausibility of the hostile view.[4]

What this means, of course, is that the burden of proof in any controversy falls largely or completely on the American side, a highly disadvantageous position when dealing with a skilled and determined propagandist. For example, on January 4, 1989, American Navy F–14 fighters shot down two Libyan MIG–23 aircraft over the Mediterranean Sea. In justifying the action, the United States claimed its pilots had acted to defend themselves from a possible Libyan attack after maneuvering five times to avoid an engagement. The Libyan ambassador to the United Nations countered with the claim that the MiG–23s were unarmed reconnaissance aircraft. The United States then provided audio and video tapes of the engagement, the latter clearly showing air-to-air missile pods on one of the Libyan fighters. According to news accounts at the time, the Libyan ambassador responded that the tapes were "fake, fake, fake," noting that "we are in the country of Hollywood." At each stage of the dispute, only the United States was expected to provide proof of its claims, a task that turned out to be impossible. As any good propagandist knows, one cannot prove a negative, and thus the United States was unable to prove that the tapes were not fakes. The Libyan ambassador, in contrast, was free to assert whatever he liked without offering the slightest evidence in support of his claims. He was required neither to provide positive proof that the tapes were fakes (e.g., by identifying the Hollywood studio that produced them) nor to explain certain apparent anomalies in the Libyan case (e.g., why the Libyans thought it necessary to send a formation of *two* aircraft on a reconnaissance mission). In short, in this as in the preceding examples, viciously anti-American propaganda was not merely reported in the American media but accorded privileged status because relayed to the American public without journalistic comment or challenge.

If it is granted that hostile foreign propaganda is both common in international discussions and prominent in American news coverage, the problem of explaining why American scholars and journalists have devoted so little attention to it in recent years acquires even greater force and urgency. Unfortunately, the issues involved in this question are complex and contentious, and there is little space to deal with them here. Thus it must suffice to note only three immediately relevant causes and leave full discussion to another occasion.

The first and most obvious reason for the decline of propaganda analysis involves a shift in political orientations. Both scholars and national journalists are part of what the *New York Times* critic John Corry has called (1986) the "dominant culture" of the American intellectual and artistic elite.[5] Traditionally progressive in political outlook, the dominant culture moved sharply left during the political upheavals of the 1960s and early 1970s. One result is that faculties in the humanities and social sciences at the more prestigious senior colleges and universities now tend to be overwhelmingly liberal or "radical" in their political views, especially in several disciplines such as philosophy, sociology, political science, history, and English which in the past have been deeply concerned with the study of propaganda (see, e.g., the analysis of the 1984 Carnegie Foundation for the Advancement of Teaching survey data provided by professors Stephen Balch and Herbert London, 1986, pp. 43–44). Among journalists too, surveys typically show self-described liberals outnumbering conservatives by ratios of three to one or more, and a 1979–80 study of 238 national journalists found that of those who reported voting, 81 to 94 percent gave their support to the more liberal Democratic candidate in each of the four preceding presidential elections (Lichter, Rothman and Lichter 1986, pp. 20–53).

It should be noted, however, that while the dominant culture is generally leftist in outlook, it is neither monolithic nor politically extreme. A substantial number of its members are scattered among the multitudinous variants of Marxism, but the majority are more accurately described as liberals. Regardless, nearly all share a common animus: detestation of the insistent anticommunism of the political Right. For Marxists, the antipathy is clean, direct, and intense, the obvious product of a fundamental clash of primary principles. The antipathy of liberals, many of whom are themselves opposed to communism, is less direct and of more recent origin. Born of the backlash against the perceived[6] injustices of McCarthyism, it rejects conservative anticommunism both as a threat to the expression of minority views and, on grounds of intellectual taste, as shrill, simplistic, rigid, and gauche.

This widely noted anti-anticommunism of the dominant culture is directly relevant to the study of propaganda. In the decades immediately following World War II, when it was possible to point to recent examples of propaganda on both the extreme Left (communism) and Right (fascism), propaganda analysis entailed no necessary political commitments: Analysts on the Right could focus on communist examples, those on the Left on fascist. But fascism was virtually eradicated with the defeat of the Axis powers in 1945, while international socialism flourished. Thus, increasingly, new examples of what had traditionally been defined as propaganda came primarily from Marxist sources, and the study of contemporary propaganda necessarily acquired an anticommunist bent. When the dominant culture shifted further left in the 1960s, interest in analyzing contemporary propaganda quite understandably declined. As noted above, what interest remained tended to focus on historical studies of fascist propaganda in the Nazi era or on propaganda redefined to include discourse in the Western democracies (as in most Ellulian and Marxist analyses).

The second reason for the neglect of traditional propaganda may stem from the simple fact that it is so common and, at least to knowledgeable observers, so obvious. Intellectuals of a certain cast have always preferred the novelty, complexity, and subtlety of the realm of ideas to the world of brute facts and mundane experiences. In the dominant culture, however, this preference has hardened into orthodoxy.[7] It is manifested in contemporary scholarship (and journalism) by an almost contemptuous hostility to accounts of the obvious or "surface" meaning of events and a corresponding fascination with "deeper," hidden (and often contrary) levels of significance. Applied to the study of propaganda, this means there is little intellectual interest in showing, say, that the U.S. position in a dispute is almost certainly true while that of the USSR is almost certainly a lie. If one bothers at all, the far more appealing challenge is to show that by some novel standard of veracity the American position can be construed as false and the Soviet true. Hence the course of much recent propaganda analysis.

No one doubts that the pursuit of novelty, complexity, and subtlety can contribute to a richer, fuller understanding of the world. But serious problems arise when these traits are elevated to the position of dominant intellectual values. For one thing, those unaware of the new rules of the game (in particular, the general public) can be misled into mistaking the exceptional for the typical and the merely possible for the probable.[8] A deeper concern is that this habit of mind may have taken a pathological turn among some intellectuals. A large and growing number of interpretive (often "revisionist") studies in the humanities and social sciences (see, e.g., Lubin 1985 or the examples of classical semiotic scholarship analyzed in Sless 1986) can be accurately characterized as both wildly speculative and counterevidential, yet are treated seriously, sometimes even reverentially, by scholars in the field. What seems to be operating here is a standard of judgment which sees an existing view as false or suspect precisely *because* it is so obviously true, and an alternative "reading" as true or uniquely insightful precisely *because* it is so improbable. This strange inversion, which might be called the *intellectual fallacy*, now comes close to dominating scholarly discussion in some areas of the humanities.

The third and most important factor in the decline of propaganda studies is a direct outgrowth of the other two. It consists of the adoption of cultural relativism as the guiding philosophy of the dominant culture. This view begins with the belief that any knowledge claim inevitably reflects the values and assumptions of the culture in which it originates. To the extent that cultures differ, they will necessarily produce different truths. Thus a claim that appears to be false and dishonest by the standards of one culture may be true and sincere by the standards of another. Further, because there are no culture-free (i.e., universal) criteria with which to judge, the truths of any given culture must be accepted as just as valid as those of any other. To insist upon the unique validity of the insights of one's own culture is to commit the dread sin of ethnocentrism, presumed wellspring of racism, fascism, and imperialism, the great evils of our age.

It is difficult to exaggerate the extent to which this viewpoint—the basis of so-called "postmodern" thought—has come to permeate nearly all levels of American intellectual discourse. Among academics in particular, relativistic judgments are pronounced with an air of unanswerable finality, as if the whole of human thought and experience allowed no other possible conclusion. By now, almost an entire generation of American students has been drilled in its precepts. One of the most common tools in this endeavor is the familiar "perception" exercise. It consists of showing a group of students one or more drawings which have been carefully crafted to be interpretable in two ways, depending on what the observer takes as figure and what as ground. For example, one drawing shows an old woman or a young woman, another two profiles or a vase. From a pedagogical viewpoint the exercise is delightful because it always works—some students see the old woman, others the young, some see the profiles, others the vase. The "pullout" is usually a discussion of how one's "mental set" organizes sensory data into a coherent whole which, although essentially arbitrary, is highly resistant to change.

The application of these ideas to traditional conceptions of propaganda is obvious and devastating. Given contradictory claims by, say, the United States and another culture, the relativist sees no valid grounds for censure or concern; both sides, it must be presumed, are merely telling the truth as they see it, and both truths are equally valid. Insistence that the American claim is uniquely true, and the opponent's false, demonstrates nothing but the benighted ethnocentrism of the accuser, and opens him to the righteous contempt of the enlightened. This is especially clear when the opponent is a Marxist, whose claims are typically grounded in a highly elaborated and fully consistent ideological structure that guarantees their validity for the relativist.

Because the doctrine of cultural relativism is both widely accepted and, it would seem, directly opposed to the conception of propaganda developed here, some attempt at refutation is in order. This turns out to be a very easy task. Despite its intellectual cachet and glittery postmodernist trappings, relativism is in fact an old and grossly flawed philosophy, its deficiencies notorious since antiquity. The most lucid and comprehensive recent discussion of these defects can be found in Professor Allan Bloom's celebrated bestseller, *The Closing of the American Mind* (1987). For present purposes it will suffice to note only four of the more obvious flaws (see Smith 1988a, pp. 42–68 for a fuller discussion).

In the first place, relativism is *self-limiting* in much the same sense as the statement, "All general statements are false." Its primary assumption is that all truths are culture-bound and coequal. This implies that relativism itself must be the product of some culture (i.e., a set of values and assumptions) and that its truths are no more valid than the truths of any other culture, including those that reject relativism. That is, by its own standards, relativism is but one of many possible viewpoints, the one that consists specifically in denying the unique validity of any viewpoint, including (by implication) its own. A person may arbitrarily choose to adopt this viewpoint, but no one is intellectually compelled to do so. So much, then, for unanswerable finality.

Second, relativism is *useless* as a practical philosophy. The whole point of the doctrine is that different cultures can produce contradictory truths. For example, the United States and the Soviet Union disagree fundamentally about who started the Korean War. According to American (observational) standards of truth, North Korea attacked South Korea; according to Soviet (dialectical) standards, South Korea attacked the North. Which of these is true? Relativism must answer "Both" and leave it at that. But for those concerned with survival, that simply is not good enough. In general, survival requires action, action requires choice, and choice requires judgments of truth and value. Should we maintain or withdraw our troops now stationed in South Korea? Increase or decrease defense spending? Develop or abandon SDI? These are far from trivial choices, and each depends in part on how we answer the question of who started the Korean War. Given that we must decide, it seems perfectly reasonable to follow American standards and conclude that the North invaded the South. Certainly we have no reason to *prefer* the Soviet view. Thus we end up exactly where we would have if no one had ever thought of relativism.

Third, relativism is flagrantly *unrealistic*, especially in its more popular applications. There is a tendency among relativists, well represented in media coverage of the Soviet Union and other hostile regimes, to treat any statement from another culture as a true expression of that culture's standards and therefore exempt from criticism. But this is absurd. Even by the standards of his own culture, the person who made the statement could always be mistaken or lying, and it would be both valid and useful for a critic to point this out. Thus relativism, properly understood, neither precludes the existence of propaganda nor denies the value of propaganda analysis.

More important, relativism assumes that different cultures do have fundamentally different standards of truth and value. While this may be true in the realm of intellectual analysis, in the real world it is false. For one thing, real cultures are so interconnected by common roots, shared subcultures, and ongoing interaction that the boundaries among them are highly indistinct. Further, all cultures face the challenge of survival in the physical world and so must adjust their truths to the constraints of an apparently immutable physical reality.

This suggests the viewpoint's central flaw. Relativism is based on the undeniable insight that we can mentally construe reality in any way we please, and that, in purely intellectual terms, all of these constructions share a fundamental coequality. Applied to the physical world this means we could have, say, Albanian laws of motion or a Nigerian speed of light. But of course we don't, for the simple reason that nature, perhaps including human nature, seems to have a fixed character that functions very much like a universal (albeit solely negative) criterion of truth whenever a mental construction is used to guide action in the world. I amy be totally convinced I can fly, and able to offer the most elegant proofs of my ability to do so, but these count for little the moment I step off a cliff. Similarly, while it is possible that different people or cultures actually perceive the world in fundamentally different ways, experience suggest that for the most part they do not. Ironically, one of the best proofs of this comes from the perception exercise described above. While it is true that students differ in which figure they see, it is equally true, and very significant, that they only see one figure or the other. I know of no instance where a student looking at the drawing of the two women claimed to see, for example, a kitten or a tree. Yet if perception were really arbitrary and free, he could see, quite literally, anything at all.

In short, real cultures, despite their manifold differences, have tended to evolve very similar standards of fact and inference.[9] Indeed, it is doubtful that a single national culture now rejects the validity of statistical inference, scientific method, sensory observation, categorical logic, or, in general, more than a handful of the traditional standards of rational argumentation listed in any introductory logic text. Given this widespread agreement, it is perfectly valid for one culture to criticize the claims of another, especially on issues of physical existence and causal implication. Further, it seems clear that the standards of any given culture can be invalid, and its claims therefore false. A spectacular example of this is now unfolding. Marxists tried for more than a century to impose on reality a mental construct that was highly elaborated and fully consistent, but which most of them now recognize as false in certain crucial respects. This recognition is the driving force behind the Soviet policies of glasnost and perestroika, which have led to the wholesale abandonment of ideological (dialectical) "truths" about history and current affairs and their replacement by new truths which seem to be derived from familiar Western observational standards.

The fourth flaw of relativism is its *antidemocratic* cast. Western liberal democracy is a sociopolitical system based on values of freedom, equality, and tolerance which seeks truth through a process of reasoned discourse. Relativism denies that these values and truths are inherently superior to those of any other system, attributing all to the operation of arbitrary preference. One effect of this is to weaken the defense of democracy against the attacks of hostile systems untroubled by relativistic assumptions. If democracy really is no better than any other system, on what grounds can it possibly be defended? Further, if rational truths really are no better than irrational, or if rational discourse produces contradictory truths, then reason itself is worthless in adjudicating disputes. This leaves but one arbiter of truth and value: force. These criticisms, of course, are far from universal. As any relativist would agree, their acceptance depends on how one feels about such concepts as democracy and reason, and the proponents of these, both now and in the past, have been relatively few. Still, we do live in a democratic society and at least some are still committed to its ideals. For them it may be useful to see just what is implied by the philosophy so widely embraced by the dominant culture of the artistic and intellectual elite.

In summary, the three factors of shifts in the political orientation of propaganda sources and critics, intellectual fascination with novelty, complexity, and subtlety, and adoption of relativism as the guiding philosophy of the dominant culture provide at least a partial explanation for the neglect of propaganda by scholars and journalists in recent years. These factors also indicate the existence of several problems which, while they do not invalidate traditional propaganda analysis, do suggest the need for reforms. In particular, the liberal concern that pejorative labels can function to suppress the expression of minority ideas calls attention to the fact that the term "propaganda" is often misused as a mere epithet to dismiss unpalatable views. Similarly, intellectual preoccupation with the margins of possibility reminds us that the issues addressed in analyzing propaganda can seldom be resolved with complete certainty. In any given case, alternative analyses and conclusions will be possible, and some apparently obvious truths can turn out to be neither. Finally, for all its flaws, relativism is right in insisting that every truth is a product of an intellectual perspective based on values and assumptions about which reasonable people can and do disagree. Thus the mere existence of contradiction or disagreement in the conclusions of different groups is no necessary sign of error or deceit.

However, the scope of these problems is strictly limited. The fact that the term "propaganda" can be misused provides no reason for abandoning it altogether. To the contrary, it seems clear that anyone who falsely calls another "propagandist" deserves the label for himself. Similarly, the circumstance that truth is seldom certain and sometimes hidden is hardly grounds for renouncing reasoned judgment or embracing the intellectual fallacy. It does mean that accusations of propaganda must be documented with great care and that even in the best of circumstances limitations of available evidence may leave some room for doubt about the accuracy of the label. Finally, while it is axiomatic that truth varies by perspective, it does not necessarily follow that all perspectives are true.[10] It does mean that the propaganda analyst should be able to defend the validity of whatever perspective he chooses, and should choose a perspective that will allow him to be tolerant of sincere disagreement but intolerant of error and deceit.

The problems of malign mislabeling, evidential limits of certainty, and perspectival limits of truth all suggest that the analysis of propaganda defined as deceitful communication is a difficult and dangerous undertaking, strewn with pitfalls for the unwary. The solution to these problems follows from developing a much more precise conception of what propaganda is and how it can be recognized. We turn to these tasks next

PROPAGANDA DEFINED

Because all definitions involve an element of arbitrary stipulation, they cannot be judged as true or false, only more or less useful. In the case of propaganda, a useful definition is one that permits unequivocal judgments of type when applied to instances of actual discourse. To this end, propaganda may be defined as *any conscious and open attempt to influence the beliefs of an individual or group, guided by a predetermined end and characterized by the systematic use of irrational and often unethical techniques of persuasion*. Each term in the definition merits separate discussion.

The stipulation that propaganda is *conscious* means only that the propagandist deliberately seeks to influence his audience. It does not imply that he consciously chooses to employ irrational and unethical techniques of persuasion. While this may often be the case, it is not invariably so.

Propaganda is *open* in the sense that there is no attempt to hide the source of the propaganda message. This distinguishes propaganda from "disinformation," which may be defined as deceitful information spread by clandestine means such as forgery, blackmail, and the use of front groups and agents of influence, the latter including journalists who knowingly or unknowingly disseminate foreign or other hostile material without revealing its source. While the two are obviously related, propaganda analysis focuses primarily on message content while disinformation analysis tends to focus on message origin and the means employed in its distribution.

The characterization of propaganda as an influence *attempt* means only that it can be identified independently of its effects. This contrasts with the view of some researchers in the broader field of persuasion, especially those working in the behaviorist tradition, who restrict the term "persuasion" to successful influence attempts (Smith 1982, pp. 3–26). There are two major problems with adopting this view in the study of propaganda. First, to justify describing a message as propaganda, it would be necessary to offer proof of its effects. Unfortunately, this is seldom possible outside the research setting and thus would greatly restrict the use and usefulness of the term. Second, in this view the same message could be seen as propaganda or not depending on its effects on different audiences. This opens endless possibilities for confusion.

Propaganda is an attempt to *influence the beliefs* of an audience. This formulation in no way contradicts the common view that propaganda is typically intended to influence action. It does serve to remind that changes in belief are almost always a prerequisite for changes in external behavior, and that sometimes the purpose of propaganda is to inhibit action, not encourage it. It also suggests that the goals of propaganda are often more modest than is commonly thought. In particular, few experienced propagandists ever seek to actually convert their opponents, choosing instead the much easier task of modifying the strength of their convictions. For example, the Soviet Union has long justified its destruction of KAL flight 007 by asserting that the aircraft was spying for the United States. Lacking any positive proof for this claim, it appears that the Soviets are less concerned with convincing the American public that the aircraft actually *was* spying, than that it *might* have been, or at least that the Soviets were justified in thinking it was. Aided by extensive and highly sympathetic treatment in the American news and entertainment media (especially the 1988 NBC docudrama *Shootdown*), the campaign seems to have been successful. Certainly there are few Americans who have not at least heard of the spy charge (Smith 1988a, pp. 93–119).

Stated in general terms, a liar is successful to the extent that he reduces belief in the truth. Any reduction is useful, because it decreases the confidence with which an opponent will act. If the goal is to paralyze opposition, it is enough to instill the belief that a lie and the truth are equally probable, or that all parties to the discussion are lying. Thus propaganda can seek either action or inaction, conviction or doubt, and its efficacy should be judged accordingly.

The stipulation that propaganda seeks to influence an *individual or group* implies that it can use either interpersonal or mediated channels of communication. This marks a break with the tradition that associates propaganda exclusively with the mass media. It is difficult to see the value of this restriction. Propaganda existed before the invention of the modern high-speed media, and most if not all of the techniques of the craft can be used with equal facility in both mass and interpersonal settings. Further, many organized propaganda campaigns such as "grassroots" movements in the United States and "study" or "struggle" sessions in the Marxist countries can be understood only if their major interpersonal components are considered. Having said this, it must still be acknowledged that most of the more dramatic, significant, and readily documented examples of propaganda are found in the mass media.

All propaganda is guided by some *predetermined end*. It is easy to make too much and too little of this point. Nearly all communication is goal-directed, so in that sense propaganda is unexceptional. But the ends of propaganda have two somewhat special characteristics. First, they are fixed. In ordinary discourse, goals often fluctuate in the course of interaction. In propaganda, however, the ultimate goals are immutable and thus unresponsive to situational variation. Second, the ends of propaganda are typically remote, in the sense that propaganda almost always seeks effects beyond the immediate occasion. These ends may be general or specific, hidden or open, sinister or benign, but they add a dimension of significance often missing from ordinary interaction.

The primary defining characteristic of propaganda is its reliance on *irrational* techniques of persuasion. There are, of course, a number of different views of rationality. For present purposes, a technique will be considered irrational if it serves to induce belief in an audience without providing adequate support for that belief. Put somewhat differently, a technique is irrational if it produces a claim that cannot survive the unrestricted critical scrutiny of reasonable men. In one form or another, this critical (or "conflict") view of rationality underlies all Western democratic institutions and constitutes one of the proudest accomplishments of Western civilization. It therefore seems particularly appropriate as a standard for judging discourse in Western democratic societies.

There is need, however, for a certain amount of care in applying this standard. Given the normal human frailties of ignorance, error, inattention, and sloth, careful examination will reveal that nearly all persuasive messages are marred by at least the occasional use of irrational techniques. It would serve little purpose to classify all of these as propaganda. Instead, the term should be reserved for those messages marked by the *systematic* use of irrational techniques. Systematic use is indicated either by the frequent occurrence of those techniques or by their occasional occurrence at critical junctures of an argument. In the extreme case, a message could be considered propaganda if it contained a single, but absolutely crucial, error.

The penultimate characteristic of propaganda is its use of techniques that are *often unethical*. As in the case of rationality, there are many opinions about the nature of ethical behavior. One very widespread view centers on the idea of the present worth, dignity, and autonomy of the individual. Its primary assumption is that each person has a peculiarly authentic perspective which must be taken into account when dealing with that person. Thus each individual is seen as an end in himself, uniquely qualified to judge what is in his own best interests, who must be fully consulted in matters affecting his fate. Applied to the realm of social influence, this view sees any conscious attempt to manipulate an individual (e.g., by the use or threat of force, by offering defective proofs, or by arousing base emotions) as unethical, either because it uses the individual merely as a means to another's end or because it denies him the opportunity to truly judge what is in his own best interest. Thus any conscious use of irrational techniques of persuasion must also be unethical. This view of the individual is central to the Western conception of popular democracy and most of the rights it confers. It therefore seems particularly appropriate as a standard for ethical judgments of discourse in Western democratic societies.

It is important to note the precise implications of this analysis. In the conception here proposed, the crucial defining characteristic of propaganda is the systematic use of irrational techniques of persuasion. An irrational technique can be used consciously or unconsciously. If used consciously, the message is also unethical; if unconsciously (e.g., through ignorance or honest error), the message may very well be ethical. Thus, in this conception, ethicality is *not* a defining characteristic of propaganda.

The stipulation that propaganda can sometimes be fully ethical is offered as an analytical refinement to the popular conception of propaganda as deceitful communication, which implies that propaganda is *always* unethical. It seems likely that nearly all propaganda is unethical to some degree.

But it creates several serious and unnecessary problems if used as a defining characteristic in formal analysis.

One problem with defining propaganda as always unethical is that it creates an unreasonable burden of proof for the propaganda analyst. To conclude that a message is unethical, it is necessary to show that the propagandist employed irrational techniques *consciously*. But even in the best of circumstances the task of establishing conscious intent is notoriously difficult. When dealing with a skilled and unscrupulous propagandist, the task is often impossible, especially because the propaganda analyst is so seldom able to directly interrogate the source. For example, there is little likelihood that any critic could prove that the Libyan ambassador was lying when he described the Libyan MiG–23s as unarmed reconnaissance aircraft. Even if the claim were shown to be false, it could still be argued that the ambassador was merely mistaken or misinformed in his assertions. Thus the effect of making unethical behavior a defining characteristic of propaganda would be to eliminate from consideration a number of important instances of irrational and misleading communication because of a lack of definitive proof of unethicality. This would benefit only propagandists.

Second, while acceptance of the ethical viewpoint adopted here is widespread, it is by no means universal. In particular, it is a central tenet of Marxist-Leninist ideology that the masses of ordinary citizens in a society can be so oppressed that they labor under a "false consciousness" in which they are incapable of recognizing their own best interests. In this circumstance, it is the role and duty of the enlightened members of the Communist Party—Lenin's "vanguard of the proletariat"—to use whatever means are necessary to induce the masses to act in their own interests. This may require manipulation (or worse), but such means can always be morally justified by the altruism of the end (i.e., liberation from oppression).

It is, of course, perfectly legitimate for someone committed to the Western democratic principle of the present worth, dignity, and autonomy of the individual to condemn the Marxist-Leninist view: The two positions are, after all, fundamentally opposed. It is also worth noting that the Marxist-Leninist view is very easily abused, and that its application in countries such as the Soviet Union, the People's Republic of China, and Cambodia has led to human death and misery on an almost unimaginable scale. Still, there is no doubt that both positions (and others) are fully coherent and can be sincerely espoused. Thus the conflict between them is ultimately irresolvable. This means that the question of whether a given message is unethical may also be irresolvable, and therefore the use of unethicality as a defining characteristic of propaganda would tend to divert attention from analysis of the message to endless disputes about the nature of ethical behavior.

A third problem is implicit in the other two. The study of propaganda has always had a strongly practical and didactic cast. We label messages "propaganda" to warn that they may not be what they seem and to invite a closer scrutiny. And we analyze examples of the craft to see how reasonable people can be misled and to teach them how such snares can be avoided. In this tradition, the question of ethical status, while often significant, is clearly secondary, for a message can deceive just as surely by accident as by design. But if ethicality is made a defining feature of propaganda, this order is reversed. If each use of the term implies a final moral verdict, peripheral issues of conscious intent and the nature of ethical behavior must become primary. When these are irresolvable, the term must be abandoned. But in so doing, we abandon also those pragmatic benefits which are the reason we engage in propaganda analysis in the first place. Thus adoption of an ethical criterion is fundamentally self-defeating.

Finally, elimination of unethicality as a defining characteristic of propaganda can have the effect of facilitating useful ethnical judgments. If unethicality is a definitive factor, the evidence of unethical behavior must be so overwhelming that it supports a *categorical* judgment. This is seldom possible in practice. If it is not a definitive factor, however, it is necessary to establish only the *reasonable probability* that the propagandist acted unethically. This is often both possible and useful, because it serves as a warning of manipulative intent. For example, the character of certain propaganda techniques (e.g., assertions contrary to obvious matters of fact) is such that the simple fact of their use provides strong (but not irrefutable) proof of conscious deceit. Similar conclusions follow from the finding that irrational techniques have been used systematically, especially when there is evidence of selection by the propagandist. Finally, given that irrational techniques have been used, the only way to avoid a judgment of unethicality is to claim that their use was the result of honest ignorance. This is a very difficult claim to accept when it is offered in defense of messages crafted with care by knowledgeable professionals such as national leaders, official spokesmen, and supposed experts in a field. In these cases, the mere existence of systematic irrationality supports a presumption of guile.

The last notable feature of propaganda is its reliance on characteristic *techniques* of persuasion. For many years, most popular and academic discussions of the topic featured some list of common propaganda devices. Brown's inventory (1963, pp. 26–28) is typical: stereotyping, substitution of names, selection, repetition, downright lying, assertion, pinpointing the enemy, and appeal to authority.

In general, this emphasis seems well placed. Unlike other forms of discourse, propaganda seeks not truth but adherence or effect, and it is therefore not a method but a body of techniques. Moreover, certain techniques of persuasion have long been recognized as irrational and thus their use in a message constitutes clear evidence of its propagandistic nature. But the various lists proposed in the past are poorly suited to guide propaganda analysis because they share the defect of focusing on techniques which are defined so vaguely that even experts disagree whether their use is irrational in particular cases. For example, of the eight techniques listed by Brown, only "downright lying" is generally unacceptable, and Brown defines it only by example (1963, p. 27). All of the others are open to widely varied interpretation. One person's stereotype is another's generalization, disputants disagree sharply over proper naming, all messages must be a partial selection from the available facts, and so on through the list. What is needed is a more precisely specified set of techniques, and one more closely in line with the actual practices of sophisticated modern propagandists. We turn to this task next.

THE TECHNIQUES OF PROPAGANDA

The number of different irrational techniques is unlimited, but all can be placed in one of four general categories: falsehoods, omissions, distortions, or suggestions. In a sense, all propagandistic claims are *falsehoods*. But it will be useful to reserve the term to denote those claims, supported or unsupported, that conflict with verifiable facts. As with all irrational techniques, a falsehood can be the product of accident or design. When uttered with full knowledge of its falsity, a falsehood becomes a lie. For most, lies and falsehoods are the paradigmatic techniques of the propagandist, and their use in a message provides the clearest possible evidence of its propagandistic nature.

Lies can take several forms, the most familiar of which is the blatant, reiterated "Big Lie" of Nazi lore. In addition to those cited earlier, one recent and obvious example[11] is the TASS statement of September 1, 1983, which claimed that KAL flight 007, after ignoring Soviet interceptors which "tried to give it assistance in directing it to the nearest airfield," then "continued its flight in the direction of the Sea of Japan." Another instance is the repeated and categorical denials by various members of the Nicaraguan government in March 1986 that its troops had entered Honduras to attack Contra forces. In both cases these statements were later contradicted by the governments which had made them.

More generally, almost every formal American criticism of the Soviet Union elicits a *tu quoque response* in which a mirror-image set of accusations is directed against the United States. For example, on January 23, 1984, President Reagan charged the Soviet Union with specific, documented violations of seven treaties governing strategic arms and chemical and biological weapons. The Soviet government responded immediately by accusing the United States of an almost identical set of specific violations, but, characteristically, offered no evidence to support them.

Another form of lie, familiar to anyone who has read Orwell's *1984*, is the *historical reconstruction*. Although all accounts of history involve a degree of selection and emphasis, Marxist states are unique among modern nations for engaging in the systematic elimination and fabrication of elements of the historical record. The classic example of historical eradication involves Soviet official Lavrenti Beria, Stalin's feared head of internal security from 1938 to 1953, a member of the central committee of the C.P.S.U. and Politburo, one of three leaders to deliver a eulogy at Stalin's 1953 funeral and, briefly, minister for internal affairs in the post-Stalin government. Within a few months of Stalin's death, however, he was accused of high treason, convicted, and executed, after which the long (and laudatory) article on him in the *Great Soviet Encyclopedia* was physically removed (Brown 1963, p. 123).

These practices are still very much in evidence. For example, historical photographs published in the Chinese press in recent years have been retouched to remove all traces of the Gang of Four, and when a joint Indian-Soviet documentary on Jawaharlal Nehru was shown on Soviet television in 1985, all footage of former leader Nikita Khrushchev had been edited out. At present, there are signs that Mr. Khrushchev may soon be "rehabilitated," but the Soviet government has now ordered the removal of all public commemorations of Leonid Brezhnev, who ruled the Soviet Union from 1964 to 1982, and Konstantin Chernenko, who held power for 13 months in 1984–85. Nor has Mr. Beria fared any better: His name is still missing from the index of the current edition of the *Great Soviet Encyclopedia*.

Instances of historical fabrication range from the crude to the sophisticated. Included in the former category are the Chinese films of captured American airmen "confessing" to germ warfare attacks during the Korean War (Kinkead 1960). At the other extreme is a monument to the victims of the Katyn massacre erected by the Polish government. In 1939, approximately 15,000 Polish army reservists were interned by the Soviet Union when its forces occupied eastern Poland in accordance with secret provisions of the Russo-German nonaggression pact negotiated by Hitler and Stalin. The pact was shattered in 1941 when Hitler ordered the invasion of the Soviet Union. In 1943, Germany reported the discovery of mass graves in the Katyn forest near Smolensk containing the bodies of more than 4,000 of the Polish internees and accused the Soviet Union of their murder. The Soviets, responding tu quoque, blamed Germany.

Popular and scholarly opinion in the West and Poland, backed by very strong circumstantial evidence, has long favored the German account (see Rurarz 1989 for a brief discussion). In 1981, groups associated with the Solidarity movement erected a monument to the victims which, by its dating of the event, clearly implied Soviet responsibility. That monument was quickly removed and, in 1985, the Polish government installed another on the same site; its inscription blames "Hitlerite fascism" for the massacre, a lie immortalized in stone. But there may yet be several more chapters in the drama. On November 6, 1988, Soviet media announced that a new monument would be erected in the Soviet Union to commemorate the "Polish officers" and "Soviet prisoners" who were "held at the concentration camp near Katyn" and "shot by fascists in 1943 when our army approached." Meanwhile, back in Poland, the Polish government announced in February 1989 that the false inscription on its monument would be removed.

A final type of lie is the *symbolic fiction*, an untruth endorsed by some supposedly disinterested and respectable party. The classic example concerns the Russian claim that the USSR is a voluntary confederation of fifteen independent republics. Few knowledgeable observers take this claim seriously, but the Soviets demanded at the 1945 San Francisco Conference that all fifteen republics be granted seats in the General Assembly of the proposed United Nations. The outcome was a "compromise" that gave full membership to the Byelorussian SSR and Ukrainian SSR and thus official United Nations endorsement of the falsehood. (It is the darkest of ironies that the Ukraine, incorporated into the Soviet Union by the Red Army and scene of the genocidal "terror-famine" of 1932–33 [Conquest 1986], should receive this spurious recognition of its sovereignty.) More recently, on January 12, 1989, the United Nations Security Council voted 9–4 in favor of a resolution proposed by Libya and the 101-nation "nonaligned" bloc which states that the Council "deplores the downing of the two Libyan reconnaissance planes" by the United States. The only negative votes came from Britain, France, the United States (all vetoes), and Canada.

A more subtle example came to light in 1985 when it was revealed that the Oxford University Press had allowed the Soviets to change a number of entries in two dictionaries published under its name for use in the Soviet Union. As a result, Marxists throughout the world can now point to authentic Oxford dictionary defintions of capitalism as "the last antagonistic social and economic system in human history, based on the exploitation of man by man, replacing feudalism and preceding communism," and of communism as "a theory revealing the historical necessity for the revolutionary replacement of capitalism by communism."

Omissions constitute the second category of irrational techniques. It must be stressed that every persuasive message will necessarily omit material relevant to its claims because no message can possibly say everything that is known about a subject. An omission is irrational and propagandistic when the missing information is both available to the message source (should he take the effort to look for it) and highly damaging to his claims Consider for example the entire description of the Korean War provided under the entry "Korea" in the current English-language edition of the official *Great Soviet Encyclopedia*.

In June 1949, by resolution of a joint plenary session of the Central Committee of the Workers Parties of North and South Korea, both parties merged into the Korean

Workers Party (KWP), which headed political and economic construction. Founded in June 1949, the United Democratic Fatherland Front (UDFF) advanced proposals in 1949 and 1950 for peaceful unification. They were rejected, however, by the South Korean authorities, who attempted to annihilate by arms the people's democratic system in the North. On June 25, 1950, the South Korean military clique launched a military action against the PDRK [North Korea]. The USA immediately intervened in this domestic Korean conflict. Several other countries also took part in the intervention, carried out under the mask of "UN forces." More than half of the armed forces fighting in the Korean War were American (American ground forces amounted to 50.3 percent, naval forces—85.9 percent, and air forces—93.4 percent).

Called upon by the KWP, the working people of the PDRK arose to take part in the Fatherland Liberation War of 1950–53. The PDRK, with the support of the USSR, the People's Republic of China (from which detachments of people's volunteers came to Korea), and other socialist countries, as well as progressive forces from all over the world, rebuffed the aggressors, who were compelled to sign a truce on July 27, 1953. (The agreement was signed by the supreme commander in chief of the Korean People's Army and the commander of the Chinese people's volunteers, on one hand, and by the commander in chief of the so-called UN troops, on the other.)

These two short paragraphs offer a veritable cornucopia of propaganda devices, a few of which will be noted below. For present purposes it is enough to note that the entire thrust of the analysis is contradicted by the indisputable fact that within a month of the outbreak of hostilities, North Korean (PDRK) forces had occupied approximately 85 percent of South Korean territory. Thus omission of this fact is irrational and propagandistic.

The third and largest category of irrational techniques consists of *distortions*. A distortion occurs whenever a message source draws an invalid or unjustifiable conclusion from the evidence he presents. It is impossible to enumerate all of the different kinds of distortions because the number of conceivable reasoning errors is unlimited. Nevertheless, several hundred of the most common have been named and described over the last 2,300 years and can be found in any good introductory logic text under the headings of formal and informal fallacies. Only a few of the more important of these can be discussed here.

Perhaps the most common group of distortions in contemporary discourse consists of *errors of statistical inference*. A striking feature of current popular debate in the United States is the widespread reliance on quantified information. Yet, paradoxically, the vast majority of Americans have little training in or understanding of quantitative methods. This statistical illiteracy extends from presidents and their advisors down to the lowliest citizens. But it is especially evident in the news reports of journalists, where elementary errors of interpretation are common, even routine, at least in coverage of such areas as economic affairs (e.g., Smith 1988c) and opinion poll results (e.g., Smith and Verrall 1985; Smith and Hogan 1987). This is not meant to disparage journalists, but only to indicate that they, like most people, often do not know what they are talking about when they discuss statistical information. And it suggests that if honest, reasonable, and well-educated people can make such errors, the possibilities for distortion and deception in the hands of skilled and unprincipled propagandists are limitless.

Several other distortions are noteworthy because they occur with such frequency in Marxist propaganda that they serve to define its nature. The first of these is the technique of *multiple assertions*. It consists of making contradictory claims to different audiences, as did the Soviet authorities in the 1970s when they provided one account of the policy of detente to their own citizens and a contradictory account to foreigners (e.g., U.S. Congress, Senate 1972). While it may be impossible to prove which of the accounts is false, they cannot both be true, thus revealing propagandistic intent.

A second technique is the use of *multiple standards*. Thus Marxists invariably evaluate socialist societies according to how far they have come since the evils and privations of prerevolutionary days, but judge capitalist societies on the basis of how far they have yet to go to realize their ideals. These themes are also a staple feature of American television coverage of socialist countries, especially Cuba (e.g., the 1986 PBS documentary "Cuba: In the Shadow of Doubt" or the contrasting reports on Cuba and Honduras on consecutive "60 Minutes" programs in January 1989). Not surprisingly, the socialist societies always seem to emerge looking superior.

The next common distortion, which might be called the *fallacy of limited alternatives*, is a more general version of the false dilemma, known since antiquity. It involves reasoning to a false conclusion by artificially restricting the number of alternatives considered possible. For example, in his two-hour news conference following the destruction of KAL flight 007, Marshal Ogarkov gave this account of Soviet actions: "When it [KAL flight 007] did not react to 120 warning shots, nothing was left for us to do but to react the way we did." Obviously, a number of other actions were possible, such as firing more warning shots, firing shots into the aircraft, or, most important, breaking off the engagement.

A final distortion might be called the *fallacy of impossible certainty*. It consists of drawing a positive conclusion about an issue on which certainty is impossible. For example, in September 1985 the Afghanistan government claimed that antigovernment guerrillas had shot down a civilian airliner using an American-made missile and that the attack was proof that the U.S. was providing sophisticated military equipment to the guerrillas. It is highly doubtful that the aircraft was a civilian airliner (it had taken off from the besieged and embattled city of Kandahar), and it is not even certain that it was shot down (it may simply have crashed due to mechanical problems). Nor is there any clear evidence that the U.S. government was supplying American antiaircraft missiles to the guerrillas at that time. Regardless, there is no possible way in the time available that the Afghan government could have identified with certainty the country of origin of the *exploded* missile supposedly used in the attack, and thus for this reason alone the argument is fallacious. That did not, however, prevent it from being reported without question in a number of American news media.

Suggestions comprise the fourth major category of irrational techniques of persuasion. The defining characteristic of a suggestion is that it presents information in such a way that the audience is likely to draw an invalid or unjustifiable conclusion. It should be stressed, however, that the information itself is often accurate or at least indisputable (as in the case of a definition).

The crudest form of suggestion is *name-calling*, which offers not proof for a claim but a mere label. For example, by calling someone a "scoundrel" the audience is encouraged to believe that he is one, although no evidence of this has been provided. A common positive variant of this is the technique of *role reference*, which describes a person in terms of one of his marginal roles in hopes that the audience will falsely ascribe the assumed characteristics of that role to the person. Examples of this practice are legion in American news coverage. For example, Marxist revolutionaries are typically described as poets, artists, teachers, writers, journalists, or clergymen, and members of the Marxist, Ethiopian-backed Sudanese People's Liberation Army are almost always referred to as "Christian" guerrillas.

Three specific forms of suggestion are especially common in Soviet propaganda designed for Western audiences. The technique of *allusion* points directly to an unstated claim that the audience is invited to accept without proof. For example, in the description of the Korean War provided by the *Great Soviet Encyclopedia*, the phrases "under the mask of 'UN forces' " and "so-called UN troops" suggest the false but unstated claim that these troops were not fighting under the aegis of the United Nations. In fact, a resolution passed by the United Nations Security Council on June 27, 1950, two days after the North Korean invasion, recommended that member nations "furnish such assistance to the Republic of Korea [i.e., South Korea] as may be necessary to repel the armed attack and to restore international peace and security in the area." This resolution avoided being vetoed only because the Soviet Union had been boycotting Council meetings since January 1950, but it committed the United Nations fully and legitimately to the South Korean side.

The technique of *apposition* is more subtle. It simply arrays a collection of materials and allows the audience to deceive itself by discovering a connection among them. Thus the entry on the Korean War ends by noting that the truce was signed by the North Korean, Chinese, and United Nations commanders. In conjunction with earlier comments about outside intervention and the predominance of American troops, this might suggest to some that the South Koreans were mere pawns who played no active part in the conflict. Of course, in fact, South Korea was fully represented in all negotiations but refused to sign the armistice because it perpetuated the division of the country. Further, the outside "intervention" was requested by the South Korean government and endorsed by the United Nations, and South Korean troops suffered far more casualties than all other U.N. forces combined and constituted a majority or plurality of all U.N. forces for much of the war.

The last type of suggestion, which might be called *asymmetrical definition*, is so central to Marxist propaganda that it requires extended consideration. It occurs whenever a message source uses a word that has a substantially different meaning to his audience than it does to him. Unless warned, audience members will naturally attribute their usual meaning to the word and thereby be misled.

The description of the Korean War from the *Great Soviet Encyclopedia* provides at least a dozen examples, of which two are particularly clear. It states that "several other countries" intervened along with the United States and that "detachments of people's volunteers" from China supported North Korea. Unlike many of the other terms used in the article (e.g., "peaceful unification," "intervened," "rebuffed the aggressors"), these are fairly straightforward descriptions of factual matters. The facts are that fifteen countries provided combat units to assist the U.S. and South Korean forces and five additional countries sent noncombat medical teams (see Hastings 1987, pp. 365–68 for a complete list of countries offering and providing aid); the Chinese "detachments" comprised several million members of the Chinese Red Army over the course of the war, of whom at least 500,000 died in battle (1987, p. 329).

Most Americans would find it very difficult to reconcile these facts with the Soviet description of them. In American English, "several" does not mean twenty, and "detachments of people's volunteers" does not connote millions of regular army troops. There are two possible reasons for this disparity. It could be that the Soviet author is asserting a different set of facts. That is, he may be claiming that only, say, three or four other nations joined the United States and that the Chinese detachments were small voluntary units similar to the Abraham Lincoln Brigade in the Spanish Civil War. If so, his statements are best described as lies or falsehoods, because there is overwhelming evidence that more than twenty nations and millions of Chinese troops were involved. The other possibility is that the problem lies not in disagreement about facts but in the use of language. That is, the author may be using "several" to denote twenty and "detachments" to describe millions. If so, an American would say he is misusing language and misleading his readers, for his words suggest something very different. But can the Soviet author be faulted for this?

Few would hesitate to condemn the author if it were known that he had deliberately chosen inappropriate language for his descriptions in order to mislead his readers. In this case, his descriptions would be simple lies. The problem is that it is very difficult to expose this kind of a lie. The definition of any word is a matter of convention and can be changed more or less at will. Thus different cultures (nations, groups, individuals) can use the same word to mean very different things and, as relativists would insist, one culture's conventional definition is just as valid as any other's. It could be that Soviet culture (or some group in that culture, or merely the author himself) defines "several" to mean twenty and "detachment" to mean millions. Therefore it could be that the author was merely telling the truth as he saw it, using language that is perfectly appropriate given the definitions of his culture. In this case, the author's descriptions might well mislead someone from another culture, but he could hardly be accused of lying. Even if he was lying, he could always claim he was using a different definition and it would be hard for anyone to disprove him.

In the absence of any firm evidence to the contrary, it must be assumed that misleading statements are the product of unusual cultural definitions rather than deceit. And it is obvious that no one could fault a person for using those definitions when addressing other members of his own culture. But the case at hand is somewhat different, for the English-language edition of the *Great Soviet Encyclopedia* is not addressed to Soviet citizens, but to members of other cultures. In such situations, other responsibilities come into force. You can mean anything you like by a word when talking to yourself or to others in your culture, but when you address me, my meanings and the meanings of my culture must be taken into account. In American culture, if you invite me to dinner I can expect to be fed, not eaten, no matter how the invitation might normally be interpreted in your culture.

This matter strikes at the core of the "East-West dialogue" fostered so assiduously over the last two decades by a broad spectrum of American politicians, journalists, and other opinion leaders. That policy is grounded in the belief that increased communication between the United States and the Soviet Union will lead to greater trust and understanding, recognition of shared interests, and a lessening of international tensions. One result has been a vast expansion in coverage of the Soviet viewpoint in the American news media. For example, the number of appearances by Soviet spokesmen on network television evening newscasts increased 550 percent (from 50 to 325) between 1981 and 1985 (Smith 1988a, p. 88). Whatever merits this may have as a conflict resolution strategy, it should be recognized that the Soviets and other Marxists are extremely careful in defining their terms, and that the definitions they propose often bear little resemblance to those assumed by the American public. Indeed, virtually all of the common terms of political discourse—peace, freedom, democracy, majority, truth, consciousness, and hundreds of others—have acquired a radically different aspect in the context of Marxist-Leninist dialectics.

The Soviets in particular are quite open about this, and anyone who takes the trouble to familiarize himself with the basic tenets of Marxist-Leninist theory will quickly see the great differences in significance these terms can acquire. For example, consider the meanings of the word "peace" distinguished by Brown (1963, pp. 121–22): "Thus 'peace', which ordinarily means a state of friendly relations with other countries, is interpreted by Communists to mean the state of affairs in a Communist country since capitalist countries are assumed to be in a state of open class war and of at least potential hostility amongst each other in their competitive struggle for survival." Therefore, if a Soviet spokesman says his country is committed to achieving "world peace," it could mean his country is committed to establishing worldwide communism, for according to Marxist-Leninist theory it is only under those circumstances that true "peace" is possible.

Or consider the following discussion of "peaceful coexistence." It is taken from an illuminating little book entitled *Whose Interests Does "Psychological Warfare" Serve*, written by one Lev Nikolayev and published by the official Novosti Press Agency Publishing House (1983). Copies of it could be found in every tourist room in Leningrad a few years ago, the Soviet equivalent of the Gideon Bible. After showing "why the struggle between proletarian [i.e., communist or Marxist] and bourgeois [i.e., capitalist or Western democratic] ideologies is inevitable," Nikolayev explains (1983, p. 12):

Lenin in his time foresaw the inevitability of the ideological struggle. In drafting the policy of peaceful co-existence he proceeded from the assumption that for a relatively long period to come socialist and capitalist countries would exist simultaneously in the world. With the uneven economic and political development of capitalist countries, socialist revolution cannot take place simultaneously all over the world and will gain ground in different countries at different times as the conditions mature that ultimately make it inevitable.

Significantly, *Lenin's concept of peaceful co-existence is valid for the entire era of mankind's transition from capitalism to socialism* [emphasis in original].

There follows a great deal more in the same vein. Under such headings as "The Uncompromizing [sic] Nature of the Ideological Struggle," Mr. Nikolayev takes special pains to ridicule the popular Western notion that peaceful coexistence implies a situation in which capitalist and socialist countries would live side by side indefinitely without attempting to transform (i.e., subvert) each other. This is unthinkable, because it would involve (1983, p. 44): "abandonment by the Communists of their struggle against capitalist views and persuasions." It is made quite clear that, to the Soviets, peaceful coexistence means only that the uncompromising struggle against capitalist imperialism will use all methods except military conquest to secure the inevitable triumph of world communism.

Pleas for "peace" and "peaceful coexistence" are the constant refrain of the endless stream of Soviet statements relayed to the American public by the American news media. A glance at any interview, speech, or commentary involving a Soviet spokesman will provide numerous examples. At worst, these could be nothing more than the soothing lies of an imperialist power bent on world conquest; the leaders of Hitler's Reich spoke in much the same way until 1939. But even if we discount the possibility of lying, it is unclear what the Soviets might mean by these (and similar) terms. Are they using them in the American sense or in the almost contradictory Marxist-Leninist sense? Although the emergence of glasnost and perestroika make it unwise to prejudge the question, it is reasonable to suspect the latter because the highly systematized nature of Soviet ideology makes it difficult for them to change important definitions such as these without seriously jeopardizing the intellectual foundations of their society. If so, then virtually the entire corpus of Soviet discourse is propagandistic because it is based on the suggestion technique of asymmetrical definition. But the only way to know this would be to demand that the Soviets specify which meanings are implied by their pronouncements. Unfortunately, American politicians and journalists almost never bother to do so. This failure alone makes the renewal of propaganda analysis imperative.

NOTES

1. I have chosen to focus this chapter on hostile foreign propaganda because the issues involved are more distinct and significant, and in order to avoid some of the entanglements of partisan politics. It should be stressed that with the rise of interest-group politics and its endless procession of "studies," "campaigns," and "movements," propaganda is even more common in domestic disputes than in international. The essay by Hogan and Olsen offers a detailed analysis of one instance of this form of propaganda.

2. As reported by the Associated Press on March 1, 1989, sociologist Igor M. Klyamkin reached a very similar conclusion in an article in the prestigious Soviet literary monthly *Novy Mir* in which he accused the Communist Party of the Soviet Union of spreading "lies" that have deceived the Soviet people for generations.

3. The national media are defined as those capable of reaching a substantial fraction of either the American public as a whole or its policymaking elite. Included in the definition are the three commercial television networks, CNN, perhaps PBS, *Time, Newsweek, U.S. News and World Report, The New York Times, The Washington Post, The Wall Street Journal, USA Today,* and the various wire services, especially the Associated Press.

4. A particularly clear example of this is provided by network television coverage of the Daniloff-Zakharov spy controversy of August and September 1986.

In response to the arrest of one of their agents (Zakharov) by the United States, the Soviet Union arrested Nicholas Daniloff, an American reporter for *U.S. News and World Report*, and accused him of espionage. Faced with an exceptionally weak Soviet case against Daniloff, journalists at all three networks offered their own ingenious (but specious) arguments in support of the Soviet side (see Smith 1988a, pp. 119–23 for a complete discussion). In the end, Zakharov pleaded "no contest" to the charge of espionage and was convicted and expelled from the United States. Daniloff was then released from custody and permitted to return to the United States. He was never formally charged with any crime by the Soviet Union.

5. The exact boundaries of the dominant culture are necessarily vague. It is used here to denote the American intelligentsia, defined as that group of individuals who deal primarily with the creation and dissemination of ideas and their application in social affairs, and who therefore establish a context of value and significance for the culture. Broadly speaking, it encompasses leaders and other interested professionals in the arts, humanities, social sciences, jurisprudence, education, and the various fields of communication, as well as certain more progressive elements in government and religion. It generally excludes those individuals, however brilliant and reflective, who deal primarily with the natural world or practical affairs, such as engineers, natural scientists, health professionals, and, of course, anyone associated with commerce. Exceptions are made, however, for those (e.g., astronomer Carl Sagan) who employ their special knowledge in the service of acceptable ideologies.

6. By choosing this word I mean only to call attention to the idea that the issues involved in McCarthyism are nowhere near as simple as the constant stream of shallow and selective media depictions of the era have claimed. Alger Hiss, it seems, was guilty as charged (see, e.g., Weinstein 1978). And while some of his methods were deplorable, Senator McCarthy's concerns were far from groundless. A great many of those he identified as communists turned out to have been just that, as established both in carefully documented contemporary accounts (e.g., Buckley and Bozell 1954) and, paradoxically, by many of the more recent and highly sympathetic media portrayals of McCarthy's "victims" (see, e.g., the 1986 PBS documentary "Seeing Red"; see also Watergate journalist Carl Bernstein's 1989 book *Loyalties*, in which he quotes his father—himself damaged by his association with the Communist Party—giving this reason why he should not write the book: "You're going to prove McCarthy right, because all he was saying was that the system was loaded with communists. And he was right."). It is also worth noting that Senator McCarthy's methods were, arguably, no more deplorable than those used by opponents of Robert Bork to block his appointment to the Supreme Court.

7. For a detailed account of the evolution of this orthodoxy from its roots in the relativistic theories of Marx, Freud, and Einstein, see Johnson (1983, p. 11 ff.).

8. This concern is the basis of much criticism of contemporary journalism, with its relentless emphasis on the atypical and negative. For a detailed analysis of the distortions this emphasis produced in television coverage of economic affairs during the Reagan era, see Smith (1988c).

9. There are also marked cross-cultural similarities in values, as discussed in Smith (1988a, p. 54).

10. It appears that there are at least four fundamentally different and autonomous philosophical "styles," each with its own ultimate criterion for truth and each embracing a range of specific perspectives. See Smith (1988b) for fuller discussion.

11. Unless otherwise noted, recent examples of propaganda are taken from contemporary wire service and national newspaper stories, copies of which are available from the author. All historical data have been verified using the 1970 edition of the *Encyclopaedia Britannica*.

REFERENCES

Aristotle. 1941. *Rhetorica*. Translated by W. R. Roberts. In *The basic works of Aristotle*, ed. R. McKeon, pp. 1317–1451. New York: Random House.

Balch, S. H., and H. I. London. 1986. The tenured left. *Commentary* 82 (October):41–51.

Barron, J. 1983. *KGB today: The hidden hand*. New York: Reader's Digest Press.

Bernays, E. L. 1928. *Propaganda*. New York: Liveright.

Bernstein, C. 1989. *Loyalties*. New York: Simon & Schuster.

Bittman, L. 1981. *The deception game*. New York: Ballantine.

———. 1985. *The KGB and Soviet disinformation*. Washington, D.C.: Pergamon-Brassey's.

———, ed. 1988. *The new image-makers: Soviet propaganda and disinformation*. Washington, D.C.: Pergamon-Brassey's.

Bloom, A. 1987. *The closing of the American mind*. New York: Simon & Schuster.

Brown, J.A.C. 1963. *Techniques of persuasion*. Baltimore, Md.: Penguin.

Buckley, W. F., Jr., and L. B. Bozell. 1954. *McCarthy and his enemies*. New Rochelle, N.Y.: Arlington House.

Conquest, R. 1986. *The harvest of sorrow: Soviet collectivization and the terror-famine*. New York: Oxford University Press.

Corry, J. 1986. *TV news and the dominant culture*. Washington, D.C.: The Media Institute.

Dailey, B. D., and P. J. Parker, eds. 1987. *Soviet strategic deception*. Lexington, Mass.: Lexington Books.

Daniloff, N. 1988. *Two lives, one Russia*. New York: Houghton Mifflin.

Dzhirkvelov, I. 1988. *Secret servant*. New York: Harper & Row.

Ebon, M. 1987. *The Soviet propaganda machine*. New York: McGraw-Hill.

Ellul, J. 1965. *Propaganda*. New York: Knopf.

Hastings, M. 1987. *The Korean War*. New York: Simon & Schuster.

Hazan, B. 1982. *Soviet impregnational propaganda*. Ann Arbor, Mich.: Ardis.

The Heritage Foundation, 1985. Soviet disinformation and the news. *Backgrounder* #465. Washington, D.C.

Hook, S., V. Bukovsky, and P. Hollander. 1987. *Soviet hypocrisy and Western gullibility*. Washington, D.C.: Ethics and Public Policy Center.

Johnson, P. 1983. *Modern times*. New York: Harper & Row.

Jowett, G. S., and V. O'Donnell. 1986. *Propaganda and persuasion*. Beverly Hills, Calif.: Sage.

Kinkead, E. 1960. *Why they collaborated*. New York: Longman.

Levchenko, S. 1988. *On the wrong side: My life in the KGB*. Washington, D.C.: Pergamon-Brassey's.

Lichter, S. R., S. Rothman, and L. S. Lichter. 1986. *The media elite*. Bethesda, Md.: Adler & Adler.

Lubin, D. M. 1985. *Art of portrayal: Eakins, Sargent and James*. New Haven, Conn.: Yale University Press.

Muravchik, J. 1988. *News coverage of the Sandinista revolution*. Washington, D.C.: American Enterprise Institute.

Nagorski, A. 1985. *Reluctant farewell*. New York: Holt, Rinehart & Winston.

Nikolayev, L. 1983. *Whose interest does "psychological warfare" serve?* Moscow: Novosti.

Oberg, J. E. *Uncovering Soviet disasters*. New York: Random House, 1988.

O'Donnell, J. P. 1988. AIDS and bum dope: A case study in disinformation. Boston University Program for the Study of Disinformation occasional paper # 2. Boston.

Pincher, C. 1985. *The secret offensive*. New York: St. Martin's.

Rurarz, Z. 1989. Lozhnost at the Katyn Forest? *The Washington Times*, February 6, D4.

Shultz, R. H., and R. Godson. *Dezinformatsia*. Washington, D.C.: Pergamon-Brassey's.

Shevchenko, A. 1985. *Breaking with Moscow*. New York: Knopf.

Sless, D. 1986. *In search of semiotics*. London: Croom Helm.

Smith, M. J. 1982. *Persuasion and human action*. Belmont, Calif.: Wadsworth.

Smith, T. J. 1988a. *Moscow meets Main Street*. Washington, D.C.: The Media Institute.

———. 1988b. Diversity and order in communication theory: The uses of philosophical analysis. *Communication Quarterly* 36:28–40.

———. 1988c. *The vanishing economy*. Washington, D.C.: The Media Institute.

Smith, T. J., and J. M. Hogan. 1987. Public opinion and the Panama Canal treaties of 1977. *Public Opinion Quarterly* 51:5–30.

Smith, T. J., and D. O. Verrall. 1985. A critical analysis of Australian television coverage of election opinion polls. *Public Opinion Quarterly* 49:58–79.

Tyson, J. L. 1981. *Target America*. Chicago: Regnery Gateway.

U.S. Congress, House. 1980. Permanent Select Committee on Intelligence. *Soviet covert action: The forgery offensive*. 96th Cong., 2d sess., February 6 and 19.

———. 1982. Permanent Select Committee on Intelligence. *Soviet active measures*. 97th Cong., 2d sess., July 13–14.

U.S. Congress, Senate. 1972. Committee on the Judiciary, Subcommittee on Internal Security. *Detente and the world revoltuionary process*. 92nd Cong., 2d sess., June 9.

———. 1985. Committee on Foreign Relations. *Soviet active measures*. 99th Cong., 1st sess., September 12–13. Part 2.

U.S. Department of State. 1986. *Active measures: A report on the substance and process of anti-U.S. disinformation and propaganda campaigns*. Publication 9630.

————. 1987a. *Soviet influence activities: A report on active measures and propaganda, 1986–87*. Publication 9627.

————. 1987b. *Contemporary Soviet propaganda and disinformation: A conference report*. Publication 9536.

U.S. Information Agency. 1988. Soviet active measures in the era of glasnost. Report to Congress. Mimeo.

Weinstein, A. 1978. *Perjury*. New York: Knopf.

6   *"Active Measures" in Contemporary Soviet Strategy*

Roy Godson

Disagreement clearly exists in the West over the importance Moscow places on the utility of overt and covert propaganda and political influence techniques as instruments of its foriegn policy. There are those who believe that these techniques continue to play a central role in Kremlin strategy. Others disagree, maintaining that the Kremlin no longer regards them as important. Based on more than six years of research, however, it seems clear that propaganda and covert political influence techniques do in fact constitute significant instruments of Soviet foreign policy and strategy. This appears to be no less true under Mikhail Gorbachev than was the case under previous Soviet leaders.[1]

Soviet use of such methods flows naturally from the Leninist concept of politics. Even prior to their seizure of power in 1917, Bolshevik leaders rejected the Western distinction between periods of war and peace. From their perspective, politics is a continual state of war carried out by a wide variety of means, only sometimes requiring military operations. Indeed, included in this approach are all means deemed effective.

Soviet leaders now use the term "active measures" (*activnyye meropriatia*) to describe an array of overt and covert techniques for influencing events and behavior in, and the actions of, foreign countries. (Prior to the 1960s, the term *dezinformatsia* was used in some Soviet circles to describe these activities.) The term "active measures," as used here, includes at-

Reprinted with permission from: Robbin F. Laird and Erik P. Hoffmann, Editors, *Soviet Foreign Policy in a Changing World* (New York: Aldine de Gruyter) Copyright © 1986 by Robbin F. Laird and Erik P. Hoffmann; and by permission of the National Strategy Information Center, Inc.

tempts to influence the policies of another government, undermine confidence in its leaders and institutions, disrupt relations with other states, and discredit and weaken governmental and nongovernmental opponents. This frequently involves attempts to deceive the target (foreign governmental and nongovernmental elite or mass audiences) and/or distort its perception of reality.

Active measures are conducted overtly through officially sponsored foreign propaganda channels, diplomatic relations, and cultural diplomacy. Covert political techniques include the use of covert propaganda, oral and written disinformation, agents-of-influence, clandestine radios, and international front organizations. In practice, these techniques often are integrated and coordinated.

While other states from time to time may employ some of these techniques, the Soviet Politburo uses them in a very different way—qualitatively and quantitatively. Soviet overt and covert techniques are much more centrally coordinated and intensive. They are also systematically and routinely conducted on a worldwide scale. Soviet leaders use covert means in most noncommunist states to enhance dramatically their themes of overt propaganda. These overt and covert political campaigns are frequently sustained over long periods of time. Few, if any, Western governments emulate these activities in peacetime.

Since the early days of the post-World War II period, the United States and the NATO Alliance have been the main targets of Soviet active measures. Kremlin leaders have consistently sought to discredit, isolate, and separate the United States from its allies and undermine NATO's defense policies. In the 1980s, the Soviet leadership attempted to prevent the modernization of NATO's intermediate range nuclear forces (INF) and the development of antimissile defenses. With respect to the latter, the Soviets conducted for several years a large-scale campaign of coordinated diplomatic moves, overt propaganda, and covert political action aimed at preventing the development and deployment of defensive systems by the United States, and the collaboration in this project by West European countries.

Because Soviet leaders, both in their doctrine and actions, emphasize the importance of active measures and devote extensive organizational and financial resources to them, it is surprising that Western scholars until relatively recently have devoted little attention to this subject.[2]

Active measures are used to promote Moscow's foreign policy goals. While specific policies reflect the situation and issues unique to a given period, the following broad objectives of Soviet foreign policy have been identified by many Western scholars (see, e.g., Nogee and Donaldson 1981; Rubenstein 1981; Mitchell 1982; Ulam 1974): (1) to preserve, enhance, and expand security in those areas under the influence of the USSR; (2) to divide Western opponents of the Soviet Union by driving wedges between them and disrupting alliance systems; (3) to retain the primacy of the USSR in the communist world; (4) to promote "proletarian internationalism" and "national liberation movements" which serve Soviet interests; and (5) to minimize risk and avoid serious involvement on more than one front at a time.

The particular instruments deployed to achieve these objectives at any given time are based on Moscow's assessment of what it calls the "correlation of forces." This is an assessment of military, economic, and political forces as well as international movements, particularly those affecting the internal affairs of noncommunist countries. According to Soviet commentary (Serjiyen 1975, p. 103):

The foreign policy potential of a state is dependent not upon its own forces and internal resources but to a considerable extent on such factors as the existence of reliable socio-political allies among other states, a national contingent of congenial classes, mass international movements, and other factors active on the world scene.

Influencing national and international political and social forces appears to constitute an important objective in Soviet strategy.[3]

An examination of the period since the 1960s demonstrates that the leadership of the CPSU has consistently regarded active measures as an important instrument to influence these forces. Active measures were used in the 1960s when the Soviet Union was militarily inferior to the West; in the 1970s during the period of detente; in the late 1970s when the Soviets came to believe the "correlation of forces" had begun to move in their favor but were still seeking to shift it even more; and also in the 1980s, when Mikhail Gorbachev was calling for a "new political thinking" and an "all-embracing concept of international security."

Most Western specialists believe that major Soviet foreign policy decisions are made by the Politburo, the apex of the CPSU. The Politburo also appears to approve general active measures programs. Since the late 1950s at least three important organizations under Politburo control apparently have planned and conducted active measures. They are the CPSU's International Department (ID), the Propaganda Department, and several sections of the KGB.[4] In September 1988, the CPSU's foreign policy apparatus was restructured into an International Policy Commission, chaired by Alexander Yakovlev.

The ID currently is headed by Valentin Falin. Previously he spent eight years in Bonn as the USSR's ambassador to the Federal Republic of Germany. Most recently he was director of the Soviet news agency Novosti. According to former KGB officials such as Stanislav Levchenko and Ilya Dzhirkvelov, it is the ID which coordinates active measures.[5] In fact, comparing the ID's scope of responsibilities to those of American government institutions, one Western specialist has argued that the ID incorporates some of the functions of the National Security Council, Congressional intelligence and foreign relations committees, the CIA, and even the departments of State and Labor (Kitrinos 1984, p. 50; see also Schapiro 1976–77).

The ID coordinates and reviews inputs concerning Soviet foreign policy and active measures from the Ministry of Foreign Affairs and various "think tanks" under the Academy of Sciences, and presents proposals to the Politburo. It also plans and coordinates active measures with similar departments in the Communist parties of other Soviet bloc countries as well as with nonruling Communist parties, major international fronts, and national liberation movements throughout the world. Moreover, the ID has responsibility for operating a number of clandestine radios that broadcast to the noncommunist world, and for supervising the activities of a worldwide network of Soviet Friendship Societies.[6]

The Propaganda Department until recently had been supervised by Yakovlev. It coordinates overt propaganda aimed at foreign audiences. (From 1978 to 1986, this responsibility was entrusted to the International Information Department [IID] of the CPSU, and prior to that time this task was incorporated into the work of the CPSU's Department for Agitation and Propaganda.) This includes controlling the foreign operations of TASS, Novosti, international radio broadcasting, periodicals and books sent abroad, and embassy information departments.[7] At this date it remains unclear whether or not the foreign policy functions of the Propaganda Department will come under Yakovlev's new commission or under the new Ideology Commission, which has assumed responsibility for this department.

Although the primary purpose of the KGB is internal security, its First Chief Directorate carries out espionage and active measures abroad. Its Second Chief Directorate works against Western intelligence in the USSR, seeking to prevent Soviet citizens from cooperating with Western governments. It also tries to recruit and influence foreign diplomats, journalists, businessmen, and other foreigners resident in the Soviet Union (Dzhirkvelov 1987, p. 165). If successful, Moscow uses these foreigners not only while they are in the USSR, but also after they return to their native countries.

In the late 1950s, the KGB began to increase its active measures operations.[8] First, a Department D (for *dezinformatsia*) was created, and then in the 1960s this was upgraded to Service A (for *activnyye meropriatia*) of the First Chief Directorate. This group assists KGB residencies (stations in Western parlance) in each country to engage in covert active measures, as well as to coordinate covert active measures with the intelligence services of other Soviet-bloc countries. According to Dzhirkvelov (1987, ch. 11), the decision to step up active measures also led to a heightened emphasis on suborning and recruiting Western and Third World journalists, in order to use them as conduits of disinformation. It was for this purpose that the Union of Journalists, with the post of Deputy General Secretary filled by Dzhirkvelov, was created.

While it is difficult to estimate the numbers of personnel involved in overt and covert Soviet active measures, available information suggests that 10,000 to 15,000 people are involved, with a budget, in the late 1970s, of $3 to 4 billion per year. In 1985 Congressional testimony, the most senior United States intelligence analyst stated that there had been no evidence of any diminution in the level of resources devoted to active measures (U.S. Congress, Senate 1985:4).

A systematic examination of several major Soviet propaganda outlets from 1960 to 1980 revealed a pattern of messages which Moscow wanted Western Europeans and Americans to hear over the twenty-year period. The "International Review" column of the authoritative Soviet daily *Pravda* was analyzed using a computerized form of content analysis to ensure that the authors did not focus selectively on themes as a result of bias. Then this basically quantitative approach was supplemented by a more qualitative assessment of selected articles from *New Times*, a world affairs weekly believed to be published by the ID of the CPSU and distributed worldwide in ten languages.

Using these methods, it was found that Soviet propaganda from 1960 to 1980 described the United States and NATO as: (1) aggressive, adventurous, and provocative; (2) militaristic, promoting arms races and cold war; (3) opposed to negotiated settlements of international issues; (4) in the throes of political, economic, and social crises; and (5) threatening communist bloc unity and conducting anti-Soviet bloc propaganda and political action.

While the United States consistently was characterized as the major threat to world peace, careful analysis of Soviet propaganda indicates that in reality the Kremlin did not perceive any direct threat or challenge to its security interests emanating from alleged U.S. aggressiveness and militarism. Moscow asserted a threat without describing how the U.S. military or the U.S. government were threatening the Soviet leadership. The incongruity between Soviet propaganda and Moscow's actual threat perception may be explained partially by considering the tactical foreign policy objectives of the Kremlin rather than its immediate security concerns (Shultz and Godson 1984, ch. 3).

By the late 1960s and the 1970s, Moscow's foreign propaganda became increasingly sophisticated. The Soviets concentrated on more themes than before. The number of elements within Western governments and societies that were targeted increased. Soviet propaganda also became increasingly flexible, enabling Moscow to respond rapidly to critical issues and events of the day. Under the leadership of Alexander Yakovlev, the U.S. government maintains, Soviet foreign propaganda has been characterized by even greater sophistication and flexibility (U.S. Department of State 1986a, pp. 25–26). Nonetheless, Soviet media outlets have continued to disseminate disinformation, both introducing campaigns and replaying covertly planted stories in non-Soviet media. For example, Radio Peace and Progress and *Literaturnaya Gazeta* have played a major role in Moscow's campaign since 1985 accusing the United States of creating AIDS. Despite Soviet promises in late 1987 to stop disinformation, campaigns have continued well into 1988 (U.S. Information Agency, 1988).

The Soviets operate secretly to promote and enhance the effectiveness of their overt propaganda. The Kremlin goes to enormous lengths to hide covert techniques, and it is not easy to detect or document them. Nevertheless, it is possible to demonstrate persuasively that the Soviets integrate overt propaganda with covert political techniques to multiply the effectiveness of their overall effort. For example, the Kremlin manipulates at least thirteen major international front organizations.[9]

The origins of the post-World War II international fronts can be traced to the Comintern (Communist International) in the 1920s. This was described by Willi Munzenberg, the Communist expert on organizing fronts: "We must penetrate every conceivable milieu, get hold of artists and professors, make use of theaters and cinemas, and spread abroad the doctrine that Russia is prepared to sacrifice everything to keep the world at peace."[10] In 1935, Comintern official Otto Kuusinen was more explicit: "We want to attack our close enemies in the rear. . . . But how can we do so if the majority of working class youth follow not us, but for instance the Catholic priests or the liberal chameleons?" The answer, according to Kuusinen, was "to create a united youth front" (Communist International 1939, p. 489).

These commentaries illuminate the tasks of front organizations. They are to employ propaganda and active measures to promote Soviet foreign policy objectives within other states by creating coalitions of communists and noncommunists (from many segments of society), including those not under Soviet control.

After World War II, responsibility for directing and coordinating the various international fronts was assigned to the Communist Information Bureau (Cominform) and then in the late 1950s to the ID of the CPSU.

One of the most important international fronts is the World Peace Council (WPC) which Moscow created in 1949. Indeed, the other important fronts, such as the World Federation of Trade Unions, the World Federation of Democratic Youth, and the International Union of Students clearly coordinate their stands with the WPC.

Moscow, of course, tries to mask its control of the fronts. In the years immediately following World War II, these organizations were based in Western capitals (until they were expelled), and Soviet officials were not appointed to top posts of these ostensibly nongovernmental organizations.

But Moscow maintains its influence by controlling the leaders and staff of the WPC and its national affiliates in almost every Western and Third World country. Also, Moscow provides most of the WPC's funds. In the late 1970s, the U.S. government estimated Soviet annual expenditure on the fronts at $63 million; approximately one-half of this is spent on the WPC (U.S. Congress, House 1980, p. 79).

Since its creation the WPC and most of its national affiliates have supported Soviet foreign policy almost unswervingly. However, they play the role of independent and nongovermental organizations in international forums such as those sponsored by the United Nations. Through their national affiliates they also influence national noncommunist peace movements in directions favored by Moscow. In the mid–1980s, mirroring the priorities of overt Soviet propaganda and diplomacy, the WPC began concentrating its attention on opposition to U.S. strategic defense programs, as previously it had followed Moscow's lead on the neutron weapon, INF modernization, and other issues.

Another technique of covert active measures used by Moscow is recruiting agents-of-influence, one of the most complex and difficult measures to document. Agents-of-influence include the unwitting but manipulated individual, the trusted contact, and the controlled covert agent. *An unwitting but manipulated person* is unaware of being directed and/or financed by the Soviet Union, because he or she is hired or directed by a trusted contact or controlled covert agent. *A trusted contact* is a Soviet term used to describe a person who may not be a formally recruited, paid, or controlled agent but who wittingly uses his or her influence to advance Soviet interests. *An agent-of-influence* is a person who is not an intelligence officer but who, when recruited, uses his or her influence to promote Soviet objectives in ways unattributable to Moscow. The agent-of-influence may be a journalist, a prominent private citizen, a government official, a labor leader, or an academic. The main objective of the influence operation is the use of the agent's position—be it in government, politics, labor, or journalism—to support and promote political conditions desired by the Kremlin.

Generally, the KGB is responsible for conducting agent-of-influence activities. The first phase entails the development of strong covert personal relationships with important figures in foreign societies. Once such a relationship has been established, the next step is to secure the active collaboration of the individual on matters of mutual interest. In return the KGB will provide remuneration tailored to meet the specific needs or vulnerabilities of the person involved.

One of a number of recent cases is that of Pierre Charles Pathe in France. Because Pathe was a prominent citizen, operated as an agent-of-influence over a long period of time, wrote a great deal, and was convicted, it is possible to trace many of his activities with a good deal of assurance.

Pathe apparently came to Soviet attention in 1958 when he wrote favorably about the Soviet Union. After accepting an invitation from the Soviet Ambassador to France, a relationship with the KGB was established. In 1961 he began to publish—with Soviet encouragement and financial support—a confidential journal/newsletter. At the same time he wrote for other journals and newspapers under the assumed name of Charles Morand.

In 1976 Pathe launched a biweekly newsletter entitled *Synthesis*, for which he received partial funding from Moscow. At the height of its popularity the subscribers included 139 senators and 299 deputies of the French Parliament, 41 journalists, and 14 ambassadors, that is, 70 percent of the Chamber of Deputies and 47 percent of the Senate, and a substantial number of important journalists and diplomats (Shultz and Godson 1984, p. 134). In 1978 his clandestine relationship with the KGB came to the attention of French counterintelligence. He was tried, convicted, and jailed.

An analysis of the seventy issues of *Synthesis* from 1976 to 1979 indicates that there were two general themes: (1) denigration of and attacks upon Western interests and policies; and (2) defense of the USSR and its allies. Pathe omitted from the publication any material which might render the USSR and its friends vulnerable to criticism, muted that criticism which could not be avoided, and included material which actively supported or defended the views of the Soviet Union and its allies.[11]

Other agents-of-influence who have been identified as such by the U.S. government include the Danish journalist Arne Petersen. Among government officials, the best-known cases are that of Arne Treholt, former head of the Norwegian Foreign Ministry Press and Information Office (who was sentenced to a twenty-year prison term for espionage on behalf of the USSR), and members of the Japanese Socialist Party whose relations with Soviet intelligence were revealed by KGB defector Stanislav Levchenko. Another example was Sidek Ghouse, the political secretary to the Deputy Prime Minister of Malaysia. He was arrested in 1981 and convicted of being a Soviet agent.[12]

Moscow uses agents-of-influence as one element of a carefully orchestrated effort. Insiders label this orchestration *Kombinatsia*. This refers to the skill of relating, linking, and combining various agents-of-influence (at various times and places) with overt propaganda to enhance effectiveness. These actions comprise one more component of the overt/covert approach employed by the Kremlin.

Forgeries are another significant weapon in the Soviet arsenal of active measures. From the earliest days of the Bolshevik regime, Moscow has used forged documents to discredit and deceive opponents. One major example was the use of forgeries in the Trust operations of the 1920s to lure important counterrevolutionaries back to Russia—to capture and death.

Moscow has used forged documents repeatedly. These forgeries appear to have been coordinated with other overt and covert operations and were closely related to specific Soviet objectives. Since the early 1960s, many forged documents have been targeted to discredit the United States and NATO. Some took the form of authentic-looking but nonetheless false U.S. government documents and communiques. Some were altered or distorted versions of real U.S. documents. Others were entirely fabricated. Apparently manufactured by the KGB's First Chief Directorate and other Soviet bloc intelligence services, they sought to portray the United States as the major threat to world peace and to create suspicion and discord in relations between the United States and its West European allies.

In the early 1960s, for example, Moscow circulated forged U.S. State Department documents designed to show that the United States was doing everything possible to sabotage all negotiations with the USSR, especially on disarmament matters. False Defense Department documents surfaced purporting to provide medical evidence that Strategic Air Command personnel were psychotic and in danger of initiating nuclear war! In the late 1970s, Moscow also began to recycle false documents initially circulated in the late 1960s and early 1970s.

Among other notable forgeries was a letter to NATO Secretary General Luns by the Supreme Allied Commander Alexander Haig stating that NATO needed to consider further use of limited nuclear weapons in wartime. Another forged letter from Luns informed the U.S. Ambassador that the Belgian government was compiling files on journalists who opposed deployment of the neutron warhead, implying that such journalists would be subject to surveillance and possibly persecution.

Forgeries have continued to be used in the 1980s. The Soviet campaign against the development of U.S. strategic defense, for example, produced at least two forgeries, both of which surfaced in 1986. One is a document alleged to be the text of remarks made by Secretary of Defense Weinberger at a secret Pentagon meeting, the other is a fabricated National Security Council outline of U.S. foreign policy priorities. Both forgeries were clearly manufactured in order to lend credence to Soviet overt propaganda claims that SDI is an offensive weapon and a means for the United States to obtain strategic superiority over the USSR (U.S. Department of State 1986b).

Forgeries are the most tangible, obvious form of disinformation, but they are only a subset—and instrument—of this larger category of actions deliberately intended to spread false or misleading information for political purposes. A major objective of Soviet disinformation is discrediting the United States. Such operations need not, but often do, employ forgeries.

For example, forgeries have been used as part of recurrent Soviet accusations conveyed in overt propaganda organs that the CIA routinely carries out assassinations and was involved in the killing of Olaf Palme and Indira Gandhi, among others. One apparent motive for such charges may be the desire to deflect suspicion of Soviet bloc involvement in political murder, as in the attempt on the life of Pope John Paul II. Accordingly, two forged U.S. Information Agency cables surfaced in 1983. The first purportedly advised organizing a conspiratorial campaign to implicate the USSR and Bulgaria in the shooting of the Pope, the second subsequently described the operation as a "resounding success."[13] At the same time, Soviet bloc publications have alleged that the CIA was actually behind the attempt on the Pope.

Another instance in which a disinformation operation included the use of forgeries is the attempt launched in the mid–1980s to discredit the United States by charging that CIA-Pentagon doctors created the AIDS virus during biological warfare experiments. The Soviet weekly *Literaturnaya Gazeta* in October 1985 cited reports in the Indian newspaper *Patriot*[14] to this effect. Soviet media channels such as TASS, Novosti, Radio Peace and Progress, *Moscow News*, and other newspapers spread this disinformation throughout the world. It then found its way into many mainstream Western media outlets such as the conservative London newspaper *Sunday Express*, and in noncommunist media in the Third World.[15]

Two bogus documents apparently hoped to further one of the major goals of this disinformation campaign: to create pressure for the removal of U.S. bases overseas by claiming that American soldiers were spreading the virus. In May 1987, a leaflet surfaced in Berlin claiming that the U.S. Army hospital was offering free AIDS tests. Soon afterwards, a forged release by the Berlin Senate press office announced that the hospital had too many cases of its own to treat civilians. The purpose of the forgeries presumably was to link AIDS in the public mind with U.S. Army personnel (U.S. Department of State 1987, p. 7). Another example was a pamphlet distributed anonymously near U.S. military bases in Spain in 1988. It warns in Spanish, German, and English that soldiers are "transmission agents of AIDS." When folded, the abstract designs on each page depict soldiers (apparently American) engaged in sexual acts with each other.

Interviews with former Soviet bloc intelligence officers who specialized in covert political techniques in the early 1960s through the late 1970s have confirmed the findings synthesized above. A former Senior Czechoslovak intelligence officer (Ladislav Bittman) and a former Soviet intelligence officer (Stanislav Levchenko) have described specific methods of planning, implementing, and evaluating Soviet active measures. They reveal the high degree of control exercised by the Kremlin over active measures conducted by the KGB and Eastern bloc services.[16] Both are convinced that Soviet leaders view these techniques as very important. They report that during the period they served as intelligence officers, the already extensive organizational and financial resources devoted to these activities were increased because Moscow was convinced of their efficacy. As a result, Soviet leaders enhanced their ability to conduct active measures on a massive worldwide scale against the United States and NATO.

Bittman reports that when he was operating under the cover of a press attache in Vienna from 1966 to 1968, he ran four or five secret agents in Austria and West Germany at any one time. Some were politicians, others journalists. The journalists were not asked to support particular Soviet policy positions but rather to undermine NATO and help create rifts among the NATO allies. During this tour, Bittman said, the Czechoslovak Disinformation Department (in which he served as Deputy Chief) focused on forgeries, rumor, and intrigue in order to deceive and mislead the West. The KGB not only provided the Czechoslovak intelligence service with general guidance but actually placed KGB advisors within the Czechoslovak service in Prague.[17]

Levchenko worked first for one of the International Department fronts in Moscow and later as a KGB officer under the cover of a *New Times* correspondent in Tokyo. There he recruited a number of politicians and journalists as agents-of-influence. In the late 1970s he was handling ten agents from all parts of the political spectrum (the democratic left to the more conservative governing party). According to Levchenko, the KGB had about 200 agents in Japan at the time. Their top priorities were to collect intelligence, to prevent further Japanese-U.S. cooperation, and to provoke distrust between Japan and the United States. Levchenko also described the financial and political means the ID uses to control the international fronts and how the fronts were coordinated with other covert and overt active measures programs.

To recapitulate:

1. Examination of the years since the early 1960s demonstrates that the Soviet leaders devoted extensive resources to discrediting, isolating, and splitting U.S. alliances through the use of propaganda and political influence activities as part of their broader political-military strategy. For these purposes, the Politburo developed a highly centralized and tightly coordinated organizational structure for planning and implementing active measures.

2. Moscow's overall propaganda message basically has remained unchanged during recent decades. Whether the Western allies have perceived East-West relations to be in a period of cold war, detente, or when, in the 1980s, Soviet spokesmen were pointing to their "new thinking," glasnost, and domestic perestroika (reconstruction) as a guide to their foreign policies,[18] Soviet overt propaganda has continued to portray the United States

and NATO in negative and defamatory terms. However, under Gorbachev many of Moscow's propaganda campaigns against the West have become more sophisticated, complex, and flexible.

3. Analysis of Soviet propaganda strongly suggests that the Kremlin does not perceive any imminent threat or danger from the United States. They rarely use foreign propaganda to warn the United States and NATO of genuine anxiety. Rather, Soviet leaders to a great extent use propaganda as part of a political-military strategy that seeks to weaken the Western alliance.

4. It is clear that Moscow actively combines overt and covert political techniques to manipulate, mislead, and deceive Western targets. When Soviet overt propaganda takes up a theme, Moscow usually plays the same message through its international fronts and agents-of-influence, simultaneously using techniques such as forgeries to further its objectives.

Will the Soviets continue to use overt and covert propaganda and political influence techniques against the United States and its allies? The answer appears to be yes. Moscow apparently has been impressed with its own programs, as can be seen by the growth in the size and scope of its active measures. Although the apparatus has recently been streamlined, a 1986 U.S. government report concluded "Soviet active measures have shown no diminution since General Secretary Gorbachev came to power" (U.S. Department of State 1986a, p. iii). This was further confirmed by a 1988 report to Congress entitled *Soviet Active Measures in the Era of Glasnost* (U.S. Information Agency 1988). Indeed, with the declining appeal of communism around the world, and the disappointing performance of the Soviet economic system, it is precisely Moscow's active measures capabilities, along with its military might, which maintain the USSR's status as a superpower.

These conclusions have important policy implications. Until recently, most Western governments have paid scant attention to Soviet active measures. Now, however, several Western governments have begun to explain them to their citizens. In the last few years, for example, educational activities have been undertaken to show journalists and politicians how the Soviets target them. The British Foreign Office occasionally issues papers on the subject, and the West German government includes a section on active measures in its annual report on subversive and terrorist organizations in the Federal Republic of Germany. In the United States, an interagency Active Measures Working Group was created in 1981. In 1986, a Permanent Office of Active Measures Analysis and Response was established in the State Department. Both attempt to sensitize the media and the public to the problem.

Nongovernmental scholars and specialists have also become involved, as evidenced by the publication of journals such as *Soviet Active Measures And Disinformation Forecast*, and the establishment of a Program for the

Study of Disinformation at Boston University. But it is unclear whether Western governments will effectively sustain such initiatives. Nor can we know the extent to which scholars and nongovernmental organizations will continue to document and analyze Soviet efforts to influence Western perceptions and behavior. It is far from certain that the West is prepared to meet the challenge posed by Soviet active measures.

NOTES

1. On the continuation of active measures as a tool of Soviet foreign policy see, for example, U.S. Information Agency (1988).

2. Much more information has become available in recent years on such operations, largely through Soviet bloc active measures practitioners who have defected to the West. Among the most important are Ladislav Bittman, Ilya Dzhirkvelov, and Stanislav Levchenko. They have heightened interest in propaganda and political influence techniques among Western governments and academic specialists. Though some continue to minimize the significance of this instrument of Soviet statecraft, it is increasingly gaining recognition as a serious and important subject of investigation and analysis.

3. For a recent examination of the Soviet understanding of the correlation of forces, see Lider (1987).

4. An overview of the active measures apparatus from the 1960s through the 1980s can be found in Shultz and Godson (1984).

5. See the interview with Stanislav Levchenko in Shultz and Godson (1984, ch. V). For more on the role of the Central Committee departments, see Ilya Dzhirkvelov (1987, ch. 5).

6. For a detailed examination of the ID, see U.S. Department of State (1986a). This report was prepared in response to a legislative requirement that the Secretary of State provide Congress with a report on active measures.

7. See "The Soviet Foreign Propaganda Apparatus," in U.S. Department of State (1986a) for a comprehensive treatment of the subject. Dzhirkvelov who served for a period as an editor of TASS, has described its purposes and methods (1987, ch. 13). For an account of how *New Times* operates, see Stanislav Levchenko (1987, ch. 5).

8. Dzhirkvelov and other defectors have discussed the decision to escalate active measures in the late 1950s. See, for example, Dzhirkvelov (1987, pp. 287–88) and Dziak (1987, ch. 8).

9. For a succinct survey of the fronts, see Spaulding (1987; 1988).

10. Based on confidential Comintern documents first published in 1924 in German by the German Trade Union Federation (ADGB) under the title "The Third Column of Communist Policy—IAH (International Worker's Aid)." Quoted in English in *Labour Magazine* (December 1924) The quotations were authenticated by Willi Muzenberg's widow, Babette Gross, in her book entitled *Willi Muzenberg—A Political Biography* (1974, pp. 121, 133).

11. A detailed analysis of *Synthesis* can be found in Shultz and Godson (1984, pp. 133–49).

12. For more on this subject, see "Agents of Influence" in U.S. Department of

State (1986a). Levchenko has stated that some of those he named are still active in the Japanese Socialist Party.

13. The cables have been reproduced in "Forgeries: An Instrument of Active Measures," U.S. Department of State (1986a, pp. 8–9).

14. KGB defector Ilya Dzhirkvelov claims to have been personally involved in the creation of this newspaper. See "Soviet Influence in Western Press?" (1987, pp. 9–10).

15. This active measures operation and the presumed motives behind it have been examined in detail in *Soviet Active Measures and Disinformation Forecast* ("AIDS: Made in the USA" 1987). See also U.S. Department of State (1987).

16. Bittman and Levchenko are interviewed in Shultz and Godson (1984, ch. 5).

17. For a description of how the intelligence services of the Soviet bloc cooperate with the KGB, see Ladislav Bittman (1985, pp. 28–33).

18. On June 1, 1987, Andrei Gromyko told visiting leaders of the Socialist International: "Soviet foreign policy is a direct continuation of domestic policy," known as perestroika which "...reflects the Soviet state's love of peace...the course towards restructuring confirms the reliability of the USSR as a partner in the system of international relations" (*Pravda*, June 2, 1987, p. 3).

REFERENCES

AIDS: Made in the USA. 1987. *Soviet Active Measures and Disinformation Forecast*, no. 5:1, 16–18.

Bittman, L. 1985. *The KGB and Soviet disinformation: An insider's view*. Washington, D.C.: Pergamon-Brassey's.

Communist International. 1939. *Seventh Congress of the Communist International*. Abridged stenographic report of proceedings, July–August 1935. Moscow: Foreign Languages Publishing House.

Dzhirkvelov, I. 1987. *Secret servant: My life with the KGB & the Soviet elite*. London: Collins.

Dziak, J. 1987. *Chekisty: A history of the KGB*. Lexington, Mass.: Lexington Books.

Gross, B. 1974. *Willi Munzenberg: A political biography*. East Lansing, Mich.: Michigan State University Press.

Kitrinos, R. 1984. International Department of the CPSU. *Problems of Communism* 33 (September–October):47–75.

Labour Magazine December 1924.

Levchenko, S. 1987. *On the wrong side: My life with the KGB*. Washington, D.C.: Pergamon-Brassey's.

Lider, J. 1987. *Correlation of forces: An analysis of Marxist-Leninist concepts*. New York: St. Martin's.

Mitchell, R. J. 1982. *Ideology of a superpower: Contemporary Soviet doctrine in international relations*. Stanford, Calif.: Hoover Institution Press.

Nogee, J., and R. Donaldson. 1981. *Soviet foreign policy since World War II*. New York: Pergamon.

Rubenstein, A. 1981. *Soviet foreign policy since World War II: Imperial and global*. Cambridge, Mass.: Winthrop.

Schapiro, L. 1976–77. The International Department of the CPSU: Key to Soviet policy. *International Journal* 32 (Winter):41–55.

Serjiyen, A. 1975. Leninism on the correlation of forces as a factor of international relations. *International Affairs*, May.

Shultz, R., and R. Godson. 1984. *Dezinformatsia: Active measures in Soviet strategy*. Washington, D.C.: Pergamon-Brassey's.

Soviet influence in the Western press? 1987. *Soviet Active Measures and Disinformation Forecast*, no. 6:1, 7–11.

Spaulding, W. 1987. Communist international fronts in 1986. *Problems of Communism* 36 (March–April):57–68.

———. 1988. Communist fronts in 1987. *Problems of Communism* 37 (January–February):82–88.

Ulam, A. 1974. *Expansion and coexistence: Soviet foreign policy, 1917–1973*. New York: Praeger.

U.S. Congress, House. 1980. Permanent Select Committee on Intelligence. *Soviet covert action (the forgery offensive)*. 96th Cong., 2nd sess., February 6 and 19.

U.S. Congress, Senate. 1985. Committee on Foreign Relations, Subcommittee on European Affairs. *Hearings: Soviet active measures*. 99th Cong., 1st sess., September 12–13.

U.S. Department of State. 1986a. *Active measures: A report on the substance and process of anti-U.S. disinformation and propaganda campaigns*. Publication 9630.

———. 1986b. Recent anti-American forgeries. *Foreign Affairs Note*, November.

———. 1987. The U.S.S.R.'s AIDS disinformation campaign. *Foreign Affairs Note*, July.

U.S. Information Agency. 1988. *Report to Congress on Soviet active measures in the era of glasnost*. Prepared at the request of the House Committee on Appropriations, June.

7   Propaganda and the Law: The Case of Three Canadian Films

J. Justin Gustainis

The role of subjectivity in human affairs is well illustrated by such adages as "One man's meat is another man's poison." However, even this familiar saying is useless unless the people employing it can agree on definitions of "meat" and "poison." Often, they do not agree. And if such a mundane goal is elusive, then complications will increase geometrically as one tries to define such complex terms as "communication," "persuasion," and "propaganda."

This chapter examines the issues arising out of the labeling of three Canadian documentary films as "political propaganda" by the U.S. Department of Justice, and the upholding of that action by the courts. It is hoped that such an examination will achieve the goals of, first, demonstrating the conflicting definitions of propaganda used by the government and the public (and some of the problems resulting from that conflict), and, second, revealing the First Amendment issues arising when material is labeled propaganda under the law. The discussion which follows will focus on the facts of the case, the reasons why the matter was controversial, and the relevant court decisions. I will conclude with an analysis of those decisions and their implications.

THE FACTS OF THE CASE

It was in January 1983 that Joseph Clarkson, who headed the Registration Unit of the Justice Department's Criminal Division, notified Canada's National Film Board that three documentary films from Canada had been declared "political propaganda." The films, all of which had been made and distributed under National Film Board auspices, were *If You Love*

This Planet, Acid Rain: Requiem for Recovery, and *Acid from Heaven* (Rothchild 1983). The films had all been available in the United States for some months prior to the Justice Department's decision.

All of the films do espouse particular points of view, although one of them does so more strongly than the others. *If You Love This Planet* is a 26-minute film on nuclear war which alternates scenes of the nuclear devastation of Hiroshima and Nagasaki with excerpts from a speech given by Dr. Helen Caldicott, a founder of the organization Physicians for Social Responsibility. In the film, Caldicott is shown describing in horrific detail the medical consequences of a nuclear explosion, exhorting the citizens of Plattsburgh, New York, to close down that city's Strategic Air Command base, and recommending that parents opposing the arms race bring their infants to Capitol Hill and confront legislators. She urges, "Set your naked toddlers loose in the Senate chambers" (McGrory 1983, p. A3). The film has been characterized as "an unrestrained attack on the Reagan administration's arms policy" (Grenier 1983, p. 70), and the director, Terry Nash, admits the work is biased—"biased against war" (Bruman 1983, p. 62). Despite (or perhaps because of) this immoderate stance, *If You Love This Planet* won the 1983 Academy Award for Best Short Documentary Film.

The other two films are less controversial. Both deal with acid rain and its effects on Canada. Although the United States is portrayed as the originator of the sulfur dioxide emissions that produce acid rain, the films also praise some American efforts to deal with the problem. John Roberts, Canada's Minister for the Environment, saw one of the films and claimed that it was *too* neutral, saying that the film should have given greater emphasis to the Canadian government's position that the United States is to blame for acid precipitation (American Library Association 1983).

The labeling of these films as "political propaganda" was effected under the authority of the Foreign Agents Registration Act (hereinafter referred to as FARA or "the act"). Originally passed in 1938 (although it has undergone three revisions since then), the act was designed to control the importation of Nazi and communist propaganda into the United States. There was concern in Congress that such material might not be properly labeled as to its foreign origins and might be perceived by American audiences as domestically produced, and hence more credible (Dorfman 1985).

Under the terms of FARA, political propaganda is defined as:

any oral, visual, graphic, written, pictorial, or other communication or expression by any person (1) which is reasonably adapted to, or which the person disseminating the same believes will, or which he intends to, prevail upon, indoctrinate, convert, induce, or in any other way influence a recipient of any section of the public within the United States with reference to the political or public interests, policies, or relations of a government or a foreign country or a foreign political party or with reference to the foreign policies of the United States or promote in the United States racial, religious, or social dissensions, or (2) which advocates, advises, instigates, or promotes any racial, social, political, or religious disorder, civil riot, or other conflict involving the use of force or violence in any other American republic or the overthrow of any government or political subdivision of any other American republic by any means involving the use of force or violence (as cited in *Meese v. Keene* 1987, p. 1866).

It was the first part of this definition which was applied to the three Canadian films. The act requires that anyone found to be distributing political propaganda (as defined above) in the United States must (1) register with the federal government as an agent of a foreign power, (2) label each copy of the material (each book, each print of a film, and so on) as lacking the approval of the U.S. government regarding its content, and (3) provide the government with a "dissemination report" indicating which groups or individuals received copies of the material.

The Canadian government made no secret of its displeasure with the application of FARA to these films. Once word of the Justice Department's decision arrived north of the U.S. border, the sparks began to fly.

THE CONTROVERSY

The controversy which developed following the government's labeling of the three Canadian films as political propaganda contained several key elements: the Canadian government, American liberals, the issue of government secrecy, and the Federal Appeals Court decision handed down by Antonin Scalia. Each of these will be considered in turn.

After the Canadian government was notified of the Justice Department's action, it lost little time in responding. The responses were both diplomatic and rhetorical. At the diplomatic level, the Canadian embassy in Washington asked the U.S. State Department to request a "clarification" of the ruling from Justice. It was hoped that the clarification would become a reversal; the hope was a vain one. Most of the rhetoric was provided by Canadian Minister for the Environment John Roberts, who characterized the labeling of the films as "bizarre and petty" (*Christian Century* 1983, p. 241) and "an extraordinary interference with freedom of speech" (American Library Association 1983, p. 264).

The American problem with Canada was exacerbated by the fact that the Justice Department decision came during a period of strained relations between the two countries. As was noted above, the two governments had been contending for several years over the question of acid rain. Canada had claimed severe harm from this phenomenon and had blamed the United States; the Reagan administration's position was that the harms were exaggerated and that the United States was not at fault.

Conflict had also taken place over a number of other issues, including Canadian lumber exports (considered by America a threat to her timber industry), Canadian natural gas prices (seen by the United States as too high), and cut-rate airline ticket prices on Air Canada flights to the United States (which were opposed by the U.S. government on the grounds that they were undercutting the prices of U.S. carriers). As a Canadian embassy representative said, "This [problem over the films] underlines the fact that there are so many issues that there can be an explosion at any moment" (Shribman 1983, p. 3).

Members of the Canadian government were not the only people to express outrage over the Justice Department's application of FARA to the films. American liberal activists reacted quickly. Some environmentalists saw the action as an attempt by the Reagan White House to stifle public discourse on the subject of acid rain. Groups opposed to the arms race believed that affixing the "propaganda" label to *If You Love This Planet* was designed to discourage discussion of arms control. Liberal politicians became involved as well. Colorado Senator Gary Hart reacted to the controversy by saying, "Thomas Jefferson would be appalled" (*Christian Century* 1983, p. 241). Senator Edward Kennedy denounced the Justice Department's action in a speech and called for a Senate investigation of the matter. Edward Markey, a Democratic congressman from Massachusetts, had *If You Love This Planet* shown over the closed-circuit television system in the House of Representatives.

The intensity of the reaction was at least partly a function of timing. The labeling of the films as propaganda occurred in the middle of a long-standing controversy over the Reagan Administration's alleged increase in secrecy. In the months preceding, the Administration had attempted to narrow the interpretation of the Freedom of Information Act (which allows the public access to many government documents), deny entrance visas to potentially troublesome speakers from abroad, and increasingly limit what government officials may say about their work, both during their government service and afterward. The point of view held by many Administration opponents was well articulated by Burt Neuborne of the American Civil Liberties Union, who said: "The Administration recognizes the relationship between information and power. They're trying to turn off information they don't like. That's all right if you're advertising soap, but it's not all right for the government" (Press and Camper 1983, p. 92).

Thus, the labeling of the Canadian films was seen by some American liberals as yet another brick in the wall of increased government secrecy. As liberal journalist Eve Pell claimed, "The business of registering foreign ideas and their disseminators may seem attractive to an administration eager to suppress informed discussion and dissent" (Pell 1984, p. 225).

In fact, much of the "new secrecy" represented only "business as usual." Many of the laws under which secrecy was being invoked by the Reagan

Administration had been on the books for years, and several of these were supported by judicial precedent—such as the Supreme Court's upholding of government action against former CIA agent Frank Snepp, who had written an unauthorized book about his CIA activities in Cambodia.

Part of the blame for making the invocation of FARA appear sinister in this case must lie with the Justice Department itself, which was apparently unprepared for the controversy that resulted. When questioned by the press, Justice Department representative John Russell claimed that categorizing of the films as political propaganda was a routine procedure, but he was unable to cite any other instances in which it had been done. The practice was, in fact, fairly common; Russell was simply not well informed about it. The confusion and frustration were compounded by other Justice Department spokesmen. Joseph Clarkson, the government attorney who made the decision to include the Canadian films under FARA, never explained to the press his precise reasons for doing so. Another representative of the Justice Department, Thomas DeCair, said that the lawyers working the Department's Internal Security section made FARA decisions "based primarily on common sense" (Peterson 1983, p. A2). This turned out to be an unfortunate choice of words, since it allowed an American Civil Liberties Union lawyer to respond. "The last one to use common sense effectively was Thomas Paine" (Peterson 1983, p. A2).

The next act in this political drama, one which revived a controversy grown cold, occurred more than three years after the events related above. In June of 1986, the U.S. Court of Appeals for the District of Columbia handed down its decision in the case of *Block v. Meese* (1986). Mitchell Block was president of Cinema Limited, a company which was the U.S. distributor of the three Canadian films. Since the suit was aimed at the Justice Department, Attorney General Edwin Meese was named as defendant, even though William French Smith had been Attorney General at the time of·the labeling of the films in 1983. Block, who was joined in his suit by the American Civil Liberties Union, the New York State Library Association, the Environmental Task Force, and the State of New York, wanted the Justice Department to rescind its categorization of the films as political propaganda. The case had originally been heard in the U.S. District Court for the District of Columbia, and had been dismissed by Judge Charles Richey. Block and his supporters appealed, which led to the Appeals Court decision of June 20, 1986.

The decision had an impact at two levels, one legal, one rhetorical. The legal aspect stemmed from the Appeals Court's upholding of the lower court's dismissal of the suit; the films were still to be considered political propaganda under the meaning of FARA. This will be discussed at length below. The rhetorical point of interest arose because the judge handing down the decision in *Block v. Meese* was Antonin Scalia. The same week that the decision was rendered, Ronald Reagan announced that Scalia was his choice to fill the latest vacancy on the Supreme Court.

The problem was one of timing. Most journalists covering the story of the Appeals Court's decision mentioned that the decision and Scalia's nomination to the high court occurred very close together. A *Washington Post* story, for example, noted that Scalia's opinion was issued the same week his nomination was announced (Lewis 1986, p. A11). *The New York Times* pointed out that the judge's decision was dated the same day as the President's announcement (June 21, 1986, p. 7).

It is possible that some opponents of the Reagan Administration read between the lines of such reports and saw the suggestion of collusion between Scalia and the President, but their suspicions were probably unjustified. Reagan certainly picked Scalia for the Court because of the judge's staunch conservatism and "strict constructionist" approach to the U.S. Constitution (as well as Scalia's reputation for brilliance). While it is likely that Scalia's opinion in this case was viewed favorably by the Administration, it probably was irrelevant to his nomination. The decision to name Scalia to the Supreme Court was made before his decision in *Block v. Meese* was announced. It is unlikely that Scalia, who has a reputation of integrity, discussed this case with anyone from the Administration before he handed down his decision. However, announcing Scalia's nomination during the same week as the issuing of his opinion supporting the government in a controversial issue was a public relations blunder. It may have suggested to some that Scalia was being rewarded for supporting Reagan administration policies, and thus fanned the flames of dispute.

Scalia's decision in *Block v. Meese* was supposed to be the penultimate act in this political and legal drama. Block appealed to the Supreme Court, which declined to hear the petition. The last bolt having apparently been shot, the case should have faded into history.

But on the opposite coast other things were happening. California State Senator Barry Keene brought suit himself against the Attorney General, claiming that he wanted to sponsor an exhibition of the films, and that association with material dubbed "political propaganda" would hurt him with the voters. Kenne took his case to the U.S. District Court for Eastern California, and won. The decision in *Keene v. Smith* (1983) included an injunction barring the Justice Department from using FARA to label any material as political propaganda.

Now it was the Justice Department's turn to appeal. A rarely employed section of the U.S. Code allows the government to appeal directly to the Supreme Court when an action of a U.S. government official is held by a lower court to be unconstitutional (Dorfman 1985, p. 446). Justice made use of this rule, and the Supreme Court agreed to hear the case. *Meese v. Keene* was argued on December 1, 1986. On April 27, 1987, the decision was announced. By a vote of 5–3 (with Scalia disqualifying himself because of his prior association with the matter), the justices held that the California court's injunction was invalid, and that FARA could properly be applied to the three Canadian documentary films. Analysis of the issues and arguments raised in these three cases follows.

THE COURT DECISIONS: ISSUES AND IMPLICATIONS

The two central questions raised in *Block v. Meese* are: (1) is the labeling of the films as political propaganda likely to affect the number of people who might buy or rent them, thus hurting Block's business, and (2) is the term "political propaganda" being used unfairly in this instance?

With respect to whether Block's film distribution business was being hurt by the Justice Department's labeling, Scalia notes that evidence had been presented to substantiate the claim that some groups and individuals had been frightened off by the "propaganda" designation. Scalia concludes that "concrete, particularized harm" had been done to Block and his company. However, he then says that the harm was not the government's fault. This conclusion was based on two premises. The first was that there was no *intent* to limit the distribution of the films. Scalia cites various ways in which governmental bodies have tried in the past to prevent films from being seen—such as limiting the times or places of exhibition, requiring a permit, or threatening legal punishment if a film were shown. He then notes that none of these mechanisms was employed in the workings of the Foreign Agents Registration Act; all that is required is that the film carry a disclaimer saying that the government does not give its approval to the film's content, and that the distributor file reports showing where the film was shown, by whom, and to how many people.

The second premise regarding the lack of government responsibility involves the meaning of the term "propaganda." Block argued that application of this label to the films implied that they contained "misstatements, half-truths, and attempts to mislead." Such assumptions, Block said, were never proven by the government, and were not true.

In his opinion, Scalia responds to this in two ways. The first response addresses the meaning of "propaganda." Scalia points out that FARA defines the term in a nonjudgmental way—it is communication designed to promote a point of view before an audience. He also notes that in the past the act had been applied to films emanating from countries closely allied to the United States, such as Israel and West Germany. Further, Scalia says that the strict, dictionary definition of propaganda is not pejorative. He cites, for example, *Webster's Ninth New Collegiate Dictionary*, which defines propaganda as involving "ideas," facts, or allegations spread deliberately to further one's cause or to damage an opposing cause." He thus concludes that to call something "propaganda" is not necessarily to demean it in the eyes of others.

In a footnote, Scalia does note that most dictionaries give a secondary definition of propaganda which *is* pejorative, since it refers to the use of lies and one-sided information. However, he says that the fault is not with the word, but in the way people use it. For this the government is not responsible.

Regarding the "propaganda" designation, Scalia's second response concerns the government's right to express an opinion. Even if the use of FARA did have the effect of implying government disapproval of the films, he says, this would not be unlawful. Government may not, in this country, unreasonably stifle free discussion of ideas. But the government does have the right to enter into such discussions, and to express its own opinions. FARA merely represents the expression of such opinion.

In the California case, *Keene v. Smith*, there was one central issue: the effect of the label "political propaganda" upon the exercise of First Amendment rights. As noted earlier, State Senator Keene claimed that he wanted to exhibit the films, but was afraid that doing so would harm him professionally, that is, would cause voters in his district to view him in such a negative light that he would be defeated when he ran for reelection. To support this contention, Keene produced a professional public opinion poll which he had commissioned. The pollster concluded that involvement with a film which had been categorized as political propaganda by the government would "have a seriously adverse effect on a California State Legislature candidate's chances [for election] if this charge were raised during a campaign." Keene also offered as support statements from politicians in California and academics knowledgeable about propaganda. All agreed that if he were to show a film considered to be propaganda, and this were made a campaign issue by a political opponent, the public's reaction to the label would hurt Keene's ability to gain political office.

The District Court, agreeing with Keene's contention, noted that the government is not supposed to take actions which interfere with or make difficult the exercise of one's rights of free speech and expression, as guaranteed under the First Amendment. The court said that, although FARA did not prevent Keene from showing the films, the law, with its use of the inherently pejorative term "political propaganda" in effect "puts the plaintiff to the Hobson's choice of foregoing the use of the three Canadian films for the exposition of his own views or suffering an injury to his reputation." The court held that the Justice Department was violating the First Amendment by using FARA to label materials as political propaganda, and issued an injunction to prevent this from happening again.

The reversal of this decision by the Supreme Court in *Meese v. Keene* was based on three conclusions endorsed by the majority of justices. The first was that the use of the "political propaganda" label under FARA does not prevent anyone from seeing those materials so labeled. The law, said the Court, does not imprint "political propaganda" on each copy of a book, film, or other artifact which comes under its purview. The term is a classification only; the film (or whatever) must only say that the government does not endorse its contents. The Court also pointed out that FARA does not prevent the distributor or exhibitor from adding a statement to the film disagreeing with the application of the law, or the meaning of political propaganda, or saying anything else. In other words, the law mandates that a particular statement be made, but also allows for rebuttal. Further, the justices claimed that FARA was not being used to restrict the free flow of information. Indeed, they said, it was the injunction issued by the District Court in California which restricted the public's access to information: "The suppressed information is the fact that the films fall within the category of materials that Congress has judged to be 'political propaganda.' "

The second major conclusion drawn by the Court involved history. There was no evidence, the opinion said, that, in the forty years FARA had been in effect, anyone had been prevented from reading or viewing any materials designated "political propaganda" under the act. Even while recognizing the importance of the evidence offered by Keene regarding the way the term "propaganda" is perceived by the average citizen, the Court said this fell far short of constituting censorship.

The third finding dealt directly with the meaning of the word "propaganda." The justices maintained that Congress has the right to use whatever language it wishes in writing legislation. Further, the term "propaganda" was defined by the act in a "neutral" way. Appearing to echo Scalia's point in *Block v. Meese*, the Court held that the government is responsible for the meaning of the words as it has defined them. If others outside the government choose to give a negative meaning to the word "propaganda," the government is not responsible.

DISCUSSION

The courts have had their say regarding the three Canadian documentary films and the Foreign Agents Registration Act. In one sense, the matter is closed. But other questions concerning the meaning and application of FARA still remain.

Congress needs to consider whether FARA still serves a legitimate purpose. It was born during a time when Nazi propaganda was active throughout the world, and the act was designed to protect the American public from lies, trickery, and exploitation. Although the Nazis have passed from the scene, propaganda (including the use of lies, trickery, and exploitation) is still with us. But the American public of the 1980s is very different from that of the 1930s. The effects of mass media are well known, education levels are higher, and audiences are more sophisticated and cynical. The level of protection deemed necessary forty years ago may not be needed today.

A second problem deals with the way FARA is applied by the Justice Department's attorneys. Under the current procedure, each organization which distributes materials in the United States on behalf of a foreign government must register with the Justice Department. Every six months, each organization must send to Justice a list of the materials it currently distributes. Justice Department lawyers, going by the titles alone, select the materials they wish to examine. They request copies of the films, books, pamphlets, or other items, and then, upon examination, decide if the materials constitute political propaganda as defined by FARA. Joseph Clarkson, who made the decision to apply FARA to the three Canadian films, testified to Congress about his decision, saying: "We know that acid rain is an issue and we selected the films based on their titles. . . . We had no description of the film. We selected it to look at it" (U.S. Congress, House 1983, p. 43).

This approach is neither systematic nor objective. It was the wide discretion given the Justice Department attorneys which aggravated the controversy. To some, who were already suspicious of the Reagan Administration's stands on acid rain, nuclear weapons, and government secrecy, it looked like a conspiracy. While there is no evidence that Clarkson's action was motivated by political considerations, or that any application of FARA has been anything but even-handed, the lack of controls on the process makes it difficult to prove objectivity when others charge bias.

A more thoughtful approach to FARA decision making would benefit both the Department of Justice and those who distribute foreign publications and films in this country. With respect to films in particular, the Justice Department lawyers should have more to go on than mere film titles. If all imported films come under their jurisdiction, they should be required to view all the films before determining which of them come under FARA.

A final problem involves an important issue of semantics. I refer, of course, to the act's use of the phrase "political propaganda." The courts have ultimately determined that FARA defines this term in a neutral fashion, and, strictly speaking, this is true. But the way it is used in everyday discourse is quite different. In this country, in this age, propaganda has assumed the status of what Richard Weaver (1953) called a *devil term*: an expression with highly negative connotations. Denton and Woodward (1985, p. 344), in discussing the term "political propaganda," note that "ominous connotations cling to this overworked phrase. It carries an enormous amount of negative weight." With respect to the alleged neutral use of the "propaganda" label, political columnist and language authority William Safire (1978, p. 573) has determined that "Despite occasional efforts to insist the word is neutral, that there is 'good' propaganda, current usage is definitely pejorative."

Both Block and Keene presented uncontested evidence that many Americans react negatively to anything which the U.S. government has labeled "political propaganda," and Keene suggested a solution which would allow FARA to function while eliminating the stigma of its application. He recommended that FARA be amended, substituting "political advocacy" for the current "political propaganda." This would be consistent with the apparent intent of Congress when the act was initially passed, would not in any way prevent the Justice Department from doing what it does now, and would avoid the problems that inevitably arise when lawyers and legislators use a word one way while average citizens employ it another way.

The Foreign Agents Registration Act may or may not be necessary to protect Americans from undue political influence. Its application in the Canadian films case has certainly caused some embarrassment to the Reagan Administration, and some diplomatic difficulties with the Canadian government. Such problems could be avoided in the future if Congress would consider whether the act is necessary, how it can be enforced fairly and uniformly, and whether the term "political propaganda" is the best way to categorize what the act is supposed to be regulating.

REFERENCES

American Library Association. 1983. Librarians question Justice Department action on Canadian films. *American Libraries* 14 (May):264.

Block v. Meese. 1986. 253 U.S. App. D.C.: 317–22.

Bruman, C. 1983. A matter of visibility. *MacLean's* 96 (April 15):62.

Christian Century. 1983. Government censorship. *The Christian Century* 100 (March 16):240–241.

Denton, R. E., and G. C. Woodward. 1985. *Political communication in America*. New York: Praeger.

Dorfman, A. 1985. Neutral propaganda: Three films "made in Canada" and the Foreign Agents Registration Act. *Comm/Ent* 7:435–468.

Grenier, R. 1983. The politicized Oscar. *Commentary* 75 (June):68–70.

Keene v. Smith. 1983. 569 F. Supp.: 1513–22.

Lewis, N. 1986. Scalia backs U.S. action on "propaganda" films. *The Washington Post*, June 21, A11.

Library Journal. 1983. NYLA joins lawsuit protesting U.S. action against nuke films. *Library Journal* 108 (April 15):778.

McGrory, M. 1983. Justice Department's boos make film subjects boffo box office. *The Washington Post*, March 1, A3.

Meese v. Keene. 1987. 107 S. Ct.: 1862–69.

Pell, E. 1984. *The big chill*. Boston: Beacon.

Peterson, C. 1983. U.S. labels three films propaganda. *The Washington Post*, February 25, A1, A6.

Press, A., and D. Camper. 1983. Keeping the cats in the bag. *Newsweek* 101 (April 18):92.

Rothschild, E. A. 1983. If you love these films. *The Bulletin of the Atomic Scientists* 39 (June/July):39.

Safire, W. 1978. *Safire's political dictionary.* New York: Random House.

Shribman, D. 1983. U.S.-Canadian relations take a testy new turn. *The New York Times*, February 26, 3.

U.S. Congress, House. 1983. Committee on the Judiciary. Subcommittee on Civil and Constitutional Rights. *Canadian films and the Foreign Agents Registration Act.* 98th Cong., 1st sess. Serial 36.

Weaver, R. 1953. *The ethics of rhetoric.* Chicago: Regnery.

8 Ideology and Propaganda: Toward an Integrative Approach
Nicholas F. S. Burnett

In his defense of historical studies in rhetorical criticism, Ernest Wrage (1972, pp. 103–11) argued that scholarship should be evaluated on its own merits, not according to the union card of its author. That defense of informed interdisciplinary inquiry may have encouraged a number of scholars to turn outside of what had been regarded as the traditional boundaries of the field of rhetoric, as it had been narrowly construed, to other disciplines involved in the study of human interaction and social theory. A comprehensive study of propaganda would seem to demand such an interdisciplinary approach, drawing on the resources and perspectives of a number of allied fields.

In the spirit of cross-boundary inquiry, I propose to examine the value of an integrated approach to the study of propaganda and ideology. While such a union would not appear on its face to be either unlikely or novel, it is a synthesis that has not been systematically pursued in the academic literature related to either concept. Although passing references are made by some writers, the exact connection between these two important areas would seem to be, at best, unclear. Thus it will be useful to begin by positing a few relevant definitions.

Propaganda will be defined as discourse in the service of ideology. Such a definition consciously subordinates the study of propaganda to an investigation of ideology for reasons that will be explicated later in this essay. In choosing discourse as the focal term in the definition, I mean only to imply that propaganda may be spoken or written and can present itself in a number of different media. *Ideology*, for purposes of this chapter, will be defined as the study of the ways in which meaning serves to sustain or alter relations of domination. That definition, adapted from a recent work by John Thompson (1984), intentionally avoids what have been characterized as noncritical conceptions of ideology—"systems of belief or thought" or "the study of the science of ideas"—in order "to preserve the negative connotation (of ideology) which has been conveyed by the term throughout most of history and . . . binds the analysis of ideology to the question of critique" (Thompson 1984, p. 4).

My intention is to consider propaganda as discourse which functions to create meanings that serve to sustain or alter relations of domination. I will first examine the rationale for integrating the study of ideology and propaganda and then consider how one of the critical frameworks that has been applied to the study of ideology might operate in a study of propaganda.

RATIONALE FOR AN INTEGRATIVE APPROACH

One obvious reason for attempting an integration of the concepts of ideology and propaganda is that the critics of each have encountered strikingly similar difficulties. Consider, first, the negative connotations that critics of either term have faced. The term propaganda, as Leonard Doob reminds us, has a uniquely pejorative meaning in our culture. "In other countries with different cultures, the word is quite respectable or at least as respectable as any of the equivalents our ingenious language and our beleaguered propagandists have devised" (Doob 1966, p. 232).

As early as 1842, Brande's *Dictionary of Science, Literature and Art* explained that the term propaganda "is applied to modern political language as a term of reproach to secret associations for the spread of opinions and principles which are viewed by most governments with horror and aversion" (Dorfman 1985, p. 452). That negative connotation seems to remain a matter of considerable dispute even today, as evidenced by a recent lawsuit in which the plaintiffs claimed that the government's use of the term "political propaganda" to describe certain films imported into the country from Canada constituted an actionable tort (Dorfman 1985).

If, as Doob (1966, p. 231) suggests, "almost any other name sounds sweeter to most people" than propaganda, we can see a similar pattern with the use of the term ideology. A number of commentators have remarked on the transformation of ideology from a positive to a predominantly negative term (Plamenatz 1970; Minogue 1985; McLellan 1986). The Count DeStutt de Tracy is generally credited with coining the term to describe his new "science of ideas" but the term quickly acquired its negative sense after Napoleon accused the Count and his followers of causing the misfortunes of the French Empire (Giddens 1982, p. 165; Thompson 1984, p. 1). Marx and Engels of course continued in this vein with their characterization of ideology as false consciousness (Tucker 1972; Manning and Robinson 1985).

The similarities at this point should be obvious: Both terms were born as innocent descriptions of social activities, each gradually attained a negative connotation, each has retained that pejorative meaning. Thompson has argued that "ideology is the thought of the *other*, the thought of someone other than yourself" (1984, p. 1). His characterization seems to echo Hummel and Huntress's description of propaganda, composed almost forty years earlier (1949, p. 1): "We are inclined to call reports which favor our own interests true; reports from the opposition are called propaganda."

Beyond the fact that the critics of these two concepts have shared similar trials and tribulations, it seems important to offer a more expansive rationale for this proposed integration. Misery may love company, but it doesn't justify a marriage. Ideology and propaganda share at least two other compelling similarities: The first is an intimate relationship to language; the second is a common concern with the problem of domination.

That the study of propaganda is tied to a study of language seems so obvious as to not require further comment; such is not the case with ideology. It is only recently that the critics of ideology have come to appreciate the centrality of language to their task. As McLellan notes (1986, p. 83):

Ideology is best viewed not as a separate system of signs and symbols that could be contrasted with—and eventually replaced by—another, e.g. science of some sort. Ideology is rather an aspect of every system of signs and symbols in so far as they are implicated in an asymmetrical distribution of power and resources.

We can understand and analyze ideology only as it is embodied and communicated through language. John Thompson (1984, p. 2) shares a similar perspective:

For increasingly it has been realized that "ideas" do not drift through the social world like clouds in a summer sky, occasionally divulging their contents with a clap of thunder and a flash of light.... Hence to study ideology is, in some part and in some way, to study language in the social world. It is to study the ways in which language is used in everyday social life, from the most mundane encounter between friends and family members to the most privileged forms of political debate. It is to study the ways in which the multifarious uses of language intersect with power, nourishing it, sustaining it, enacting it.

The second characteristic shared by propaganda and ideology is the domination of one individual or group by another. That domination need not be class-related or solely economic. By domination, I mean the attempt by one group or individual to exert a controlling influence over another group or individual. We may speak of the domination that may exist in the relations between men and women, employers and employees, or teachers and students. In addition, those battling against asymmetrical relationships participate in an ideological struggle as well. In those cases, the revolutionary propaganda of radical feminists, labor leaders, or student protesters is no less ideological because it is seeking to reverse the terms of dominance.

In this case, the tables are turned—domination is obviously a part of the study of ideology as Thompson has defined it; with propaganda, the connection may be less obvious. A number of commentators have equated the study of propaganda with the study of persuasion and attitude change (Martin 1958, pp. 10–20). Fraser (1957, p. 1), for instance, defines propaganda as "the activity, or art, of inducing others to behave in a way which they would not behave in its absence." Such definitions may be themselves deceptive because they fail to feature the motives of the propagandist. Jowett and O'Donnell have argued that "the elements of deliberateness and manipulation along with a systematic plan to achieve a purpose that is advantageous to the propagandist, however, distinguish propaganda from a free and open exchange of ideas" (1986, p. 16). Jowett has gone on to claim that while there are a variety of definitions offered by scholars of propaganda, the consensus reveals an agreement that "propaganda was distinguished from mere 'persuasion' by the elements of deliberateness and manipulation" (Jowett 1987, p. 101).

Clearly, the power exerted by the propagandist coupled with the intent to deliberately deceive those with whom he chooses to communicate results in the kind of combination that is featured in studies of ideology. Jacques Ellul (1965, p. 27) has spelled out the domination intrinsic to propaganda:

To be effective, propaganda must constantly short circuit all thought and decision. It must operate on the individual at the level of the unconscious. He must not know that he is being shaped by outside forces (this is one of the conditions for the success of propaganda), but some central core in him must be reached in order to release the mechanism in the unconscious which will provide the appropriate— and expected—action.

Of all the writers on propaganda surveyed for this essay, Ellul may have been the first to recognize a relationship between propaganda and ideology. Although Ellul accepted a more traditional definition of ideology that lacks the implicit notion of critique discussed earlier, his work shows a remarkable sensitivity for the critical project. For Ellul (1965, p. 116), ideology is "any set of ideas accepted by individuals or peoples, without attention to their origin or values." It is, however, in Ellul's categories of propaganda that we find support for a rapprochement between the study of ideology and propaganda. Ellul argued that among the categories of propaganda were political and sociological propaganda as well as the propaganda of agitation and the propaganda of integration. In each case, the former term in each pair describes the more overt and classic kind of propaganda. Political propaganda describes those techniques of influence employed by a government, a party, an administration, a pressure group, with a view to changing the behavior of the public (Ellul 1965, p. 62). Similarly, the propaganda of agitation bears "the stamp of the opposition" and is normally used to describe the efforts of those working against the government or the established order (Ellul 1965, p. 72). Neither of these categories seems particularly innovative; most traditional critics of propaganda would include these activities within their narrow definitions of the field. It is rather in the latter two categories of each pair that we find support for an integration between propaganda and ideology. Sociological propaganda, Ellul argues (1965, p. 64), is "a progressive adaptation to a certain order of things, a certain concept of human relations, which unconsciously molds individuals and makes them conform to society." Similarly, Ellul (1965, p. 75) describes the propaganda of integration which "aims at making the individual participate in his society in every way. It is a long-term propaganda, a self-reproducing propaganda that seeks to obtain stable behavior, to adapt the individual to his everyday life, to reshape his thoughts and behavior in terms of the permanent social setting." It is precisely this kind of analysis which suggests that the study of propaganda and the study of ideology share significant, heuristically valuable commonalities.

In a recent review essay, Garth Jowett (1987) attempted to isolate some of the causes of the decline in "propaganda studies" during the 1960s and 1970s. Jowett argues that scholars, faced with few systematic treatments of the subject, problematic definitions, and a lingering negative connotation associated with the field, have seemed reluctant to focus much attention on propaganda research. One way to reinvigorate such studies might be to provide a set of fresh analytic tools, a new vocabulary for discussing propaganda. Having made the argument that an integration between studies of propaganda and ideology seems justified, we need to consider what kind of analysis such a move would license. What are the advantages of such a conceptualization? How can an appreciation of ideology inform our study of propaganda?

APPLICATION OF THE INTEGRATIVE APPROACH

Among the recent studies of ideology, John Thompson has produced an investigation which draws on a number of European scholars' works. He identifies three central processes through which ideology operates in the social sphere (1984, pp. 130–31):

In the first place, relations of domination may be sustained by being represented as legitimate.... A second way in which ideology operates is by means of dissimulation. Relations of domination which serve the interests of some at the expense of others may be concealed, denied, or blocked in various ways. ... A third way in which ideology operates is by means of reification, that is, by representing a transitory, historical state of affairs as if it were permanent, natural, outside of time.

Thompson (1984, p. 131) is extremely careful to note that these three processes are neither exhaustive nor mutually exclusive. "There may be other *modus operandi* which are vitally important in certain circumstances and which would have to be elucidated through theoretical and empirical analyses. . . ." He further suggests that the various modes may overlap, that reification legitimates and that legitimation dissimulates. Thompson seems convinced however, that these three—legitimation, dissimulation, and reification—are the principal modalities through which ideology operates. It is my intention to examine the usefulness of these three processes as a new critical framework for the analysis of propaganda. It should be noted that this is only a small portion of the vast critical framework that Thompson provides and that his and other scholarly studies should be mined for possible application to propaganda studies. The more we know about how ideology operates through language, the more we will eventually know about propaganda.

Earlier in this chapter, I alluded to an incident in 1983 in which the Justice Department, under the terms of the Foreign Agent Registration Act (FARA), classified three films as political propaganda. FARA was passed in 1938 to deal with the problem of foreign "subversive" communication but the Department of Justice has interpreted the Act to apply to any attempt by foreign nationals or their agents to influence the American public. Once a film, for instance, is found to meet the statutory requirements of FARA, the Justice Department requires that a label be attached to the film indicating that it was prepared by a foreign government and that registration does not indicate approval of the contents of the material (U.S. Congress, House 1983, p. 6). Controversy arose when the Justice Department decided that two films critical of the Reagan Administration's policies on acid rain and a third film featuring a speech by antinuclear activist Dr. Helen Caldicott, all produced under the auspices of the National Film Board of Canada, fell under the provisions of the Act. There was a strong reaction against the move in the American and, not surprisingly, the Canadian press. Lawsuits were filed on behalf of the distributors of the film, who claimed that the Justice Department's actions had materially affected their ability to market the film. Most troublesome to the American Civil Liberties Union, which provided counsel for one of the suits, was the fact that FARA also required that notification be provided to the Justice Department of all those individuals and groups showing the films (see Dorfman 1985; U.S. Congress, House 1983).

What makes this an interesting case study for our purposes is that not only did the Justice Department's actions cause a considerable public controversy, but the subject of the controversy itself was the identification of discourse as propaganda. We shall now move to a consideration of how Thompson's three processes might be seen as operating in the Canadian film dispute.

Legitimation

Critics of ideology have spent a good deal of time dealing with the problem of legitimation (Habermas 1975; Mueller 1973; Therborn 1980; Clark and Dear 1984). It is not my intention at this point to provide any sort of comprehensive overview of this material. Suffice it to say that domination operates far more successfully when those who are being dominated either don't realize that they are being oppressed (robbed, perhaps, of the true value of their labor) or that such domination is natural or necessary. Thompson has argued that legitimation involves a two-step process of misrecognizing dominance as such and thereby recognizing it as legitimate (1984, p. 59). On the other hand, it is necessary to delegitimize any threats to the existing order by casting them as unnatural or dangerous.

In the present case, when the Justice Department's actions were questioned, when their legitimacy was challenged, they responded by falling back on one of the strongest sources of legitimacy available to them—the law (Clark and Dear 1984, pp. 175–94). In the hearings held in the House of Representatives investigating the Canadian film dispute, agents of the Department of Justice repeatedly defended their actions as entirely consistent with the provisions of FARA (U.S. Congress, House 1983, pp. 2–53). Even as critics were charging that the practices of the Justice Department amounted to unconstitutional infringement on the First Amendment, the Justice officials were able to claim that they had merely followed the rule of the law. That position was confirmed in June 1986 when the U.S. Court of Appeals—another powerful legitimating instrument—ruled that the Department of Justice had in fact operated within the law and found that the relevant provisions of FARA passed constitutional muster (U.S. Court of Appeals 1986).

In addition to the legitimacy claims offered by the Department of Justice, a powerful argument of delegitimation also operated in the controversy. A key complaint in both the lawsuit and in the Americal Civil Liberties Union testimony before Congress was that the labeling, per se, amounted to government intrusion into the marketplace of ideas and hence a violation of the First Amendment. Susan Shaffer of the ACLU claimed that "the term 'political propaganda' has negative connotations, no matter how benign the statutory defintions may be. It stigmatizes those in this country who disseminate the material and improperly denigrates the aesthetic, artistic, or educational value of the work itself" (U.S. Congress, House 1983, p. 55). Although that argument was ultimately rejected by both the U.S. Court of Appeals and the U.S. Supreme Court as being insufficient to justify invalidating the statute, it remains a potent strategy. To call something propaganda—a charge of wrongdoing, an arms control proposal, or a film from a foreign country—is to label it in such a way as to make a more thorough and reasoned response unnecessary. Debate stops; the sincerity of the speaker is immediately called into question and the dialogue breaks down. Edwin Newman, head of the Usage Panel of the American Heritage Dictionary, agrees. "Whatever its origin, propaganda has become a 'dirty word'. . . . When something is labeled propaganda, it should be looked at closely and with suspicion. Indeed, calling something propaganda amounts, for all practical purposes, to saying that it is not worth considering, that it is to be dismissed" (cited in Dorfman 1985, p. 453). Clearly, questions of legitimacy are at the core of this and similar discussions of propaganda.

Dissimulation

The representation of a sectional or individual interest as a more universal interest forms the core of the process of dissimulation. It is a cloaking of the true aims or goals of the policy put forward in such a way that the true interests of the authors are concealed. In terms of the present case study, the stated goal of the Foreign Agent Registration Act was "to identify foreign agents engaged in the dissemination of propaganda, to require them to make a public record of the nature of their relationship, and to require them to label political advocacy of foreign origin so that hearers and viewers in the United States would realize the source of such materials" (U.S. Congress, House 1983, p. 3). A critic focusing on matters of dissimulation might argue that the stated purpose of the act could be a cover for a more important, unstated goal of stigmatizing the political advocacy of foreign governments. What better strategy for providing a built-in rebuttal to a piece of political advocacy from a foreign (and perhaps unfriendly) nation than to provide a label that identifies the message as "political propaganda?" Such an interpretation seems even more plausible when the legislative history of the Act is taken into consideration. Representative Don Edwards, in opening the congressional investigation of the matter, stated that "the Foreign Agent Registration Act was enacted initially in 1938 in response to pre-World War II concern about Nazi propaganda. The statute's legislative history makes it clear that its original focus was subversive activities" (U.S. Congress, House 1983, p. 1). The stated goal of the Act allows the Justice Department to claim that rather than interfering with the marketplace of ideas, FARA enhances the marketplace by ensuring all messages will be clearly labeled as to source of origin— information that can only aid the critical consumer of these messages.

The government is not the only party capable of engaging in dissimulation. While the American Civil Liberties Union lent its support in the name of upholding freedom of speech for all citizens, it seems possible that this liberal organization saw not only threatened rights but also an excellent chance to embarrass the conservative Reagan Administration. More cynical critics might argue that the ACLU saw the whole controversy as a chance to gain public attention and aid in its fund-raising efforts. Whether any of these suppositions are in fact true is not as important as the fact that by using the ideological process of dissimulation we are brought to a point where we can at least ask these questions. Being sensitive to possible dissimulation appears to be another valuable tool for the analysis of propaganda.

Reification

Of the three processes identified by Thompson, the most difficult to conceptualize may be reification. Anthony Giddens has explained that "the interests of dominant groups are bound up with the preservation of the status quo. Forms of signification which 'naturalise' the existing state of affairs, inhibiting recognition of the mutable, historical character of human society thus act to sustain such interests" (Giddens 1982, p. 195). A timely example of reification involves our recent celebration of the bicentennial of the U.S. Constitution. Much praise and self-congratulation about the importance of that document seemed to gloss over the historical facts concerning the changes—truly enormous ones—that have occurred in both the document itself and the interpretation of it. Little mention was made that the original document had neglected to deal with the moral outrage of slavery and that meaningful free speech rights did not evolve until the early twentieth century. By presenting the Constitution as if it had always been a successful guarantor of rights and freedoms we give in to the process of reification. For all our discussion of history, we seem to have precious little historical sense.

But reification goes beyond the mere freezing of time to include all matters of reductionism and metonymy. Thompson (1984, p. 137) explains that "representing processes as things, deleting agency and constituting time as an eternal extension of the present tense: all of these are so many syntactic ways to reestablish the dimension of society 'without history' at the heart of historical society." One of the key points of contention during the hearings on the Canadian film dispute had to do with the fact that, ultimately, the decision to review and subsequently subject a foreign film to the label of political propaganda was a subjective one. A single lawyer, working within the Registration Unit of the Department of Justice with no clear guidelines, made the ultimate determination. It was, critics claimed, a subjective decision of a censor. The Justice Department was anxious to refute that characterization, claiming instead that the process for reviewing the films was standardized with little room for subjective judgments (U.S. Congress, House 1983, p. 5). By eliminating the agency of the censor, the Justice Department hoped to portray the entire process as regulated and consistent.

When a rhetor presents a situation in such a manner as to disguise the historical character of the topic or the situation in which it is being considered, it is possible that the process of reification is being employed. Emphasizing the here-and-now or wrenching a practice from its historical context may constitute additional strategies by which propagandists practice their trade.

CONCLUSION

I have attempted to provide a rationale for an integration of the concepts of propaganda and ideology. More importantly, a critical framework used in the analysis of ideology was demonstrated to provide valuable insight into discovering the propaganda associated with the Canadian film controversy. It should be remembered that Thompson's three processes represent only a small part of his analytic scheme; other critics of ideology may have equally valuable critical frameworks for the critic of propaganda. Students of propaganda must be willing to investigate the literature of ideology in an effort to continue this process of discovery and intellectual growth.

REFERENCES

Clark, G. L., and M. Dear. 1984. *State apparatus: Structures and language of legitimacy*. Boston: Allen and Unwin.

Doob, L. 1966. *Public opinion and propaganda*, 2nd ed. Hamden, Conn.: Archon.

Dorfman, A. 1985. Neutral propaganda: Three films "made in Canada" and the Foreign Agents Registration Act. *Comm/Ent* 7:435–68.

Ellul, J. 1965. *Propaganda*. New York: Knopf.

Fraser, L. 1957. *Propaganda*. London: Oxford University Press.

Giddens, A. 1982. *Central problems of social theory*. Berkeley: University of California Press.

Habermas, J. 1975. *Legitimation crisis*. Boston: Beacon.

Hummel, W., and K. Huntress. 1949. *The analysis of propaganda*. New York: Dryden.

Jowett, G. 1987. Propaganda and communication: The re-emergence of a research tradition. *Journal of Communication* 37:97–114.

Jowett, G., and V. O'Donnell. 1986. *Propaganda and persuasion*. Beverly Hills, Calif.: Sage.

Manning, D., and T. J. Robinson. 1985. *The place of ideology in political life*. London: Croom Helm.

Martin, L. J. 1958. *International propaganda*. Minneapolis: University of Minnesota Press.

McLellan, D. 1986. *Ideology*. Minneapolis: University of Minnesota Press.

Minogue, K. 1985. *Alien powers: The pure theory of ideology*. London: Weidenfeld and Nicolson.

Mueller, C. 1973. *The politics of communication*. London: Oxford University Press.

Plamenatz, J. 1970. *Ideology*. New York: Praeger.

Therborn, G. 1980. *The ideology of power and the power of ideology*. London: Verso.

Thompson, J. 1984. *Studies in the theory of ideology*. Berkeley: University of California Press.

Tucker, R. (ed.). 1972. *The Marx-Engels reader*. New York: Norton.

U.S. Congress, House. 1983. Committee on the Judiciary. Subcommittee on Civil and Constitutional Rights. *Canadian films and the Foreign Agents Registration Act*. 98th Congress, 1st sess., Serial 36.

U.S. Court of Appeals. June 18, 1986. *Block* v. *Meese*. Slip opinion no. 83–672.

Wrage, E. 1972. Public address: A study in social and intellectual history. In *Methods of rhetorical criticism*, ed. R. L. Scott and B. L. Brock, pp. 103–11. Minneapolis: University of Minnesota Press.

9   Deceptive Advertising and the Power of Suggestion

J. David Kennamer

Advertising may be the most visible form of "propaganda" in the United States, since most mass media are wholly or in major part supported by advertising revenues, and many would argue that advertising is the engine that drives the most powerful and most consumer-centered economy in the world.

In another chapter in this volume, Smith has proposed that propaganda takes four forms: falsehoods, omissions, distortions, and suggestions. This last category is perhaps the most subtle and sophisticated form, and the form that is most relevant to advertising, especially the category of advertising that has been labeled "deceptive but true." Such advertisements demonstrate the "power of suggestion" since deception occurs not in what they say, but in the inferences they lead receivers to draw. They depend heavily on the interaction of the advertisement with the receivers' prior knowledge, beliefs, and expectations.

This is a good example of the general principle presented by Nisbett and Ross (1980) that much of perception is "theory-driven" rather than "data-driven." As has been demonstrated in recent years in the work of cognitive psychologists, these "theories" take the form of frames, schemata, stereotypes, and scripts, all of which refer to commonly held organizations of expectations concerning categories of events, people, and other types of experience. To greatly oversimplify, memory seems to consist largely of patterns of expectations derived from experience and provided by our cultures concerning commonly encountered situations, so that every event is not confronted as if it were original and unique. Perception and comprehension are thus dependent on a sort of "pattern recognition" (Winograd 1977).

Among such expectations are those identified by H. P. Grice (1975, 1978) and termed "conversational maxims" and "conversational implicatures." These are expectations about the structure of conversations and the meanings that are inferred from the use of various linguistic conventions in ordinary conversations. The purpose of this chapter is to relate these expectations about the patterns of conversation to the study of advertising, specifically the ways in which these expectations can be systematically manipulated by advertisers so that readers, hearers, or viewers of such ads may be deceived. Another goal of the chapter is to illustrate a general mechanism by which suggestion may function by using inference and implication to evoke or induce impressions that may then become remembered as information by receivers.

CONVERSATIONS AND INFERENCES

Suggestion is a very useful technique in advertising, since it allows ads to leave the impression that they have made claims, when in fact, at the level of the advertising copy, they may claim almost nothing. Therefore the advertiser cannot be held accountable if products or services do not live up to expectations.

The process works because the advertisements lead more or less logically to some sort of inference. Harris (1981, p. 87) defines an inference as "any construction of meaning that a hearer or reader draws from a passage where he or she goes beyond what is explicitly given." The important term in this definition is "construction." The process is carried out primarily by the receiver of the message who builds meaning out of the interaction of the message with the contents of cognitive systems of beliefs and knowledge.

Stereotypes, expectations, schemata, scripts, and frames all refer to unspoken, but commonly assumed, bodies of "knowledge" existing among large numbers, if not the majority of, the members of a given society or cultural group. Such knowledge is the basis of many of these inferences and vastly enriches the communication process. The existence of such conventional ways of behaving and speaking and thinking, and the common knowledge among participants that such conventions exist, allows a great deal of submerged communication—communication that occurs not at the linguistic level, but at a more fundamental level of what words, and the ways in which they are combined, *signify* or *symbolize*, rather than in what they actually *say*.

The following example, in the form of an everyday conversation between mother and daughter, is provided by Winograd (1977, p. 82).

Mother: Where is your boyfriend going to stay when he visits?
Daughter: We have a couch in the living room.

As Winograd notes, the daughter's reply, taken in isolation, is perfectly true, but if the boyfriend has no intention of actually sleeping on the sofa, regardless of where it is located, then "the daughter has not made a false statement, but has violated the conversational convention that a question be followed by a relevant response" (1977, p. 82). This mother–daughter exchange is an example of how such conventions can be violated by the speaker with the purpose of deceiving the hearer.

Grice has described a number of conversational conventions that speakers use and hearers expect. These conventions add layers of meaning to conversations and can also be manipulated for various effects, among them deception. Grice says that most everyday conversations are guided by what he calls the "Cooperative Principle," which states: "Make your conversational contribution such as is required, at the stage at which it occurs, by the accepted purpose or direction of the talk exchange in which you are engaged" (1975, p. 67).

Grice (1975, p. 67) further specifies a set of maxims which he says are subordinate to this Cooperative Principle and, to the extent that they are observed, tend to reinforce it. For example, under a principle he calls "Quantity," he writes: "Make your contribution as informative as is required (for the current purposes of exchange)." Furthermore, "Do not make your contribution more informative than is required." Another maxim states, rather tersely, "Be relevant." For example, in the mother-daughter conversation above, the assumption, deriving from what Winograd calls "conversational schemas," is that the daughter's reply is relevant to the mother's question. As Grice (1975, p. 68) says, "I expect a partner's contribution to be appropriate to immediate needs at each stage of the transaction; if I am mixing ingredients for a cake, I do not expect to be handed a good book."

In many instances, as Grice points out, the meaning of an interchange derives largely from the fact that such conversational conventions have been followed, or have been purposefully ignored or violated, rather than in the linguistic content. He calls such instances conversational "implicatures" and notes "since the truth of a conversational implicatum is not required by the truth of what is said (what is said may be true, what is implicated may be false), the implicature is not carried by what is said, but only by the saying of what is said or by 'putting it that way' " (Grice 1975, pp. 74–75). It follows that if the receiver assumes that the sender of the message is following the Cooperative Principle or one of its maxims, but the sender is not and does not alert the receiver to this fact, then he or she may be guilty of deceptive communication. As Grice writes, the speaker "may quietly and unostentatiously *violate* a maxim; if so in some cases he will be liable to mislead" (1975, p. 69). Examples from advertising will illustrate Grice's points.

ON BEING TOO WELL INFORMED

Anderson (1985) points out that a sentence requires both assertions and suppositions. The assertion is the point of the sentence, the new information to be communicated or emphasized. The supposition is what the speaker can assume the other person knows about the subject. This knowledge allows the speaker to satisfy, or to violate, Grice's Maxim of Quantity.

This maxim is a good one to use to illustrate how advertisers can manipulate these conversational principles to create implicatures which may mislead consumers. An example is provided by ads that, instead of saying a product contains aspirin, say instead it contains "the pain reliever most recommended by doctors."

Coleman (1983, p. 224) explains: "The use of a more indirect term like a definite description in place of the name 'aspirin' implies that the ingredient is something very technical which the layperson could not identify or understand." We have been told more than we need to know. All we need to know to evaluate the product is that its major ingredient is simple aspirin. It can be assumed that everyone knows what aspirin is; this is the relevant supposition. Using the description in its place implies that this supposition is not relevant. Therefore, neither is it relevant to assume that the advertisement is referring to aspirin. The ad does not lie, but it deceives nonetheless. As Grice (1975, p. 67) notes, hearers may be misled "as a result of thinking there is some particular point in the provision of the excess information."

A very vivid example comes from an American Express advertisement of the 1970s in which spokesman Karl Malden intones: "What to do? Get American Express Travelers' Checks. If *they're* lost, you can get a full refund at over 600 places" (Berkoff 1981, p. 193). By mentioning the refund feature with such prominence the ad implies that this is unique to these travelers' checks, when in fact other companies also give refunds. In addition, Coleman (1983) points out that the information leading to an inference may not be included in what is said but in how it is said, in what are termed "prosodics." For example, placing the stress on "they're," in referring to the American Express checks, would reinforce the tendency to infer that they are unique in regard to their refund policy.

This is a clear case of being told more than we need to know, a violation of Grice's Maxim of Quantity. The refund statement is true enough; it is the mere statement of it (along with the placement of the stress) that leads to an implicature, and to deception.

A more innocent example comes from Coleman (1983, p. 228): "The air freshener you don't have to hide." The ad does not *say* that other air fresheners are ugly and therefore must be put out of sight, but it doesn't have to. The mere fact of saying that this one does *not* have to be hidden implies that unsightliness is a serious fault of air fresheners generally. Cooper (1982, p. 126) notes that the use of negation, as in this case, is often a violation of this quantity maxim, "because usually to say something did not happen is to say something more than is required."

This ad also depends upon the close connection between the concepts of "hide" and "ugly." If you have to hide something, it must be shameful, dangerous, or . . . ugly. An air freshener in normal use is neither dangerous nor shameful, so because of these semantic associations between the concepts, the hearer infers that if they must be hidden, other air fresheners must be ugly.

Advertisers can also very easily and effectively manipulate Grice's Maxim of Relation—that we expect people to say things that are relevant to the conversation. In addition, assuming the speaker is following the Cooperative Principle, it can be assumed that the juxtaposition of two statements in space and/or time will create the appearance of such coherence, regardless of the linguistic relation of the statements. Cooper refers to this as the "text coherence convention" and defines it as "the presumption that all propositions in a single text are somehow related" (1982, p. 123). This helps explain the implication resulting from the mother-daughter conversation noted earlier.

Berkoff (1981, p. 194) describes a newspaper advertisement for a utility showing a chemist testing water used to cool one of the utility's nuclear power plants. The copy reads: "The water our power plants use is just as clean coming out as going in. It's my job to make sure of it." There are a number of ways in which this ad can deceive. It may very well be true that the water is as clean coming out as going in, but "it's substantially warmer than it was before being diverted to the utility's use, and this warmer water can have the effect of changing entire ecosystems" (Berkoff 1981, p. 194). In other words, the water is polluted by heat. The advertisement violates the Maxim of Relation since the information provided is irrelevant to the question, which concerns the degree to which this industrial concern pollutes the environment. The utility in this case attempts to polish its image as a good corporate citizen, but does it by providing information that is not only irrelevant to the question, but also diverts attention from the real issue. It is a nonobvious non sequitur.

The ad accomplishes this deception in part by depending upon a particular supposition concerning a common definition of pollution, one that probably does not include heat. In other words, the advertisement depends upon and even purposely accesses an inappropriate supposition for the assertion that is being made. This seems to be a clear example of the manner in which advertisers can manipulate conversational implicatures and belief system structures, and the manner in which these rely on each other, to create deceptive but true advertisements.

THE INCOMPLETE COMPARATIVE

One of the most common of inference processes is described by Harris (1981, p. 83) as filling in "empty 'slots' in the overall structure" of a stimulus, a process that seems very much consistent with the process of conversational implicature. Consider the following example taken from Monaco and Kaiser (1983, p. 268):

An independent survey showed that 8 out of 10 farmers think that Ford makes a better truck.

Does it follow that:

Farmers think that Fords are the best trucks made?

Or even that:

Ford makes the best pickup?

Neither of these conclusions follows explicitly from the original statement, although casual hearers may interpret it in these ways. The key is the use of the incomplete comparative: Ford makes a better truck; better than what? The use of the term "better" leads one to expect an object of comparison. When it isn't provided, the hearer is likely to provide it.

Coleman (1983, p. 227) refers to this phenomenon as "closure," defined as "the tendency people have, when faced with an incomplete sequence such as a comparative with no standard, to supply the missing material themselves, and then to perceive the item to have been complete from the start." Shimp (1978, p. 26) reports, for example, that when student subjects heard "Mennen E goes on warmer and drier," they were very likely to *think* they had heard "Mennen E goes on warmer and drier than any other deodorant on the market."

Grice's Maxim of Quantity seems to be particularly apt here. By purposefully leaving out the object of comparison, the advertiser has clearly not made his contribution "as informative as is required." If receivers are to make sense of the messages, they themselves must provide the information necessary to complete it. Given that these incomplete comparatives *do* mention a product, then the obvious and logical comparison is to other members of that product category. Otherwise the statement is nonsense.

DECEPTION IN THE "REAL WORLD"

Laboratory experiments such as the one described above have repeatedly provided evidence that advertising can deceive through processes of implication and inference. But such situations have questionable "ecological validity," since they do not recreate the typical viewing, listening, or reading situation. The major difference is that they force attention to the advertising messages. Monaco and Kaiser (1983, p. 277) write:

The shift from program to commercial is a discriminative stimulus to direct attention away from the TV; and anything we remember about the commercial should be attributed to incidental learning. The start of an experiment, however, is a signal to the subject to direct attention *toward* the commercial. And even if the subject is not specifically directed to do so, he/she probably has a stronger inclination to try to remember the content of the commercial than does the consumer, at home.

The fact is that users of the media seldom give advertisements their full attention. Seeing advertisements is not the primary reason for watching television or reading newspapers and magazines. As Bettman (1986, p. 263) points out, "The typical consumer environment is potentially subject to a great deal of interference." The upshot of this might well be that under conditions of less than full attention, with little motivation to study the message, and with demands from other stimuli, such deception might be even more likely. Harris, Dubitsky, and Bruno conclude that this is indeed the case, based on the results of a study in which fictitious ads were embedded in a "Face the Nation" radio broadcast. They summarize (1983, p. 256): "It is not surprising that identification of implied claims would be even more difficult in the context of a program because more time elapsed between stimulus and test and because subjects' attention was probably directed primarily at the program, not the commercials, as it is in real life."

SUGGESTION AND THE ORGANIZATION OF MEMORY

The issues presented to this point demonstrate the effectiveness and to some extent the mechanisms of suggestion as a form of propaganda. It is effective because the receiver of the messages does most of the work, with some encouragement, of course, by the sender of the message. An example is provided by the very successful and frequent use of stereotyping in advertising. In a cognitive and communicative sense, stereotypes are highly efficient and economical. If a stereotype is a conventionalized set of attributes surrounding a social concept or category, then the presentation of the concept will ensure that the receivers will, themselves, provide those associated attributes. When an advertiser has 30 seconds to develop a plot and characters in order to make a point, then what more effective technique than to get the receiver to do most of the work? The provision of one of the set of attributes "suggests" the rest to the receiver.

This process is illustrative of a model of memory organization that seems to be dominant in cognitive psychology, the associative network. Anderson (1985) describes memory as being organized in propositional networks, with concepts being linked to other concepts through relationships of various sorts and of various strengths. Mitchell refers to such concepts as "packets of information" within which "the strength of the associative links are stronger than between packets" (1983, p. 29). For example, the definition of water pollution discussed above could be such a packet, with a weak or nonexistent link to water temperature.

An update of an automotive example provided by Mitchell (1983, p. 21) will serve to illustrate the point. The attributes that would accrue to the Ford Escort might include "small," "economical," and "popular." While a packet is a fairly discrete unit, it does have connections to other packets and indeed may be a unit of a larger packet. For example, the Escort packet is a subunit of the "small car" and "Ford" packets. Commonly held beliefs about Fords and about small cars will therefore attach to the Escort.

Thus when it is discovered that the Escort is a small car, it may also be assumed to be dangerous in an accident. When it is discovered to be a Ford, itself a subpacket of "American-made," beliefs about Fords and American cars more generally will be added to the evaluation of the Escort. Advertising may not include such information, but the consumers may provide it themselves when confronted with the advertising.

The purpose of advertising is to create or modify these packets by adding favorable attributes, deleting unfavorable attributes, or by creating or removing relations among attributes and among packets. Much of Ford advertising in recent years, for example, has hammered away at the quality issue—"Quality Is Job One"—trying to separate its products from the general stigma that has become attached to American-made cars concerning quality.

Sometimes the goal is to link two concepts into the same packet, with the result that they "may become so tightly linked that they become a single chunk of information" (Mitchell 1983, p. 21); consider, for example, natural = nutritious.

Gardner (1975, p. 2) provides a summary: "Most promotional strategies attempt either to change existing beliefs about a product or brand (i.e., how these beliefs are evaluated) or to introduce a new belief or make an existing belief more salient or important." The American Express advertisement cited earlier is a clear example of the advertiser trying to introduce the belief that it is unique among travelers' check providers in its refund policy. In this case it is done by suggestion, created in part by violations of Grice's maxim of conversation.

MAKING SENSE OF NONSENSE

Berkoff notes that advertising people often advise: "Don't sell the steak; sell the sizzle" (1981, p. 191). Rather than extolling the objective benefits or features of a product, advertising induces in the consumer the images and feelings supposedly to be derived from the use of the product. This is why cigarette ads so often use glamorous and sexy models, and why soft-drink ads so often show attractive young people engaging in active good times. An inspired example of the genre is the Sunkist orange soda commercial showing handsome and athletic young men surfing to a Beach Boys "Good Vibrations" sound-alike sound track.

Such "sizzle" ads are apparently becoming more and more common. The legal and regulatory environment that has developed in recent years has resulted, according to Shimp, "in a reduction in the amount of 'hard data' in ads and a trend toward the use of nebulous, evasive, and subjective claims, which may presumably mislead receivers in a subtle manner" (1983, pp. 195–196). In other words, because of sophistication on the part of consumers, the vigilance of consumer protection organizations, and action on the part of federal and state regulatory agencies, advertisers have gotten the word that they can't get away with outright fraud. As a result, deception is more likely to fall in the category of suggestion, the interaction of the message with "what's in receivers' heads."

Garfinkel notes, for example, that fast-food restaurants and cereal brands quite commonly use this "nonobjective" sort of advertising. He observes that such attributes as "atmosphere," "taste," "convenience," and "crunch" are empty of any "real" information and that truth "may not even be a concept which is applicable to the given information" (1983, p. 188). When Orson Welles emoted for Paul Masson Wines, "We shall sell no wine before its time," he seemed to make some claim about the quality of the wines, based on assumed links between the age of a wine and its quality. However, absolutely no objective claim was actually made.

On close inspection, much of what advertisers bombard us with is simply nonsense, sophisticated nonsense, but nonsense nonetheless; and nonsense would be, by Grice's definition, "uncooperative," in that it is largely irrelevant and uninformative. Since we do not expect people to talk nonsense to us, we make an effort to make sense of what is said; we construct a meaning based on the structure of the message and the concepts it evokes. In so doing we may be drawn to conclusions that are not explicitly stated and which may be deceptive.

DECEIVING OURSELVES (WITH A LITTLE HELP FROM OUR FRIENDS)

The approach taken in this chapter is firmly in the mainstream of recent models of the communication process, which lay a large part of the "responsibility" for the outcome of communication on the receivers of the messages. Presenting a message to an audience is seen as being necessary but not sufficient to ensure communication. The audience members may not attend to it very closely, they may not remember it, or they may perceive it in a way that was unintended by the sender. And different receivers may interpret the same message in completely different ways (McCombs and Becker 1979). The key to effective and efficient communication lies, apparently, in designing messages that fit the "fields of experience" of audience members (Gamble and Gamble 1986). This is another way of saying simply that the sender and receiver must share many beliefs about the world, and they must also know that they share these beliefs. Among these beliefs are those held about the structures and content of ordinary conversations, both the meaning of the structures chosen and the meaning of the concepts referred to or evoked.

This emphasis on the role of receivers in assigning meaning to the messages sent to them indicates that in one sense we "deceive ourselves" when confronted with the kind of advertising messages discussed in this chapter. We do this largely by making inferences as to the meaning of messages that are not warranted by the actual information provided. We jump to conclusions on limited information, we fill in gaps in information, and we expand information beyond what is given.

However, if one knows that others will interpret something in a manner that leads them to erroneous conclusions, is it misleading to present it to them anyway? Grice would certainly argue that a purposeful violation of the Cooperative Principle by a message sender, without the knowledge of the receiver, constitutes deception on the part of the sender. And Gardner provides the following example. "Suppose detergent manufacturers discovered that just putting red and blue crystals in some detergents resulted in a significant number of housewives attributing more cleaning power to those detergents with crystals than those without. Therefore, the simple statement that Brand X had blue crystals would be deceptive even though no claims about increased cleaning power were made" (1975, p. 42).

So in a certain sense we do deceive ourselves, but we may be "set up" by advertisers who create messages of a form and content that make it likely that we will draw specific, possibly misleading, conclusions about the products involved. Thus, suggestion is a particularly potent form of propaganda because it takes advantage of systematic weaknesses in what are normally very functional processes of inference drawing, processes that serve us well in most circumstances of everyday life. Perhaps the first mistake is assuming that the world as presented in advertising bears any resemblance to the world in which everyday life is actually conducted.

REFERENCES

Anderson, J. R. 1985. *Cognitive psychology*. 2nd ed. New York: W. H. Freeman.
Berkoff, R. 1981. Can you separate the sizzle from the steak? *Journal of Popular Culture* 15(2):191–200.

Bettman, J. R. 1986. Consumer psychology. In *Annual Review of Psychology*, vol. 37, ed. M. Rosenzweig and L. Porter, pp. 257–89. Palo Alto, Calif.: Annual Reviews.

Coleman, L. 1983. Semantic and prosodic manipulation in advertising. In *Information processing in advertising*, ed. R. J. Harris, pp. 217–40. Hillsdale, N.J.: Lawrence Erlbaum.

Cooper, M. M. 1982. Context as vehicle: Implicatures in writing. In *What writers know: The language, process and structure of written discourse*, ed. M. Nystrand, pp. 105–28. New York: Academic Press.

Gamble, M. W., and T. K. Gamble. 1986. *Introducing mass communication*. New York: McGraw-Hill.

Gardner, D. M. 1975. Deception in advertising: A conceptual approach. *Journal of Marketing* 39:40–46.

Garfinkel, A. 1983. A pragmatic approach to truth in advertising. In *Information processing research in advertising*, ed. R. J. Harris, pp. 175–94. Hillsdale, N.J.: Lawrence Erlbaum.

Grice, H. P. 1975. Logic and conversation. In *The logic of grammar*, ed. D. Davidson and G. Harman, pp. 65–75. Belmont, Calif.: Dickenson.

———. 1978. Further notes on logic and conversation. In *Syntax and Semantics*, Vol. 9, *Pragmatics*, ed. P. Cole and J. L. Morgan, pp. 113–28. New York: Academic Press.

Harris, R. J. 1981. Inference in information processing. In *The Psychology of Learning and Motivation*, Vol. 15, ed. G. H. Bower, pp. 81–128. New York: Academic Press.

Harris, R. J., T. M. Dubitsky, and K. J. Bruno. 1983. Psycholinguistic studies of misleading advertising. In *Information processing research in advertising*, ed. R. J. Harris, pp. 241–62. Hillsdale, N.J.: Lawrence Erlbaum.

McCombs, M. E., and L. B. Becker. 1979. *Using mass communication theory*. Englewood Cliffs, N.J.: Prentice-Hall.

Mitchell, A. A. 1983. Cognitive processes initiated by exposure to advertising. In *Information processing research in advertising*, ed. R. J. Harris, pp. 13–42. Hillsdale, N.J.: Lawrence Erlbaum.

Monaco, G. E., and D. Kaiser. 1983. Effects of prior preference, inferences, and believability in consumer advertising. In *Information processing research in advertising*, ed. R. J. Harris, pp. 263–88. Hillsdale, N.J.: Lawrence Erlbaum.

Nisbett, R., and L. Ross. 1980. *Human inference: Strategies and shortcomings of social judgment*. Englewood Cliffs, N.J.: Prentice-Hall.

Shimp, T. A. 1978. Do incomplete comparisons mislead? *Journal of Advertising Research* 18(6): 21–27.

———. 1983. Evaluative verbal content and deceptive advertising: A review and critical analysis. In *Information processing research in advertising*, ed. R. J. Harris, pp. 195–216. Hillsdale, N.J.: Lawrence Erlbaum.

Winograd, T. 1977. A framework for understanding discourse. In *Cognitive processes in comprehension*, ed. M. A. Just and P. E. Carpenter, pp. 63–88. Hillsdale, N.J.: Lawrence Erlbaum.

10 Smoke and Mirrors: A Confirmation of Jacques Ellul's Theory of Information Use in Propaganda

Stanley B. Cunningham

INFORMATION AS PROPAGANDA

Jacques Ellul (1957; 1965, pp. 84–87, 112–16) makes the chilling claim that, in contemporary technological society, information and propaganda are virtually indistinguishable. This "indistinguishability" or "inseparability" thesis is of a piece with Ellul's theory that in technological society propaganda is ubiquitous, an ineliminable sociological phenomenon which is far more comprehensive than any series of isolated episodes or discrete campaigns. Propaganda is woven into the very fabric of our society. Furthermore, as spelled out by Ellul, this relationship of inseparability is more than just one of juxtaposition and mix. Rather it takes on the character of an impersonal dialectic which implacably unfolds whenever communication is dominated by the practical dictates of *la technique*. Resistance seems almost futile. Even as the genuine informant is drawn to expose or neutralize the propagandist's message, he or she is ineluctably compelled to adopt the strategies and techniques of the propagandist. In short, propaganda always prevails because it begets counterpropaganda even within the camp of the well-motivated counterinformant. Even well-educated audiences are just as susceptible to this sort of influence.

Ellul's indistinguishability thesis has attracted its fair share of criticism, but it was strikingly instantiated in 1982, for example, when Philip Nicolaides, deputy program director of Voice of America (VOA) penned the following thoughts to the director of VOA (as quoted in Bethel 1982, p. 24):

We are, as all the world understands, a propaganda agency. . . . Since the word "propaganda" still suffers from negative connotations, let's agree that the generally acceptable substitute is "information."

This terminological and semantic equation within a U.S. government agency, of course, is not something anomalous. Indeed, the world has long come to know or at least suspect that departments or ministries with "information" in their titles are propaganda outlets: the U.S. Information Agency; Britain's wartime Ministry of Information; Information Canada (1970–76); the Republic of South Africa's Bureau of Information.

It is important, however, to appreciate what Ellul is saying and what he is not saying about the information/propaganda coupling. He is not saying that the *concept* of information is identical with the *concept* of propaganda. He is saying that in practice information and propaganda are difficult to sort out from one another. Accordingly, the issue, as some seem to assume, is not one of conceptual identity, but rather one of indistinguishability in the real order.

Paradoxically, however, Ellul's thesis is difficult to confirm, even for the most studious and analytic, because the difficulty in sorting our propaganda from information is made to be self-warranting. That seems to be why critics such as Thomas Steinfatt (1979) are inclined to view Ellul's thesis as something more tautologous than informative. In point of fact, however, Ellul's thesis seems to have a lot more going for it if we look a bit more closely at the linkages between propaganda and some rather commonplace epistemic and para-epistemic features.[1] As writers from Goebbels to Ellul have pointed out, propaganda could not succeed without the complicity of truth, facts and information, and the *appearance* of a commitment to these.

1. Ellul, for instance, argues that propaganda, like public opinion, depends upon information as a sort of propaedeutic because "it is information that creates the problem that propaganda will exploit and to which it will claim to offer solution" (1957, p. 72; see also 1965, pp. 84–87, 112–16, 144–47). It even presupposes a minimal degree of formal education.

2. Although propaganda is conventionally and stereotypically equated with falsehoods and lies, modern propaganda behaves with far greater restraint and sophistication. Typically, it relies upon facts (where "fact" is understood to mean any proposition, portrayal, or description which truthfully accords with reality). Whenever possible, the maxim "tell the truth" was as much a requirement for Goebbels as it was for USIA. Melor Sturua, a U.S.-based Soviet correspondent, puts it this way (as quoted in Lapham 1984, p. 14):

For propaganda to succeed, the fact itself must be true. If the fact is true, then it is possible to believe the interpretation. . . . Our cliches are based on your cliches. We print what you write about yourself.

3. The use of truth in the hands of the propagandist is always selective and manipulative. Truth, historically cherished as the supreme value of the human intellect, has been eclipsed by its utility. Leo Bogart (1976, pp. 128–29) in describing the mind-set of USIA and Daniel Lerner (1980, pp. 386–87) in talking about symbol manipulation in the context of political management both use the phrases "campaign of truth" and "strategy of truth." Altheide and Johnson, in their analysis of the organizational report as the principal unit of propaganda on the contemporary scene, point up the nearly imperceptible conversion of truth from an end to a means (1980, p. 23):

What has been overlooked is the essential aspect of propaganda—the practical use of information. . . . The practical use of truth is characteristic of most organizations in our modern age. . . . Bureaucratic propaganda uses truth for organizational goals.

4. As part of that project of demoting the truth, propaganda unabashedly exploits the appearance of science, rationality, and objectivity. Ellul (1965, pp. 53–57, 87), Altheide and Johnson (1980), and Wheeler (1976), to mention only a few, have convincingly argued that there is something about the use of numbers and statistics that is persuasive because they so easily reinforce beliefs in the reader/receiver that what is being reported is scientific, objective, and therefore God's truth.

In sum, modern propaganda both in reality and in theoretical commentary is characterized by a very close alliance with or incorporation of some central, highly prized epistemic values: information and knowledge; truth and facts; certainty and objectivity. It is further enhanced whenever these epistemic values are embedded within such culturally esteemed practices as debate, discussion, and scientific research; or when it is associated with such para-epistemic dispositions as thoughtfulnes and reflection, and with the social values of openness, cooperation, courtesy, and civility—all of which add up to give a total impression of fair play and reasonableness in persuasive discourse. The indistinguishability thesis has to do with not just information, but with a whole family of epistemic and para-epistemic values and practices which give propaganda the appearance of genuine knowledge and understanding.

Accordingly, given these sorts of linkages, and keeping in mind Ellul's depiction of propaganda as being a widespread social phenomenon, the indistinguishability thesis begins to sound more and more credible. It is, after all, perfectly congruent with the points itemized in Nos. 1 to 4. Even so, government agencies and titles aside, it is still a thesis which *ex hypothesi* is made difficult to confirm. As Ellul himself has asked (1957, p. 64), "where exactly is the boundary between propaganda, a massive affirmation of simplified facts, and information made up of general formulas, elementary themes, over which the reader has not the slightest control or power?"

It is useful, then, to identify and isolate those texts where the indistinguishability thesis can be confirmed and instantiated, especially when the epistemic and para-epistemic linkages can be thrown into relief.

Now, while propaganda more often than not is analyzed at the level of political and governmental communication, Ellul's thesis is meant to apply equally at all levels of everyday information flow, including commercially sponsored texts. A recent sequence of tobacco company *nonproduct* advertisements offers both a wieldy unit and a concrete illustration of Ellul's information/propaganda claim. Published by the R. J. Reynolds Tobacco Company (RJR) in 1984–86, the ads in this series appeared in a number of high-profile mass-circulation magazines (e.g., *People, Time, The New York Times Magazine, Seventeen, Young Miss, Parade* [the weekly insert magazine]). The series comprises sixteen carefully crafted ads which attempt to allay public criticism and distrust directed against smokers and secondhand or environmental tobacco smoke (ETS). The ads do this by openly raising a number of concerns about the negative aspects of smoking. In this sense they appear to be roughly analogous to public service announcements published by brewers and distillers about drinking abuse or the hazards of drinking and driving. What is distinctive about the RJR ads, however, is the way in which they secure readers' approval by championing a cluster of epistemic and para-epistemic values, thereby projecting a sustained aura of rationality, reasonableness, and fairminded exchange.

The sixteen ads may be divided into four categories—an arrangement which is not intended to reflect the chronological order of their appearance. Two of the very first to appear promote the theme of public debate; seven deal with the interconnected issues of secondhand smoke or passive smoking, smoking in public, and scientific findings about ETS; four ads are dedicated to smoking and young people. Finally, there is a fourth catchall category which includes ads that are not easily assimilable to the first three groups. One of these ads ("Of cigarettes and science" [e.g., *Time*, February 3, 1986, p. 73]) raises questions about the reliability of scientific studies which say that heart disease is caused by smoking. It could just as easily be included within the second category dealing with ETS studies, but it happens to be the only ad which, at least indirectly, addresses the issue of physical harm to the smokers themselves. Another ad ("Workplace smoking restrictions: A trend that never was" [e.g., *Parade*, March 9, 1986, p. 12]) minimizes news media reports which play up restrictive policies in the corporate sector. This too could just as well have been included in the second group of seven, but it raises as well the distinctive issues of corporate policy and regulation. The third ad (e.g., *Parade*, June 17, 1984, p. 15), one of the earliest to appear in the series, is the anomalous member of the series because more than the others it exemplifies the conventional admonitions of some public service advertisements. In large characters the title announces "What not to do in bed." There follows a litany of perfectly legitimate and even cute behaviors: "You can read . . . listen to music . . . and yes, you can snuggle. . . . " It ends with a stern prohibition against lighting up because, it adds with a deft touch of wordplay, if you should doze off "all your dreams can go up on smoke."

TALK AND MORE TALK

The title of the first ad to appear in the series (e.g., *Time*, February 6, 1984, p. 2) announced a public debate: "Can we have an open debate about smoking?" Smoking issues, it points out, are so emotional and complex that "it's hard to debate them objectively." Indeed, many now believe that there is "nothing to debate," that "the case against smoking is closed." This, we are told, is far from the truth. The many negative reports about smoking and health have met with too little or no challenge. Studies which link smoking with disease have "regularly ignored significant evidence to the contrary." Accordingly, RJR believes that this alternative evidence will be of interest because "reasonable people who analyze it" will come to see that the issue is not a closed one, but an "open controversy." Some may suspect Reynold's motives, but the company believes that its earlier silence on these questions has caused doubt, distrust, and the mistaken impression that it has nothing to say. (The reader now senses an implied obligation to remedy these epistemic defects.) This is why RJR will speak out now and in the future in order to "discuss" and "explore" several important issues. The undertaking is admittedly controversial, but there are "lots of questions," "no simple answers," "more than one side," and the need for open debate.

The project, then, is one of debate, discussion, exploration, analysis, controversy, and speaking out. The values championed are those of reasonableness, objectivity, openness, and evidence. The real participants in the debate are Reynolds' unafraid spokespersons and reasonable persons like ourselves who can analyze the evidence. The goal, however, is a little harder to settle on. Exploration and analysis normally suggest a quest for determination and truth, but in this case it may only be the more indeterminate state of always seeing the other side and rekindling open-ended controversy.

The second ad (e.g., *Time*, February 20, 1984, pp. 64–65) in the debate-announcement category is a tour de force because it promotes the motif of unresolved debate both in form and content. The ad is structured as a dialogue in two columns between nonsmokers and smokers: on the left, "a message from those who don't to those who do;" and on the right, "a message from those who do to those who don't." Equal weight and fairness in this exchange seem assured: Each column has the identical number of lines and the same number of corresponding short and one-line paragraphs. Each side starts off with a statement of uneasiness: "We're uncomfortable" (the nonsmokers); "We're on the spot" (the smokers). Both columns include statements of unhappiness, claims, disavowals, and pleas; and there is a close linear correspondence in the flow and positioning of each of these rhetorical types or arguments. Each side concludes with an identically worded plea for understanding and respect: "We know you've got rights and feelings. We just want you to respect our rights and feelings as well."

The nonsmokers confess to feeling uncomfortable, frustrated, and powerless because they have been exposed to the annoyance of secondhand smoke, because their privacy has been violated, and because whenever they speak out to complain they are regarded as "bad guys." Nonsmokers are not fanatics, they disavow any wish to deprive others of enjoyment, or to be cast in the role of enemies. Their penultimate plea is for more consideration and responsibility from smokers.

Smokers, on the other hand, feel put on the spot, confused, and singled out. Smoking, they argue, is a "very personal choice," something that gives enjoyment and is "perfectly legal." Nevertheless, their injuries are no less real than those of nonsmokers: They have been "segregated," "discriminated against," "legislated against," and verbally abused in public. They disavow criminality in their actions, and any intent to offend or any desire for confrontation. Smokers are simply doing something they enjoy and— brace yourself—"trying to understand your [i.e., the nonsmokers'] concerns."

In structure and layout, then, the two messages pose as a serious dialogue between two equally defensible points of view. The tenor of give and take, evident in the use of claim and acknowledgment, suggests reasonableness and balance. Identical line quantities, identical rhetorical types, the same concluding paragraph, and the identical positioning of corresponding messages—all these reinforce the impression that the smoker's case is equivalent in every respect to that of the nonsmoker. To this end, typographical format is just as much the message as the content. To take all this in, however, is also to recognize that this "debate" is calculated to remain just where it began—in a state of open and unresolved controversy.

Still, as Orwell remarked, some are more equal than others. In point of fact, the language of the smokers' grievances seems to have an edge over that of the nonsmokers'. "Segregated," "discriminated against," "legislated against," and public verbal abuse, with all the sociohistorical freight these words carry, sound more offensive and certainly more unjust than the annoyance of secondhand smoke, invasion of privacy, and being perceived as "bad guys." The harsher descriptions of the smokers' unhappiness carries with it the subtext that they are more vulnerable and have been more victimized than their abstaining cousins. Finally, the fact that a right-hand column is normally read *after* a left-hand column also means that the smoker's side has all the advantages of having the last word.

Other ads in the series sustain the motif of controversy and open-ended debate. "How to handle peer pressure" (e.g., *Seventeen*, March 1985) exploits a sort of thesis ("tactics") versus antithesis ("answer") model to get its message across. Many of the ads (e.g., "Passive smoking, active controversy" [e.g., *Time*, June 10, 1985, p. 46]) keep alive the element of controversy. Another ad in the second category urges smokers and nonsmokers "to talk to one another." "Smoking in public: a radical proposal" (e.g., *Time*, August 19, 1985, p. 52) promotes the dialogue/debate motif as well as the social virtues. While it stresses the theme of common courtesy in the interaction between smokers and nonsmokers, it also reinforces the element of reasonableness in social discourse. Relying upon such techniques as playful irony and hyperbole, the ad envisages a dialogue in which a smoker pauses before lighting up and asks "Excuse me, do you mind if I smoke?" The nonsmoker, stunned by this unexpected courtesy, replies "I don't mind as long as you don't let your smoke blow in my face." Confronted with this "flagrant tolerance," the smoker adds "I'll do my best. Let me know if the smoke bothers you." The nonsmoker replies "I will—and thanks for asking." Significantly, the smoker once again has the last word: "Thanks for being so understanding." This kind of interchange, the ad concludes, could lead to "a sudden outbreak of civil decency" or "even escalate into full-scale friendliness."

Though only hypothetical, this exchange takes a step in the direction of redeeming the smoker's image. After all, smoking can be seen as an occasion for practicing the virtues of politeness and thoughtfulness, courtesy and friendliness. The language of this message is also scripted in such a way as to dilute the smoker's responsibility for causing offense. Grammatically, offense is vested in the noun "smoke" and its associated verb forms: " . . . smoke blow in my face;" " . . . if the smoke bothers you." The smoker's agency, by contrast, is reduced to the more passive role of allowance: " . . . as long as *you* don't *let* your smoke blow in my face."

ENVIRONMENTAL TOBACCO SMOKE (ETS) AND SCIENCE—AND MORE TALK

Seven ads, nearly half the series, tackle the issue of secondhand or passive smoking. Most of these titles, involving wordplay, promise a movement away from fiction and in the direction of truth: "Secondhand smoke: the myth and reality" (e.g., *Time*, May 14, 1984, p. 85); "Secondhand smoke: let's clear the air" (e.g., *Time*, April 30, 1984, p. 16); "Smoking in public: let's separate fact from friction" (e.g., *Time*, March 19, 1984, p. 58); "Passive smoking, active controversy" (e.g., *Time*, June 10, 1985, p. 46); "The secondhand smokescreen" (e.g., *Time*, May 27, 1985, p. 5).

The first three of these five titles are closely similar in their physical layout and in the arrangement of arguments. Each begins by acknowledging the conflict between smokers and nonsmokers, and the belief or questionable reports that secondhand smoke causes disease. In each of the three, the third paragraph consists of the identical counterclaim: "There is little evidence—and certainly nothing which proves scientifically—that cigarette smoke causes disease in nonsmokers." This is immediately followed by concessions that this statement may seem biased, that "skeptics might call this the wishful thinking of a tobacco company," or that "you don't have to take our word for it."

The central part of each of the messages is taken up by two or three paragraphs in which factual counterevidence is cited, and there is very nearly the same pattern in presenting that evidence. First, the respectability of evidence is ensured in terms of the "scientific judgment of some of the leading authorities in the field" or the "findings and views of independent scientists." Second, credibility and objectivity are enhanced by remarking that these sources include "some of the tobacco industry's biggest critics" or "outspoken critics of smoking," or by citing supporting counterevidence offered by "one of the tobacco industry's sharpest critics." Third, the authorities cited are either highly placed senior officials or the reports of respected organizations: two U.S. Surgeons General; the chief statistician of the American Cancer Society; the director of the National Heart, Lung and Blood Institute; a 1983 statement by the unnamed organizer of an international conference on environmental tobacco smoke; and finally, a scientific study by the Harvard School of Public Health. Fourth, and not surprisingly, the reports or statements cited deny or greatly minimize the connection between ETS and disease in nonsmokers. Smoke is reported as having "very little, if any effect," or as bringing about "little or no physiological response." Evidence of any connection "has not been established" or "remains sparse, incomplete, and sometimes unconvincing."

Collectively, these three ads diagnose a major cause of the controversy as being "rumor and rhetoric." One of them speaks as well of unproved allegations and unfounded attacks. Another relates the controversy to our human tendency to magnify unproven claims out of all proportion into a "frightening myth." The annoyance, then, of ETS is neither a governmental nor a medical problem: "It is a people problem!" The moral implications are spelled out for us. Smokers and nonsmokers should "not yell, preach, threaten, badger, or bully." What is needed is *talk*, more tolerance, and respect for each other's rights and feelings. What is also needed is sticking to the facts, hearing all sides of these controversies, and sorting out realities from myths.

Other ads in this category, especially "Passive smoking: An active controversy" and "The second-hand smokescreen," also identify professional symposia and experts who minimize or negate the health hazards of ETS. These same two messages pinpoint the enemy: "sensational media coverage;" "media [which] have remained almost silent;" "one-sided coverage;" "the same old war on smoking in a new guise;" "a zealous group of anti-smokers;" "scare tactics."

Another ad from the group, "The most inflammatory question of our time" (e.g., *Time*, April 29, 1985, p. 11), draws attention to antismoking legislation and the feeling of threat experienced by smokers. There is the unmistakable implication (in "The second-hand smokescreen") that a "flurry" of scientific research in these areas has really been motivated by a desire to make smoking appear socially unacceptable—a theme that is raised again.

While category two focuses upon ETS, one ad, "Of cigarettes and science" (e.g., *Time*, February 3, 1986, p. 73), directly tackles the question of research into effects upon the smokers themselves. A little officiously it lectures the reader on how scientists should handle evidence and results, and about how "statistical association" is not the same as *causation*. However, dubious science, with questionable motives, can be found in the smoking-effects research sector. "Thus scientists have developed a theory: that heart disease is *caused* by smoking. Then they performed various experiments to check this theory." We are left to infer that these scientists operate in bad faith. RJR, on the other hand, sees greater virtue in a ten-year project that was massively funded by the U.S. federal government. As reported by RJR, the Multiple Risk Factor Intervention Trial—with the reassuring acronym of MR FIT—found no significant evidence that smoking caused heart disease. (Whether RJR's reading of this and other scientific reports is accurate is another issue altogether.) Even so, RJR notes with disapproval, antismoking scientists have not abandoned or modified their original theory. Such unheeding theory should more accurately be labeled "belief," "opinion," or "judgement," "but *not* scientific fact" (emphasis in original).

RJR deplores a double set of scientific principles. If only simplistically, it concludes: "Science is science: Proof is proof. That is why the controversy over smoking and health remains an open one."

In formulating this chapter of the debate, the Reynolds Company might seem at first glance to be on the defensive, but in reality it turns out to have the forces of light and reason on its side. This sort of impression management takes place because the smoking and science ads, as well as others in the series, employ a number of conventional propaganda techniques—the sort that have been itemized, say, in Hugh Rank's Intensify/ Downplay schematism (Ohlgren and Berk, 1977, pp. 118–34). For example, at work are such techniques as repetition, the use of testimonials, minimizing, and dismissal ("there is *little* evidence . . . *nothing* which proves scientifically . . ."), format and composition, clever wordplay, a populist ethos ("it is a *people* problem"), pinpointing the enemy, emotionally laden and persuasive language, and so forth. But even more compelling, the ads skillfully ally themselves with a network of epistemic and para-epistemic features in such a way as to give RJR and the smoking sector a positive image. Authorities and scientists even from the opposition can be enlisted to support its side of the controversy. How can you not be right when you attempt to sort out reality from myth, fact from f(r)iction; when you work at clearing the air and setting the record straight; when you express a scrupulous regard for the canons of science, proof, and research? How can bias and skepticism prevail when you also encourage talk, tolerance, and respect for others' rights and feelings? By contrast, what we find on the other side of this controversy or friction is less than applaudable: rumor and rhetoric, questionable reports, unproven allegations, unfounded attacks, misconception, frightening myth—in sum, "little evidence—and certainly nothing which proves scientifically—that cigarette smoke causes disease in nonsmokers." Here too we also find zealous, research conducted in bad faith, media misbehavior, and the specter of corporate and government regulation.

The use of these persuasive techniques seems to have another function. There is only one ad ("Of cigarettes and science") that ostensibly deals with the issue of possible harm to smokers themselves. By contrast, the *seven* ads in category two constitute their own sort of smokescreen. By concentrating upon the admittedly less conclusive findings about second-hand smoke, these messages amount to a diversion: They deflect readers' attention away from the known harm suffered by smokers.

YOU'VE COME A LONG WAY, BABY!

Four ads focus on the issue of young people and smoking: "How to handle peer pressure" (e.g., *Seventeen*, March 1985); "We don't advertise to children" (e.g., *Time*, April 9, 1984, p. 91); "Some surprising advice to young people from RJ Reynolds Tobacco" (e.g., the *New York Times Magazine*, May 27, 1984, p. 81); "Does smoking really make you look more grown up?" (e.g., *Parade*, June 16, 1985, p. 4). Each one explicitly discourages smoking among the young: "Don't smoke"; "we don't want young people to smoke"; "we think young people shouldn't smoke." Why this surprising message from a tobacco company? Because smoking is an "adult custom," and the "decision to smoke" or not smoke is one that should be made by adults. It is also one that should be made "when you don't have anything to prove." Young people, then should "think it over" because while they may not be old enough to smoke, they are "old enough to think." Why the hurry, one ad asks: "There is plenty of time later on to think about whether or not smoking is right for you."

This is why one of the ads ("How to handle peer pressure") identifies five pressure tactics used by peers to nudge youngsters into smoking. This is also why RJR insists in another ad that "We don't advertise to children."

Its product ads, it asserts, are "brand advertising"—messages designed to encourage those who already smoke to swtich to one of its brands. Research shows, the ad argues, that the influence of cigarette advertising upon young people is "insignificant: kids just don't pay attention to cigarette ads."

The pivotal issue in these ads, then, is sound choice and RJR's concern with how to safeguard it. The tactics of peer pressure identified by RJR, for instance, are just those sorts of tactics which compromise choice. They are ultimately those of blandishment (being "cool" or unwisely trusting your friends' inducements) or the powerful motive of fear—fear of being "a chicken" or "a nerd" if you don't already smoke, or fear of parental discovery if you do decide to smoke. The counterstrategies provided by RJR are clear-headed rejoinders aimed at securing independence of choice and adult maturity in young people's behavior: "It takes a lot more guts to do your own thing than to just go along with the crowd. . . . How can I expect them [my parents] to treat me like an adult if I sneak around and act like a kid." RJR wryly reflects upon a crazy world in which adults want to look younger while the young try to look more adult. With commendable sobriety, it reminds its reader that "a fifteen-year-old smoking a cigarette looks like nothing more or less than a fifteen-year-old smoking a cigarette." There are, then, a number of virtues at work in these ads: courage; honesty; a healthy disregard for mere appearance; genuine friendship (which does not lead others astray); a sense of humor—in short, a robust maturity. With reason and values, then, this tobacco company distances itself from the abuse of its product.

Nobody, it would seem, would really object to the virtues and character traits championed in these four ads. Indeed, in early July 1985, a mother wrote in to advice columnist Ann Landers asking her to print one of these ads "in the interest of fairness" (*The Windsor* [Ontario] *Star* July 4, 1985, p. C3). Ms. Landers not only complied, but raised the ante when she wrote: "I applaud the R.J. Reynolds Tobacco Co. for running that ad. . . . What an ideal time to declare one's independence and vow nevermore to be a slave to the tobacco habit."

Ann Landers's imprimatur, of course, publicly endorses the image of social and moral concern that RJR wants to wear. But her concluding remark on "independence" should also help to alert us to the fact that some deeper and more imperceptible messages are also at work here. On the surface, a number of useful strategies and disavowals have been adduced to safeguard American youth. Autonomous choice and its allied virtues are the cherished ideals on which that protection is grounded. By the same token, smoking itself is also redeemed, if only partially, by disassociating it from adolescent misbehavior and by situating it within the higher order of adult decision and choice. However, that protection of the young is little more than temporary and provisional. The decision to smoke (or not to smoke) is not one that RJR wants absolutely to abort, but only to *postpone* until adulthood. Finally, these ads, like those in category two, are also diversionary. Because smoking is depicted as an adult custom anchored in free and thoughtful choice, because it is interpreted in such epistemic and para-epistemic terms as "thinking" and "choice" and "decision," its powerfully addictive and involuntary nature is skillfully muted. To smoke or not to smoke—*that* is the question. Not once in these ads is the specter of kicking the habit ever raised.

CONCLUSION

Collectively, the RJR series of nonproduct ads illustrates Ellul's claim that in today's society information and propaganda are difficult to separate. One can, of course, easily recognize in them a number of conventional propaganda strategies; but as much and more than these specific techniques it is really RJR's systematic use of, and ostensible commitment to, a network of epistemic and para-epistemic values that work the magic of their influence upon readers. Because RJR appears open to reason and science, anxious to discuss and debate, ready to provide alternative evidence, and vigilant in its social and moral concerns—because of all of these we, the reading public, are encouraged to believe that we are party to informative discussion with reasonable spokespersons. But beneath that veneer of reason and dialogue lies a less perceptible agenda of persuasion and assuagement. That hidden agenda seems more calculated to prolong talk interminably and to turn our attention away from some harsher truths about smoking. In short, notwithstanding surface-level avowals and debate formats, these ads do not truthfully inform so much as they *use* truth and half-truths in their overall process of assuaging public anxiety and redeeming the smoking sector's image. To recognize this, however, is to appreciate the difficulty in separating information from propaganda in today's communication ecology.

The RJR ads may indeed portend a new tack in future commercial messages. As risky pleasure products come under greater scrutiny and constraint, their producers may increasingly communicate to the public a message that is self-serving and self-redeeming but one which is packaged in the appearance of such "motherhood" values as information and the social virtues.

NOTE

1. "Epistemic" refers to primary cognitive states or events such as opinion and belief; knowledge and thinking; facts, truth, and certainty; and also falsity. "Para-epistemic" denotes a range of values, attitudes, and practices which accompany and qualify the primary epistemic events, or within which the latter are embedded: for example, controversy, debate, and discussion; analysis; science, research, and

proof; objectivity; rationality and reasonableness; tolerance, fairness, and thought-fulness; choice and decision.

REFERENCES

Altheide, D. L., and J. M. Johnson. 1980. *Bureaucratic propaganda*. Boston: Allyn and Bacon.

Bethel, T. 1982. Propaganda warts. *Harper's*, May 19–25.

Bogart, L. 1976. *Premises for propaganda: The USIA's operating assumptions in the cold war*. New York: Free Press.

Ellul, J. 1957. Information and propaganda. *Diogenes* 18:61–77.

———. 1965. *Propaganda*. New York: Knopf.

Lapham, L. H. 1984. The propaganda man. *Parade*, July 4, 14–15.

Lerner, D. 1980. Revolutionary elites and world symbolism. In *Propaganda and communication in world history*. Vol. 2, ed. H. Lasswell, D. Lerner, and H. Speier, pp. 371–94. Honolulu: University Press of Hawaii.

Rank, H. 1977. Learning about public persuasion: rationale and a schema. In *The new languages: A rhetorical approach to the mass media and popular culture*, ed. T. H. Ohlgren and L. M. Beck, pp. 118–34. Englewood Cliffs, N.J.: Prentice-Hall.

Steinfatt, T. M. 1979. Evaluating approaches to propaganda analysis. *Et Cetera* 36:166–77.

Wheeler, M. 1976. *Lies, damn lies and statistics: The manipulation of public opinion in America*. New York: Dell.

11 The Rhetoric of "Nuclear Education"

J. Michael Hogan and David Olsen

The National Education Association (NEA), with some 1.7 million members, is among "the largest, best organized, and most energetic interest groups in the United States" (Finn 1983, p. 29). In the early 1980s, the group devoted much of its political energy to the campaign for a freeze on nuclear weapons. Meanwhile, ostensibly in its professional capacity, the NEA promoted so-called "nuclear education" and developed a curriculum guide for junior-high-school classes: *Choices: A unit on conflict and nuclear war* (UCS et al. 1983).

As local school boards and even state legislatures began mandating "nuclear education" (Dieringer 1985, pp. 1–2, 4; Alsop 1983), opponents of the freeze began to protest. Even President Reagan, in obvious reference to the NEA and *Choices*, lashed out at "those who have promoted curriculum guides that seem to be more aimed at frightening and brainwashing American schoolchildren than . . . stimulating balanced, intelligent debate" (Salholz, Lord, and McDonald 1983, p. 78). Thus arose the central question about "nuclear education": is it genuinely "educational" or is it "propaganda" for a nuclear freeze? This essay addresses that question, exploring the public rationale for "nuclear education," the rhetoric of *Choices*, and the role of "nuclear education" in the larger public dialogue over nuclear weapons.

THE RATIONALE FOR "NUCLEAR EDUCATION"

Although the "nuclear age" has been with us for over forty years, some educators have decided only recently that children "require a different kind of education for the nuclear age" (Wagner 1983, p. 24). An epidemic of nuclear fears among children supposedly broke out with the election of Ronald Reagan, and these fears are said to be creating a new generation of aimless pessimists. Helen Caldicott, perhaps the best-known advocate of "nuclear education," presents some of the testimony freeze advocates offer as "proof" of this "growing problem" in her book *Missile Envy* (1985, pp. 334–35):

Piper Herman, at Swampscott Junior High School, age twelve, said, her voice trembling, "I just get so scared thinking that tomorrow I might not wake up, and that would just be the end. . . . Catherine Rich, age twelve, from Swampscott, said, "I had nightmares of the bombs slowly floating towards me. I could feel my blood spurting all over the place. . . . Susan Sweeny, age seventeen, said, "As for a career, it seems like it is a waste to go to college and to build up a career and then get blown up someday.

Proponents of "nuclear education" buttress such anecdotal evidence with survey data. Educators for Social Responsibility (ESR), a group in the forefront of the freeze campaign, conducted a survey of 2,000 students and found that 90 percent believed there would be a nuclear war, and 87 percent did not think they would survive it (McGrory 1983, p. A3). Similarly, a survey of 1,000 young people in the Boston area (sponsored by the American Psychiatric Association) found, in Caldicott's words, that "almost all" believed they would "never grow up, never get jobs, never get married or have children of their own" because they would "be killed in a nuclear war" (Caldicott 1982, p. 4).

According to the "nuclear educators," the problem is compounded by a sense of powerlessness among children. Lacking sufficient understanding of both nuclear issues and the political system, students do not realize that they will help decide America's nuclear policies as adults in a representative democracy. Thus a second rationale for "nuclear education" is suggested: education for citizenship. Paul Fleisher, a Richmond, Virginia teacher who participated in the testing of *Choices*, acknowledges that the subject of nuclear war might sometimes be "uncomfortable and frightening." But, Fleisher concludes: "Our republic works best when an informed public considers the important issues of the day from all perspectives. . . . As educators, our task is to give students the skills and knowledge that they need to become effective citizens" (Fleisher 1985, p. 216).

Critics doubt that "nuclear educators" are truly motivated by concern for children's fears or their education in citizenship. Observing that virtually all of the nuclear curricula have been developed by groups involved in the campaign for a nuclear freeze, they consider such programs, quite simply, political propaganda. Some of the "nuclear educators," such as the Jobs with Peace Education Task Force, make very little effort to avoid or to deny such charges. As a political group created specifically to protest against the Reagan Administration, Jobs with Peace has no business, save political business, developing educational curricula, and its leftist, anti-Reagan stance is thinly disguised in its materials (see Jobs with Peace Education Task Force 1982). The NEA, on the other hand, is an organization of professional educators, citing curriculum development as a "professional" function and claiming that its materials are not politically biased. *Choices*, the NEA can argue with at least prima facie persuasiveness, is an "educational" document, not political propaganda.

The distinction between "education" and "propaganda" is very slippery, of course. But the "nuclear educators" themselves often draw the distinction, contrasting "truly educational" with "pseudoeducational, propagandistic" information on war and peace (Sloan 1983, p. 9). The editors of a special edition of *Social Education* devoted to "nuclear education" elaborated on some of the key differences (Reardon, Scott, and Totten 1983, p. 473):

Indoctrination is the antithesis of education, and, as such, it should be anathema to every teacher. Education has at its heart a free and open exchange of ideas. It avoids the preaching of dogma, and the suppression of conflicting opinions. . . . We need to teach the factual truth about the nuclear world and the consequences of nuclear war.

As we turn to an analysis of the NEA's *Choices*, we shall employ the rationales and definitions of the "nuclear educators" themselves in framing our questions. Is the rhetoric of *Choices* really designed to assuage the "numbing paralysis of fear" and the "sense of powerlessness" among children (Reardon, Scott, and Totten 1983, p. 474)? Is the curriculum "balanced" and "factual," offering not "the preaching of dogma" but a "free and open exchange of ideas" and conflicting opinions? In short, does *Choices* "educate" rather than "propagandize"? A close reading of the document raises a number of very serious doubts.

CHOICES: APOCALYPTIC NARRATIVE AND POLITICAL MISINFORMATION

Contrary to the rationales offered for "nuclear education," the NEA's *Choices* does not appear designed to lessen children's fears or to prepare them for responsible citizenship. In fact, it seems almost deliberately created to do precisely the opposite: to increase fear and pessimism among children, to misinform them about the issues, and to foster alienation from the political system.

At the heart of most "nuclear education" is a genre of apocalyptic narrative popularized by the "bible" of the nuclear freeze movement, Jonathan Schell's *The Fate of the Earth* (1982). "Nuclear educators" embrace Schell's contention that nuclear warfare should be discussed in "human" rather than "statistical" terms. Thus they treat children to obscenely vivid descriptions of what nuclear bombs do to human bodies. Somehow they have concluded that the way to cure the alleged epidemic of fear among children is to bombard them mercilessly with gruesome scenes of people being vaporized, burned, crushed, melted, irradiated, or otherwise pulverized out of existence by a virtually inevitable nuclear holocaust.

Choices begins with Harvard Professor John E. Mack expounding on the curious logic behind "nuclear education" in a message to teachers. Mack reports that "young, and even very young, children are . . . afraid of dying in a nuclear war," and that "the experience of living with the threat of imminent annihilation" has had "a significantly adverse impact on the emotional lives of young people." Yet the good doctor says that youngsters are "grateful" for "information they receive on these subjects that is presented in a meaningful and objective manner." Acknowledging that "much of what is contained in this unit is difficult and often unpleasant to contemplate," he argues that it nonetheless will help "young minds visualize and experience the nuclear reality in a way that is not threatening" (UCS et al. 1983, p. 4).

Choices' definition of "not threatening" becomes evident immediately, as lesson 1 exposes children, "perhaps for the first time," to "the destructive power of the atomic bomb." Acknowledging in "teacher notes" that "the unit does not pursue the reasons for targeting populated cities," it emphasizes instead the "unbelievable ruin" wrought by the U.S. bombing of Japanese cities, as portrayed in two "personal accounts" by survivors of the attack. The first describes how people near ground zero "literally evaporated and only their shadows remained," and how "others were turned to charred corpses." It details how those who survived were "badly burned" and doomed by the "large black drops" of a radioactive, "deadly rain." It describes the "endless line of injured people" marching through the black rain and the "burning flames" toward the outskirts of the city. The burns made their "skin hang down"; their hands looked like "those of ghosts" (1983, pp. 11, 14–16).

The second narrative details the experiences of a fourteen-year-old Japanese youngster, bringing the horrors closer to home for the junior-high-school classes. Recounting his first impressions upon regaining consciousness, the fourteen-year-old tells of his "frantic effort" to find his mother and his five-year-old sister in the darkness:

Terribly frightened, I thought I was alone in a world of death and groped for any light. My fear was so great I did not think anyone would truly understand. When I came to my senses I found my clothes in shreds. . . . It was quiet, very quiet, an eerie moment. I discovered my mother in a water tank. She had fainted. Crying out, "Mamma, Mamma," I shook her to bring her back to her senses. After coming to, my mother began to shout madly for my sister, 'Eiko, Eiko!"

Thus the story ends, with no word on the fate of the five-year-old (1983, p. 16).

The emotional assault peaks in lesson 4, with discussion of the much greater destructive power of modern nuclear weapons. The first worksheet of the lesson compares the power of the Hiroshima bomb with modern weaponry. Today's total nuclear arsenal, it points out, has 1 million times more power than the bomb dropped on Hiroshima ("One million times larger is a lot—it's hard to understand! Can you figure out how many miles long a line will be that is a million times longer than one inch?"). It then compares an eight-inch representation of the MX missile with a one-quarter inch version of the Hiroshima bomb. Commenting on the difference, the worksheet states: "One warhead in the new MX missile is about 25 times stronger than the Hiroshima bomb. Each MX missile alone carries ten warheads! . . . Plans now call for 100 MX missiles: how many Hiroshima bombs would that be?" Students then move to another worksheet detailing "the long-term effects on those who are not immediately killed by the explosion" in a nuclear attack. The worksheet emphasizes how radiation would cause even people living "far away from an explosion" to "lose their appetite and hair," to become "constantly nauseated," and to "eventually die." They conclude the lesson by contemplating the effects of a one-megaton bomb dropped on their own home town. Students use a compass to draw concentric circles on a map of their city, detailing the proportions of family and friends that would be dead, burned, or blinded at familiar locations (1983, pp. 34, 37–39).

Choices supplements its grotesque consideration of nuclear effects with a discussion of the "issues" surrounding the decision to drop the bomb. In a "factual account," the children are told that President Truman also had "choices": one group of "advisors" argued that a mere demonstration of the weapon, perhaps on an "uninhabited island," would induce surrender. But for reasons that remain a mystery, Truman chose to disregard the more humane alternative, preferring instead to use atomic weapons "on people" for "the first time" in history (1983, p. 15).

Choices' apocalyptic narratives and its interpretation of Truman's decision clearly raise questions of balance, if not of factual accuracy. One wonders, for example, why the unit explicitly sidesteps the reasons for targeting the two cities, why Japan's surprise attack on Pearl Harbor is not even mentioned, or why there are no equally gruesome descriptions of, say, the Bataan Death March. One also might question *Choices'* interpretation of Truman's decision to drop the bomb, with its obvious grounding in the New Left revisionism of Gar Alperovitz and others (see Hogan 1985, p. 345). It *is* true that the United States first used atomic weapons, of course, and *Choices*' interpretation of Truman's decision has at least *some* intellectual credibility as the product of a popular, albeit controversial, school of academic historiography. But clearly *Choices* fails to provide a balanced treatment of history; it emphasizes only the suffering of the Japanese in World War II, and it simply ignores the American government's explanation for the bombing.

Other lessons in *Choices* are likewise politically unbalanced, as they further develop the theme that the United States is the major villain in the nuclear arms race. In one lesson, *Choices* treats the arms race as essentially a technological rather than a political phenomenon, and it graphically illustrates how the United States has been responsible for nine of twelve technological "firsts." This lesson not only lays historical blame for the arms race on the United States, but it also implies the futility of any new weapons development and suggests that the arms race would end if the United States simply stopped developing new weapons. Still another lesson emphasizes that the Soviet Union, but not the United States, is bordered by "unfriendly countries," and that Russia has lost about 31 million people in war compared to only 1 million for the United States. The suggestion, of course, is that Russia is more understandably militarized; its policies are more defensive in nature and justified by its history (UCS et al. 1983, pp. 15, 44, 47, 64–65).

Critics have pointed out that *Choices* makes "no reference to the ideology of Marxism-Leninism, to the brutal Soviet regime, or to the Soviet Union's imperial expansion since 1945" (Lefever 1985, p. 217). Barry Goldwater complains that the unit fails to even "mention the numerous acts of Soviet aggression on its own people and neighboring countries" (Goldwater 1983, p. A20). While emphasizing America's technological superiority, *Choices* also neglects to point out that the United States "neither struck nor threatened to strike" even when it enjoyed a nuclear monopoly (Lefever and Hunt 1983, p. 728). None of these criticisms challenge the truth of *Choices*' historical claims (the Soviets have indeed lost more men in war and the United States did in fact pioneer most nuclear technology). But again, one might question the balance of *Choices*. Even the orthodoxy of the liberal establishment assigns at least *some* blame to the Soviets for the escalating arms race.

Choices' lesson on American budget priorities raises more serious questions, as the factual errors are so grievous as to suggest conscious misinformation. Developing the argument that money for defense deprives Americans of domestic services, *Choices* contains a "game" on budget priorities in which the students first divide twenty "tokens" by priorities such as health care, parks, schools, roads, police, and the military. They then contemplate the "fact" that the actual budget of the United States distributes, in effect, nine of the twenty tokens to the military, leaving only one for "social needs" (education, food, jobs, and social services), two for health ("medical research" and "programs for the elderly, handicapped, and poor"), one for science and politics, and so on (UCS et al. 1983, pp. 58–59). The outcome is predictable, of course, with students undoubtedly shocked at how many tokens pile up for the military.

Simple arithmetic tells us that *Choices'* budget game attributes 45 percent of the budget—nine of twenty tokens—to the military. This, of course, is simply not true. Defense spending in recent years has consistently run between 26 and 29 percent of the federal budget. One might add that *Choices* says nothing about Soviet military spending. The fact that the Soviets consistently spend about 14 percent of their gross national product on the military, compared to less than 7 percent for the United States, certainly puts the matter in a much different light (U.S. Department of Commerce 1985, pp. 331, 336). Also, *Choices* presents "national defense" as a monolithic category, while categories of domestic spending are divided into more specific subcategories ("Social Needs," for instance, is divided into education, food and nutrition, job training, and social services). This masks two important facts: that a large portion of the "National Defense" category is comprised, not of weapons procurement, but of personnel costs and retirement pay, and that strategic nuclear forces typically account for less than 20 percent of the defense budget (Garfinkle 1984, p. 106). Finally, *Choices* encourages students to think that federal military spending is at the expense of such vital domestic needs as public schools, police, and firefighters. The truth, of course, is that funding for police and firefighters is almost entirely local, and public schools get 92 percent of their funding from state and local revenues (Maeroff 1983, p. C4).

Choices' lesson on the balance of nuclear forces is also blatantly misleading and constitutes, in effect, propaganda for a nuclear freeze. Totally ignoring the raging controversy over the matter at the heart of the nuclear debate, *Choices* presents the "fact" that the United States is far ahead of the Soviets in total nuclear forces: the United States has 9,500 warheads, a worksheet in lesson 7 notes, while the Soviets have but 7,500. The worksheet also includes maps of the two countries showing missile-submarine bases, major airfields, missile-launching sites, and missile-testing centers. In completing the worksheet, students are asked to compare the two countries in terms of major airfields and missile-launching sites. In doing so they discover again that the United States has a significant advantage: U.S. airfields outnumber Soviet airfields 44 to 21, while U.S. missile-launching sites outnumber those of the Soviets by 10 to 5 (UCS et al. 1983, pp. 64–66).

The lesson comparing maps of the two countries displays the most obvious bias in *Choices'* materials on the nuclear balance. Aside from the fact that the number of bases or launching sites really says nothing about nuclear capabilities, students are asked to compare only airfields and missile-launching sites—areas in which the United States has an advantage—while nothing is said about missile-submarine bases or missile-testing centers. The maps show that the Soviets enjoy a 3 to 2 advantage in the former, and a 4 to 2 advantage in the latter.

A more subtle but much more significant problem is that *Choices* employs *only* the number of warheads as *the* measure of total nuclear capabilities. Yet as the Harvard Study Group on Nuclear Weapons points out, it is totally meaningless to compare the number of nuclear weapons without considering their characteristics: their accuracy, their vulnerability, their destructive power, and the like (Carnesale et al. 1983, pp. 115–26). The Soviets, for instance, pack more than twice as much destructive force (7,868 to 3,505 megatons) in their numerically smaller arsenal (Talbott 1982, pp. 19, 22).

Measuring "who's ahead" in the arms race is an extremely complicated business, of course, and a junior-high-school curriculum cannot be expected to resolve all the controversies. But if *Choices* were truly educational, one would expect to find at least some acknowledgment that the matter *is controversial*. Obviously, the President, the Secretary of Defense, and a host of defense experts do not consider it a "fact" that the United States is far ahead of the Soviets. It is little wonder that opponents of the freeze, such as Barry Goldwater, were "outraged to read that the highly debatable question on nuclear superiority" had been "resolved" by *Choices* (Goldwater 1983, p. A20). Even the *Washington Post* chastised the NEA: "The materials show us far ahead of the Russians. The matter is surely debatable, but arguments to the contrary are buried in a reprinted article in the appendix" (Political teaching 1983, p. A14).

By misinforming students about the issues in the nuclear debate, the NEA raises serious doubts that it aims to "educate" children for responsible citizenship. Those doubts grow as one considers *Choices*' message about politicians and the political system. Rather than teaching children about the political process, *Choices* "educates" children to be politically cynical and alienated from their government. A number of lessons teach, in essence, that politicians—and especially American politicians—generally lie about the arms race and, by implication, that they are almost universally in favor of destroying the world. In lesson 8, childen are taught how to recognize "propaganda"—"opinion in the form of fact"—in the nuclear debate. As the first exercise in a worksheet for the lesson, the students critique a newspaper report of President Reagan's televised "dense pack" speech in November 1982. Another exercise attributes a fictitious statement on law-and-order, first to President Kennedy, then to Adolf Hitler. The intent of the lesson is unmistakable: to teach children that even the President of the United States might make "propagandistic" statements and that they should "evaluate the meaning of something apart from who said it" (UCS et al. 1983, pp. 72–73, 76).

Choices' final two lessons follow logically from its lesson in political cynicism. Celebrating dreams of political utopia and antiestablishment political activism, they incite kids to reject and rebel against the corrupt political world of their parents. "The wild dream is the first step to reality," lesson 9 proclaims, before recommending songs that might "encourage creativity." *Choices* first recommends John Lennon's "Imagine"—a controversial attack on religion and patriotism as the evils behind war. *Choices* also recommends Pete Seeger's "Ain't Gonna Study War No More"—a pacifist anthem calling for total abolition of the military. Moving from utopian visions to political activism, lesson 10 suggests (1983, pp. 79–80, 84) such activities as investigating "the role the military plays in the community": "Are weapons produced at a local plant? Is research and development in progress at a local university? Are weapons stored at a nearby base?" *Choices* stops short of stirring the little radicals to storm the fences of the local weapons depot. But at schools with "nuclear education," as Ronald Alsop reports, "students are forming nuclear-awareness clubs and staging rallies reminiscent of Vietnam era activism" (Alsop 1983, p. 1).

As Deputy Undersecretary of Education, Gary L. Bauer called *Choices* "leftist indoctrination aimed at turning today's elementary students into tomorrow's campus radicals" (cited in Hoffman 1983, p. A10). Yet even this view seems a bit naive, for the NEA is not content to wait for the next generation to embrace its political agenda. The NEA has a much more immediate goal: to enlist the emotional and moral force of children in its campaign for a nuclear freeze. *Choices* does not *prepare* children for political activism. It suggests that children protest *now* by organizing rallies in their communities, exploiting local media, raising money for "an organization . . . that the class wants to support," or gathering signatures to place a freeze referendum on the local ballot. A story evoked at the outset and again at the conclusion of the unit, "The Hundredth Monkey," communicates the essence of this message. In the story, the elder monkeys ignore a "social improvement" (washing potatoes before eating them) discovered by their children until the hundredth youngster achieves the "new awareness." The lesson? When "only a limited number of people know of a new way, it may remain in the minds of only these people. But there is a point at which if only one more person tunes in to a new awareness, the idea is strengthened so that it reaches almost everyone!" The story concludes: "Your awareness is needed in preventing nuclear war. You may be the 'Hundredth Monkey' " (UCS et al. 1983, pp. 20, 82–84).

Choices encourages teachers to consult outside readings, but it is careful to recommend only those readings, audiovisual materials, and political organizations that echo its message. Almost all of the dozens of resources cited for further study "are intricately bound up with the peace movement" (Maeroff 1983, p. C4). Of fifteen audiovisual resources, only two (both films by the American Security Council) could be called pro-defense. The list of thirty books and articles is also dominated by the literature of the "peace movement," with only three "hawkish" works listed. Of the thirty-three organizations listed in *Choices*, twenty-five are found in the national directory of the "peace movement," the *American Peace Directory* (Institute for Defense and Disarmament Studies 1984, pp. 10–42), and five or so others probably *should* have been included. It is little wonder that teachers who have used *Choices* often display an almost unbelievable ignorance of the issues and differing viewpoints in the contemporary nuclear debate. One teacher who tested the unit reportedly contended that the materials were "justifiably biased in favor of a nuclear freeze" because "nuclear war is wrong" (Political teaching 1983, p. A14).

Perhaps more disconcerting than the content of *Choices* itself has been the NEA's response to criticism of the curriculum. Calling *Choices* a "conservative document" and a "piece of Americana," the NEA's Sharon Robinson insists that it is "ideologically neutral." "To those who suggest that *Choices* is propagandistic," Robinson absurdly responds, "we would ask only that they read the document," as if none of the critics had done so (Robinson 1983, pp. 487–88). Other NEA officials have responded in propagandistic fashion themselves, deflecting substantive criticism with ad hominem attacks, reverse Red-baiting, scapegoating, and allegations of conspiracy. When American Federation of Teachers President Albert Shanker criticized the NEA's involvement in the nuclear freeze movement, the NEA's Gary Watts responded that "Shanker is well-known as one of the country's most hawkish union leaders" and accused him of "right-wing, McCarthy-like tactics" (Bernstein 1983, p. 1). The NEA's Bob McClure found *Human Events* a useful scapegoat, accusing the "reactionary right wing newspaper" of instigating a "concerted effort of the far right to get *Choices*." Proclaiming it the policy of the NEA to "react with fact," McClure proved otherwise by dismissing all critics as favoring "propaganda" to "indoctrinate young people" (telephone interview with David Olsen, April 24, 1986).

It is troubling enough that the nation's largest organization of professional educators perceives some logic in trying to calm the fears of young people by assaulting their emotions with grotesque scenes of atomic death and destruction. It is even more troubling that they misinform children about the issues, and that they teach them to reject the politics of their parents and to celebrate utopian and antiestablishment political views. But perhaps most troubling of all is the fact that the NEA's leaders are either incapable of understanding all the furor or they simply refuse to respond responsibly.

Contrary to the NEA's conspiracy theory, the "far right" has not been alone in condemning *Choices*. Some of the harshest criticism has come from the *Washington Post*, which editorially concluded: "This is not teaching in any normally accepted—or, for that matter, acceptable—sense. . . . It is, quite simply, political indoctrination" (Political teaching 1983,

p. A14). It is true that Barry Goldwater and other conservatives have been in the forefront of opposition to *Choices* and to "nuclear education" in general. But one need not be conservative to agree with Goldwater that if *Choices* were "truly an educational tool, it would present both sides of the case giving equal weight to each viewpoint" (Goldwater 1983, p. A20).

"NUCLEAR EDUCATION" AND THE FREEZE DEBATE

Not all mental health experts and educators agree with those "experts" who "gravely" report that kids are increasingly fearful of nuclear war and that "this fear is ruining their lives" (Krauthammer 1984, pp. 10–11). Harvard child psychiatrist Robert Coles writes that "in years of work with children and youth all over this country, . . . I have not met the children Dr. Caldicott and others described" (Coles 1985b, p. 22). Joseph Adelson and Chester E. Finn, Jr., agree that the problem is exaggerated, calling the research on children's nuclear fears "amateurish." Most of the evidence consists of "anecdotes rather than data," they argue, and the surveys are "essentially worthless" (Adelson and Finn 1985, pp. 29–30).

Even assuming that *some* kids in *some* areas are indeed troubled by visions of the holocaust, there remains the question of who is to blame. Advocates of "nuclear education," of course, are quick to blame Reagan's arms buildup for traumatizing the children. Helen Caldicott argues that kids "just have to listen to President Reagan make a speech renaming the MX missile 'the Peacekeeper' to realize they are living in an insane world" (Caldicott 1985, p. 334). A much more believable hypothesis, however, is that children pick up such fears from their parents and teachers. "Again and again," Coles argues, "I find that the children who have taken this issue to heart are from well-off families whose parents are themselves involved in the nuclear freeze movement" (Coles 1985a, p. 61). And both the children's testimony and the survey research evoked by the "nuclear educators" point to their own programs as the most likely source of such fears.

As the kids speak of Hiroshima and the "human effects" of the bomb, or when they claim to "feel sorry for the Russians" (Caldicott 1985, pp. 334–35), it seems clear that they have learned more from "nuclear education" than from Ronald Reagan. Similarly, survey research shows that kids have little confidence in what the President, military leaders, or even the clergy tell them on this subject. The data show kids to be more likely than the adult population to be sympathetic toward the Soviets, to favor more radical measures such as unilateral disarmament, and to reject the argument that America's deterrent must be strengthened (Sussman 1984, pp. A1, A16–17). Again, these hardly seem attitudes developed spontaneously while witnessing the President on television.

Advocates of the freeze have strong political motives for frightening children. Talk of traumatized children has proven a useful tool for recruiting concerned parents. Listening to the "medical experts" of the freeze campaign, we learn that kids are "tremendously reassured" by their parents' political activism. Freeze advocates are fond of telling the story of a teacher who discovered only one child in her class unafraid of nuclear war. When asked why he was not scared, the little boy replied: "Because my Daddy is out every night trying to prevent it" (Yudkin 1984a, p. 25).

Most significantly, freeze advocates have convinced many parents that involving the children themselves in protest is effective therapy. As a result, the campaign has gained a potent political weapon: the emotional and newsworthy spectacle of innocent children crying out against the Reagan arms buildup. Focusing upon the prominent role of children in demonstrations staged by the nuclear freeze campaign, major news media have provided positive, even celebratory coverage. In reports from the freeze rally in New York on June 12, 1982, even the *New York Times* gushed about the children. "If there was one single symbol of [the freeze rally]," Anna Quindlen reported, "it was a small child. There were hundreds, perhaps thousands of them, . . . a testimonial to the oft-stated belief that marching for an end to the nuclear arms race meant marching for a future for future generations" (Quindlen 1982, p. 43). Never mind that children, as a rule, do not attend political demonstrations of their own accord. In the *Times'* coverage we witness children leading the march and serving up quotable profundities. "This is very important," nine-year-old Gregory Barger reportedly said of his "first demonstration." "If there is a nuclear war, a lot of us children will die, and some of us could be very important to the future of America" (McFadden 1982, p. 42).

Other parents have encouraged their children's involvement in such groups as the Children's Campaign for Nuclear Disarmament (CCND). "Inspired" by Helen Caldicott, the CCND is best known for organizing a letter-writing campaign, traveling to Washington, and reading thousands of anti-Reagan letters in front of the White House. One typically angry letter asked the President: "Who will cry for me when I am dead from your pro-war actions?" Another echoed *Choices'* lesson on budget priorities: "How can you say you're for peace when most of our economy is going towards the military" (Yudkin 1984b, pp. 24–25)? At one point, schoolchildren were "spontaneously" sending more than 100 such letters a day to the White House (Hentoff 1983, p. 30).

Some children have even been dragged before congressional committees to testify about their nuclear neuroses and the need for a freeze. "I think about the bomb just about every day now," a sixteen-year-old girl told the House Select Committee on Children, Youth, and Families at hearings in September 1983. "It's hard to live with the possibility that we might not ever get a chance to grow up." At the same hearings, twelve-year-old Gerald Orjuela lectured the committee on Hiroshima: "Parts of people literally melted under the blast. A bone was sticking out from the socket where there once was an arm. The shadows of people left imprinted on the floors and walls when the heat flash vaporized them. Pitiful piles of entrails that were once known as human beings." The presumably typical, unrehearsed youngster mocked the President's rhetoric ("Is it right to call a nuclear missile 'peace keeper?' ") before concluding that America was "criminalizing Newton, Dalton, Einstein, Lucretius, and Democritus, great pioneers in the Atom." That left it for eleven-year-old Jessica Fiedler to instruct the committee on the policy needed to save the children: "I think we should put a freeze on nuclear weapons" (U.S. Congress, House 1984, pp. 21–26).

Perhaps some children are indeed frightened by the prospects of nuclear war. Perhaps "nuclear education" of some sort could prove beneficial. But how are children reassured by contemplating how people melted at Hiroshima, by memorizing half-truths and falsehoods about the issues of the nuclear debate, or by learning that their political system holds no hope of a solution? How are children soothed by the sort of shock treatment Alsop witnessed in a "nuclear classroom" in New Jersey? "A six foot bomb was assembled from papier-mâché and chicken wire, air raid sirens were sounded, and students screamed and writhed on the ground as they pretended to be blinded or killed by the fiery blast" (Alsop 1983, p. 24).

The NEA's *Choices* clearly fails to serve the rationale offered for "nuclear education," and by the "nuclear educators' " own definitions, it is clearly "propagandistic." The teachers who promote such curricula are either well aware that they are politicizing American education, or (perhaps worse) they are incapable of understanding the differences between "education" and "propaganda." Whatever the explanation, "nuclear education" gives new meaning to the phrase "a nation at risk." Considering "nuclear education," as Adam Garfinkle suggests, "a parent could not be faulted for wondering whether a public school is still a safe place to send a child" (Garfinkle 1984, p. 32).

REFERENCES

Adelson, J., and C. E. Finn, Jr. 1985. Terrorizing children. *Commentary*, April, 29–31.

Alsop, R. 1983. "A" is for atom: Nuclear war becomes hot topic in schools, stirs up controversy. *The Wall Street Journal*, May 24, pp. 1, 22.

Bernstein, H. 1983. Teacher unions swing right and left in battle. *Los Angeles Times*, July 11, 4:1.

Caldicott, H. 1982. Growing up afraid: The 37th summer of the bomb. *Family Weekly*, August 8, 4–7.

———. 1985. *Missile envy: The arms race and nuclear war*. New York: Bantam.

Carnesale, A., P. Doty, S. Hoffmann, S. P. Huntington, J. S. Nye, Jr., and S. D. Sagan. 1983. *Living with nuclear weapons*. New York: Bantam.

Coles, R. 1985a. Children and the bomb. *New York Times Magazine*, December 3, 44–50, 54, 61–62.

———. 1985b. The freeze: Crusade of the leisure class. *Harper's* March, 21–23.

Dieringer, L. 1985. The challenge of legislation and school board resolutions. *Forum* (Educators for Social Responsibility), Fall, 1–2, 4.

Finn, C. E., Jr. 1983. Teacher politics. *Commentary*, February, 29–41.

Fleisher, P. 1985. Teaching children about nuclear war. *Phi Delta Kappan* 67:215–17.

Garfinkle, A. M. 1984. *The politics of the nuclear freeze*. Philadelphia: Foreign Policy Research Institute.

Goldwater, B. 1983. NEA's nuclear "Choices." *Washington Post*, June 18, A20.

Hentoff, N. 1983. Student letters to Reagan on war stir their own tempest in Senate. *The Wall Street Journal*, September 14, 30.

Hoffman, D. 1983. NEA criticized for curriculum on nuclear war. *Washington Post*, June 8, A10.

Hogan, J. M. 1985. The rhetoric of historiography: New Left revisionism in the Vietnam era. In *Argument and social practice: Proceedings of the fourth SCA/AFA conference on argumentation*, ed. J. R. Cox, M. O. Sillars, and G. B. Walker, pp. 340–59. Annandale, Va.: Speech Communication Association.

Institute for Defense and Disarmament Studies. 1984. *American peace directory 1984*. Cambridge, Mass.: Ballinger.

Jobs With Peace Education Task Force. 1982. *Crossroads: Quality of life in a nuclear age*. Boston: Jobs with Peace Education Task Force.

Krauthammer, C. 1984. Kid's stuff. *New Republic*, February 13, 10–11.

Lefever, E. W. 1985. Teaching history and politics in the age of nuclear arms. *Phi Delta Kappan* 67:217–18.

Lefever, E. W., and E. S. Hunt. 1983. Education, propaganda, and nuclear arms. *Phi Delta Kappan* 66:727–28.

McFadden, R. D. 1982. A spectrum of humanity represented in the rally. *New York Times*, June 13, 1:42.

McGrory, M. 1983. Administration fires back with its own schoolbook on A-war. *Washington Post*, June 9, A3.

Maeroff, G. I. 1983. Curriculum addresses fear of atom war. *New York Times*, March 29, C4.

Political teaching. 1983. *Washington Post*, April 5, A14.

Quindlen, A. 1982. About New York. *New York Times*, June 13, 1:43.

Reardon, B., J. A. Scott, and S. Totten. 1983. Nuclear weapons: Concepts, issues, and controversies. *Social Education* 47:473–74.

Robinson, S. 1983. Of history, peace, and choices. *Social Education* 47:487–88.

Salholz, E., with M. Lord and D. H. McDonald. 1983. Teaching about nuclear war. *Newsweek*, July 18, 78.

Schell, J. 1982. *The fate of the earth*. New York: Knopf.

Sloan, D. 1983. Preface: Toward an education for a living world. In *Education for peace and disarmament: Toward a living world*, ed. D. Sloan, 1–14. New York: Teachers College Press.

Sussman, B. 1984. Young people in area fear a nuclear war. *Washington Post*, February 19, A1, A16–17.

Talbott, S. 1982. Living with mega-death. *Time*, March 29, 19–22.

UCS et al. See Union of Concerned Scientists.

Union of Concerned Scientists, Massachusetts Teachers Association, and National Education Association. 1983. *Choices: A unit on conflict and nuclear war.* Washington: National Education Association.

U.S. Congress. House. 1984. Select Committee on Children, Youth, and Families. *Children's fears of nuclear war.* 98th Cong., 1st sess., September 20.

U.S. Department of Commerce. 1985. *Statistical abstract of the United States, 1986.*

Wagner, T. 1983. Educating for responsibility in a nuclear age. *Media and methods* 20 (November):24–25.

Yudkin, M. 1984a. When kids think the unthinkable. *Psychology Today*, April, 18–25.

———. 1984b. Young activists. *Psychology Today*, April, 24–25.

Bibliography

Afanasayev, V. 1978. *Social information and the regulation of social development*. Translated by P. I. Krotkov and I. P. Medova. Moscow: Progress Publishers.

Agitation. 1973–83. *Great Soviet encyclopedia*. Vol. 1:137–38. New York: Macmillan.

Altheide, D. L., and J. M. Johnson. 1980. *Bureaucratic propaganda*. Boston: Allyn and Bacon.

Balfour, M. 1979. *Propaganda in war: 1919–1945*. London: Routledge & Kegan Paul.

Baritz, L. 1985. *Backfire: A history of how American culture led us into Vietnam and made us fight the way we did*. New York: Morrow.

Benn, D. W. 1985. Soviet propaganda: The theory and the practice. *The World Today* 61:113–16.

Bernays, E. L. 1923. *Crystallizing public opinion*. New York: Boni and Liveright.

————. 1928. *Propaganda*. New York: Liveright.

Bernays, E. L., and F. Lundberg. 1938. Does propaganda menace democracy? A debate. *Forum* 99:341–45.

Bittman, L. 1981. *The deception game*. New York: Ballantine.

————. 1985. *The KGB and Soviet disinformation*. Washington: Pergamon-Brassey's.

————, ed. 1988. *The new image-makers: Soviet propaganda and disinformation*. Washington: Pergamon-Brassey's.

Bogart, L. 1976. *Premises for propaganda: The USIA's operating assumptions in the cold war*. New York: Free Press.

Bramsted, E. K. 1965. *Goebbels and National Socialist propaganda: 1925–1945*. East Lansing: Michigan State University Press.

Brown, J.A.C. 1963. *Techniques of persuasion*. Baltimore: Penguin.

Bytwerk, R. L. 1983. *Julius Streicher: The man who persuaded a nation to hate Jews*. Briarcliff Manor, N.Y.: Stein and Day.

Corry, J. 1986. *TV news and the dominant culture*. Washington: The Media Institute.

Dailey, B. D., and P. J. Parker, eds. 1987. *Soviet strategic deception*. Lexington, Mass.: Lexington Books.

Daniloff, N. 1988. *Two Lives, one Russia*. New York: Houghton Mifflin.

Doob, L. W. 1935. *Propaganda: Its psychology and technique*. New York: Henry Holt.

————. 1966. *Public opinion and propaganda*. 2nd ed. Hamden, Conn.: Archon.

Dorfman, A. 1985. Neutral propaganda: Three films "made in Canada" and the Foreign Agents Registration Act. *Comm/Ent* 7:435–468.

Dziak, J. 1987. *Chekisty: A history of the KGB*. Lexington, Mass.: Lexington Books.

Dzhirkvelov, I. 1987. *Secret servant: My life with the KGB and the Soviet elite*. London: Collins.

Ebon, M. 1987. *The Soviet propaganda machine*. New York: McGraw-Hill.

Ellul, J. 1957. Information and propaganda. *Diogenes* 18:61–77.

————. 1965. *Propaganda*. New York: Knopf.

Fraser, L. 1957. *Propaganda*. London: Oxford University Press.

Grachev, A., and N. Yermoshkin. 1984. *A new information order or psychological warfare?* Translated by D. Beliavsky. Moscow: Progress Publishers.

Grice, H. P. 1975. Logic and conversation. In *The logic of grammar*, ed. D. Davidson and G. Harman, 65–75. Belmont, Calif.: Dickenson.

————. 1978. Further notes on logic and conversation. In *Syntax and Semantics*. Vol. 9. *Pragmatics*, ed. P. Cole and J. L. Morgan, 113–28. New York: Academic Press.

Harris, R. 1986. *Selling Hitler*. New York: Pantheon.

Harris, R. J., ed. 1983. *Information processing research in advertising*. Hillsdale, N.J.: Lawrence Erlbaum.

Hazan, B. 1982. *Soviet impregnational propaganda*. Ann Arbor, Mich.: Ardis.

Hogan, J. M. 1985. The rhetoric of historiography: New Left revisionism in the Vietnam era. In *Argument and social practice: Proceedings of the fourth SCA/AFA conference on argumentation*, ed. J. R. Cox, M. O. Sillars, and G. B. Walker, 340–59.

Hook, S., V. Bukovsky, and P. Hollander. 1987. *Soviet hypocrisy and western gullibility*. Washington: Ethics and Public Policy Center.

Hummel, W., and K. Huntress. 1949. *The analysis of propaganda*. New York: Dryden.

Jowett, G. 1987. Propaganda and communication: The re-emergence of a research tradition. *Journal of Communication* 37:97–114.

Jowett, G. S., and V. O'Donnell. 1986. *Propaganda and persuasion*. Beverly Hills: Sage.

Kecskemeti, P. 1973. "Propaganda." In *Handbook of communication*, ed. I. D. Pool, F. W. Frey, W. Schramm, N. Maccoby, and E. B. Parker, 844–70. Chicago: Rand McNally.

Lasswell, H. D. 1933. Propaganda. In *Encyclopedia of the social sciences*, Vol. 12, ed. E.R.A. Seligman, 521–28. New York: Macmillan.

Lasswell, H. D., and N. Leites. 1949. *Language of politics*. Cambridge: M.I.T. Press.

Lefever, E. W., and S. E. Hunt. 1983. Education, propaganda, and nuclear arms. *Phi Delta Kappan* 64:727–28.

Levchenko, S. 1988. *On the wrong side: My life in the KGB*. Washington: Pergamon-Brassey's.

Lippmann, W. 1922. *Public opinion*. New York: Macmillan.

Martin, L. J. 1958. *International propaganda*. Minneapolis: University of Minnesota Press.

Mock, J. R., and C. Larson. 1939. *Words that won the war*. Princeton: Princeton University Press.

Muravchik, J. 1988. *News coverage of the Sandinista revolution*. Washington: American Enterprise Institute.

Oberg, J. E. 1988. *Uncovering Soviet disasters*. New York: Random House.

Panfilov, A. 1981. *Broadcasting pirates or abuse of the microphone: An outline of external political radio propaganda by the USA, Britain and the FRG*. Translated by N. Bobrov. Moscow: Progress Publishers.

Prokhorov, Y. 1976. The Marxist press concept. In *International and intercultural communication*, ed. H. Fischer and J. Merril, 51–58. New York: Hastings House.

Propaganda. 1973–83. *Great Soviet encyclopedia*. Vol. 24:269–70. New York: Macmillan.

Qualter, T. H. 1962. *Propaganda and psychological warfare*. New York: Random House.

Roetter, C. 1974. *The art of psychological warfare*. New York: Random House.

Shevchenko, A. 1985. *Breaking with Moscow*. New York: Knopf.

Shultz, R. H., and R. Godson. 1984. *Dezinformatsia*. Washington: Pergamon-Brassey's.

Smith, T. J. 1988. *Moscow meets Main Street: Changing journalistic values and the growing Soviet presence on American television*. Washington: The Media Institute.

Sproule, J. M. 1987. Propaganda studies in American social science: The rise and fall of the critical paradigm. *Quarterly Journal of Speech* 73:60–78.

Tyson, J. L. 1981. *Target America*. Chicago: Regnery Gateway.

U.S. Congress, House. 1980. Permanent Select Committee on Intelligence. *Soviet covert action: The forgery offensive*. 96th Cong., 2d sess., February 6 and 19.

———. 1982. Permanent Select Committee on Intelligence. *Soviet active measures*. 97th Cong., 2d sess., July 13–14.

U.S. Congress, Senate. 1972. Committee on the Judiciary, Subcommittee on Internal Security. *Detente and the world revolutionary process*. 92nd Cong., 2d sess., June 9.

———. 1985. Committee on Foreign Relations. *Soviet active measures*. 99th Cong., 1st sess., September 12–13, part 2.

U.S. Department of State. 1986. *Active measures: A report on the substance and process of anti-U.S. disinformation and propaganda campaigns*. Publication 9630.

————. 1987a. *Soviet influence activities: A report on active measures and propaganda, 1986–87*. Publication 9627.

————. 1987b. *Contemporary Soviet propaganda and disinformation: A conference report*. Publication 9536.

Vaughn, S. 1980. *Holding fast the inner lines*. Chapel Hill: University of North Carolina Press.

Wheeler, M. 1976. *Lies, damn lies and statistics: The manipulation of public opinion in America*. New York: Dell.

Index

About the Contributors

TED J. SMITH III is an associate professor in the School of Mass Communications at Virginia Commonwealth University. A graduate of Michigan State University, he received his Ph.D. in Communication in 1978. He has authored or edited five books and more than twenty scholarly articles in the areas of persuasion theory and research, news and public opinion, communication theory, and organizational communication. His most recent books are *Moscow Meets Main Street*, a study of television coverage of the Soviet Union, and *The Vanishing Economy*, an analysis of economic coverage during the Reagan era. He and his wife Rosemary make their home in Richmond, Virginia.

NICHOLAS F. S. BURNETT is an assistant professor and Director of Forensics in the Department of Communication Studies at California State University at Sacramento.

RANDALL L. BYTWERK is Professor and Chairman of the Department of Communication Arts and Sciences at Calvin College.

STANLEY B. CUNNINGHAM is a professor in the Department of Communication Studies at the University of Windsor, Canada.

ROY GODSON is an associate professor in the Department of Government at Georgetown University and Director of the Washington office of the National Strategy Information Center.

J. JUSTIN GUSTAINIS is an associate professor in the Department of Communication at the State University of New York at Plattsburgh.

J. MICHAEL HOGAN is an associate professor in the Department of Speech Communication at Indiana University.

GARTH S. JOWETT is a professor in the School of Communication at the University of Houston.

J. DAVID KENNAMER is an associate professor in the School of Mass Communications at Virginia Commonwealth University.

J. FRED MACDONALD is a professor in the Department of History at Northeastern Illinois University and General Editor of Praeger's Media and Society book series.

VICTORIA O'DONNELL is Professor and Chair of the Department of Speech Communication at Oregon State University.

DAVID OLSEN is a doctoral candidate in the Department of Communication Studies at Northwestern University.

J. MICHAEL SPROULE is an associate professor in the Department of Communication Studies at San Jose State University.